Praise for Larry Kelley's
Lessons from Fallen Civilizations

I0039134

"In reading Larry Kelley's book, I have found new hope that my country will be liberated and the Persian people freed from the foreign tyranny of Islam."

Roya Teimouri
Human Rights Activist

"In *Lessons From Fallen Civilizations* Larry Kelley reminds us how important history is in informing and instructing the future. As the book suggests, history is written by the winners. To this point, though it has lost battles, Western Civilization has been winning the war. That may change. As Kelley documents, loss will be catastrophic. That said, Kelley is no defeatist. The book is solidly written, rich in useful detail, and a must read for those who want to keep the writing of history in our hands."

Jack Cashill
Best-selling author of *Deconstructing Obama*

"Western CIV 101 before the imams of political correctness took over our campuses. Larry Kelley's *Lessons from Fallen Civilizations* is a sweeping tour de force that reminds us that civilization as we know it is a fragile miracle that modern day barbarians could easily sweep away with the help of a complacent polity if we fail to protect and defend it."

Kenneth R. Timmerman
Best-selling author of *Countdown to Crisis:*
the Coming Nuclear Showdown with Iran

"In developing his unique list of immutable principles that govern the fall of great Western Civilizations, Kelley makes a compelling contribution in the effort to reverse America's decline. His prescriptions for countering the Islamic threat generally and the Iranian theocracy specifically are dead on. If I were elected President next November, I would order each of my cabinet secretaries to read *Lessons From Fallen Civilizations* by inauguration day."

Jerome Corsi
Best-selling co-author of *Unfit for Command*

"The West is at a crossroads. If you want to really understand how other cultures fell, why the United States is at a precipice, who the real threat is to our survival, and what we must do to avoid the fates of Greece, Carthage, and Rome, listen very closely to what Larry Kelley is telling you in *Lessons From Fallen Civilizations*. Our Founders understood well these messages from history—so should we."

Chris Field
Executive Editor, *The Blaze Magazine*

"America was forged from a different model of government, endowing the individual with personal freedoms and responsibilities. But Americans have failed to pay attention to those immutable laws that either allow nations to thrive or cause empires to crumble. America is under attack, incredibly subject to the same forces and philosophies that have led to the collapse of other once great cultures. Will America survive? Larry Kelley compellingly shows us that history is repeating itself. This time America is in the cross hairs and if we don't act fast, we'll lose."

Sue Farley
Best-selling author of *Trust Are You Kidding?:*
Pitfalls of the Current Trust System Exposed

LESSONS FROM FALLEN CIVILIZATIONS

VOLUME 2: THE WAY FORWARD

The United States is Losing the War on Terror.
What Are the Steps to Restore America's Strength?

LARRY KELLEY

Copyright © 2016 Larry Kelley. All rights reserved.

No portion of this book may be reproduced mechanically, electronically, or by any other means, including photocopying, without written permission of the publisher. It is illegal to copy this book, post it to a website, or distribute it by any other means without permission from the publisher.

DISCLAIMER
The purpose of this book is to educate. The author and/or publisher do not guarantee that anyone following these techniques, suggestions, tips, ideas, or strategies will engender success. The author and/or publisher shall have neither liability nor responsibility to anyone with respect to any loss or damage caused, or alleged to be caused, directly or indirectly by the information contained in this book.

ISBN: 978-0-9983167-2-7 (2nd Edition: 2017)

Dedication

For my loving wife, Debbie,
and my sons, Brendan and Austin

and

For the female warriors of the Kurdish Peshmerga -
the heroines of the coming Islamic Reformation

Table of Contents

Preface

Preface

By the spring of 2016, in the waning months of the Obama Administration, Americans could not help but sense that their government's malfeasance had reached the level of criminality. Appalling figures released by their government showed that ICE (The Immigration and Customs Enforcement Agency, a division of the Department of Homeland Security), in the previous year, had released from US prisons 19,723 criminal illegal aliens, including 208 convicted murderers and 900 convicted sex offenders. Not deported, but released. Criminal illegals were at large in virtually every US state. This group accounted for 64,197 convictions and 8,234 violent crimes.[1]

Meanwhile, across America's unsecured southern border near Juarez and adjacent to El Paso, Texas, Mexican drug traffickers were helping ISIS terrorists cross into the country to explore targets for future attacks. Among the jihadists was a Kuwaiti named Shayk Mahmood Omar Khabir, an ISIS commander who had trained hundreds of al Qaeda fighters in Pakistan, Afghanistan, and Yemen, and was training thousands of mostly Yemenis and Syrians in a base near Juarez. He even bragged to an Italian newspaper that the US border was so open that he could "get in with a handful of men and kill thousands of people in Texas or Arizona in the space of a few hours."[2]

Also in early 2016, the Investigative Project on Terrorism (IPT) released a report which noted that Muslim terrorists were killing nearly 30,000 people per year as compared to 2010 when terrorism's death toll was 3,284. The number of Islamic terror attacks in the US and around the world mushroomed to 10,088 in 2015 from 1,440 in 2010. These were roughly 800% increases. The report further disclosed Secret Service logs showing Esam Omeish, an outspoken supporter of the Muslim Brotherhood and close associate of the deceased terrorist Anwar Awlaki, had visited the White House nine times.[3]

This book is a commentary on the massive losses the West has suffered at the hands of resurgent militant Islam, the consequent dangers America faces due to the failures of the Obama presidency, and what future American presidents and the US allies must do about it.

Introduction

Can a Bankrupt America
Survive the Current Islamic
Threat?

Can a Bankrupt America Survive the Current Islamic Threat?

"Three Thousand Lives Wasted" – A Slip of the Tongue?

On February 11, 2007, at a campaign rally at Iowa State University, Barack Hussein Obama announced his candidacy for the presidency. During his speech he chose to emphasize his opposition to the Iraq war which, by then, the bulk of his Democrat party considered lost. "We ended up launching a war that should have never been authorized and should never have been waged - and to which we now spent $400 billion and have seen over 3,000 lives of the bravest young Americans wasted."

Earlier that same year, the freshman Senator from Illinois was appointed chair of the Senate Foreign Relations Subcommittee on European Affairs. But by that time he had begun running for president and subsequently failed to hold a single policy hearing, a fact that his Democrat opponent, Hillary Clinton, raised continuously in her losing presidential campaign. His gaff - "wasting of 3,000 lives" would have sunk a fledgling aspirant to the White House had it been uttered by a Republican. Yet it would be the first in a long run of Obama's statements and deeds which deeply offended American soldiers and their families, especially those families which had lost a son or daughter in the wars in Iraq and Afghanistan.

A few days later, with his staff in full damage control mode, Obama walked his remarks back in an interview with the *Des Moines Register*, "Their sacrifices are never wasted; that was sort of a slip of the tongue as I was speaking," he said. "What I meant to say was those sacrifices have not been honored by the same attention to strategy, diplomacy, and honesty on the part of civilian leadership."[4]

Four years after Obama's first election, on the eleventh anniversary of the 9/11 attacks, on September 11, 2012, the US Consulate in Benghazi, Libya was attacked by an al Qaeda affiliate, Ansar al Sharia. That night our ambassador to

Libya, Chris Stevens, and three ex-special forces contractors were killed. The new policy of using a "light footprint" to protect our people in Muslim countries was completely repudiated.

As Mark Moyar writes in *Strategic Failure*, "Attacks on Western Installations and personnel in Benghazi surged in late 2011 and the first half of 2012. During June of 2012, Islamist militiamen in Benghazi attempted to assassinate the British Ambassador, causing the British to shut their consulate, and they blew a hole in the US diplomatic compound."[5]

On July 9, Ambassador Stevens sent a request to the State Department, with copies to the most senior Pentagon officials, asking for an additional 13 security personnel to guard his two installations in Tripoli and Benghazi, citing that safety of his staff was his "most pressing concern." Marine Lieutenant General Neller, the Joint Staff's Director of Operations, seconded Stevens' request, offering the Administration several military force options. In addition, Carter Ham, Commander of the US Military's Africa command added his recommendation that more troops be sent. As Moyar writes, "The State Department's leaders in Washington rejected Neller's offer (as well as Ham's) and told Stevens not to ask for more military forces again."[6]

So shockingly impotent had America become under its 44th president, that on October 18, 2012, six weeks after the Benghazi attacks, *New York Times* correspondent David Kirkpatrick was able to sit down with Ahmad Abu Khattala at a Libyan luxury hotel overlooking the Mediterranean Sea, a short distance from Benghazi. Khattala was a known Ansar al Sharia leader whom numerous eye witnesses had seen directing the attacks on 9/11/12. In fact, it was widely known that he wandered openly around the city mocking the US and proudly gave interviews to Muslim media tacitly admitting his leadership in the attack. Kirkpatrick had no difficulty in locating him and gaining an audience. When he asked the terrorist if he led the attacks, he gave a smirking non-answer, stating that he was not a member of al Qaeda but that he would be "proud to be associated with its religious zealotry."[7]

The End of the Arab Spring

wo years after Obama's election, on December 17, 2010, a Tunisian fruit vendor, Mohammad Bouazizi, set himself on fire after government thugs had confiscated his small supply of fruit and had beaten him. On the fifth anniversary of the fruit vendor's immolation, the Wall Street Journal's Sohrab Ahmari wrote a piece entitled *The End of the Arab Spring*.

The incident sparked an uprising that within weeks would topple Tunisia's venal aristocracy. Protests spread to Egypt, Libya, Yemen and Syria. Despots from Morocco to Mesopotamia felt the heat of the popular anger. Many couldn't withstand it.[8]

In Egypt, seeing the massive protests in Tunisia, millions of Egyptians flooded the streets of Cairo until the dictator and long-term ally of the US, Hosni Mubarak, sent in the military only to find his generals sided with the protestors. The country had not been governed by a popularly elected ruler for all of its vast 4,000-year history. Sadly, that first man elected by a plurality of Egyptians, Mohammad

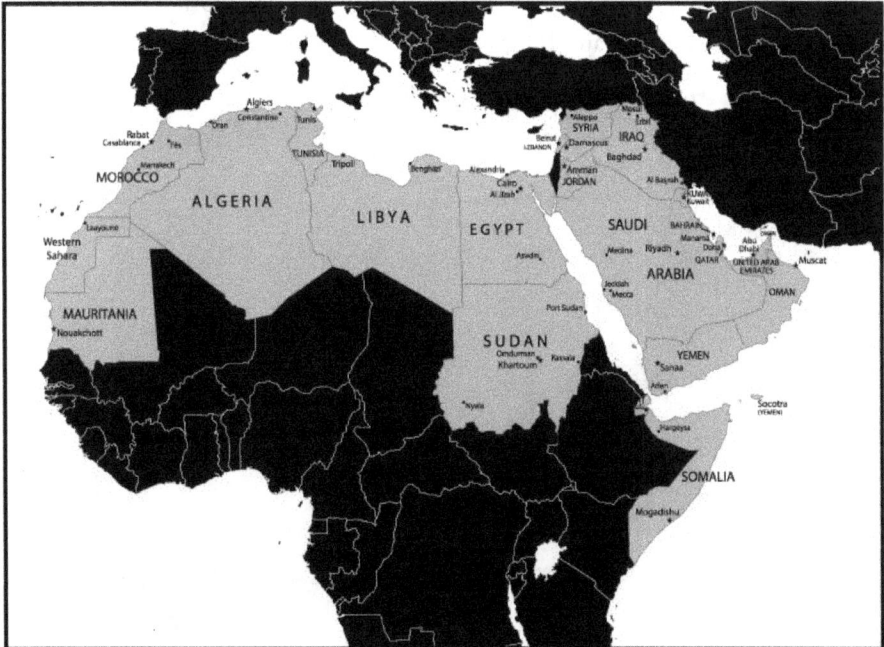

Political map of Northern Africa and the Middle East

Morsi, a man of the Muslim Brotherhood and favored by Obama, governed so badly that just 13 months later millions again poured into the streets and deposed him, resulting in military rule.

In Yemen, the country quickly disintegrated into tribal/sectarian warfare where the resident Shiite minority, the Houthi's, ultimately overran into the presidential palace and forced President Hadi to flee to Saudi Arabia. This in turn caused the neighboring Sunni states, headed by Saudi Arabia, to intervene, hoping to prevent Iran from making the failed state one of its Shiite satellites.

Libya, by late 2015, had become a lawless, failed state where smugglers and ISIS operated freely and openly.

In Syria, the so-called "Arab Spring" ignited a civil war that resulted in a new incubator of world-wide Islamist terrorism, an invasion of Europe, and by 2016, 250,000 killed.

Tunisia, ironically, became the one exception in the sense that its people not only toppled their dictatorial government but created a fledgling democracy which survived two election cycles. Yet, by 2016 it had become the world's top exporter of fighters to the Islamic State (ISIS).

Why Great Civilizations Fail & What That Means to Us

My first book, *Lessons from Fallen Civilizations*, was my response to the original 9/11 attacks on the World Trade Center Towers and the Pentagon. It was a ten-year effort, triggered by 9/11 but also built on the fact that all great civilizations fail, presumably, as will the US... someday.

Two years after the book appeared, in August of 2014, a *Wall Street Journal/NBC* poll found that 76% of adult Americans lacked the confidence that their children's generation will have a better life than they have - an all-time high. Some 71% of adults thought the country was on the wrong track. 60% believed the US was in a state of decline.

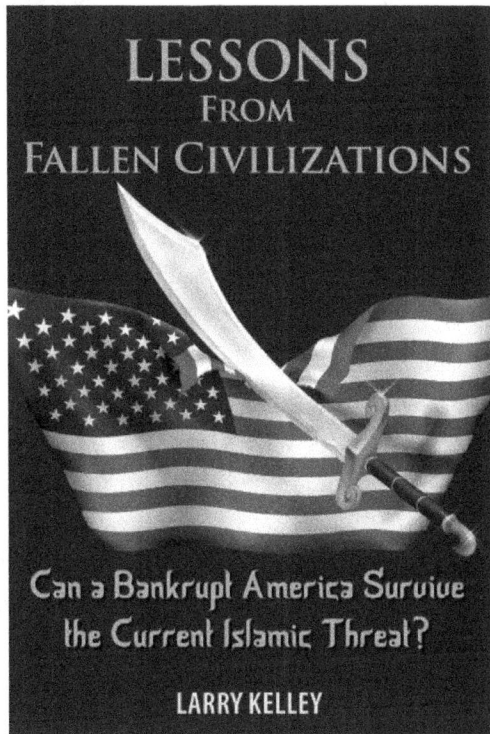

LESSONS
FROM
FALLEN CIVILIZATIONS

Can a Bankrupt America Survive
the Current Islamic Threat?

LARRY KELLEY

Evidence that our own civilization was drifting toward failure was in abundance. During the last century, at the close of World War II, Nazi Germany and Imperial Japan had been bombed into rubble and both Britain and France lost their empires in the conflict. It could be argued that France and Britain, and even Germany and Japan, were still great civilizations given the relatively large land masses they controlled. But by the second decade of the twenty-first century, my answer was: no, they were no longer great civilizations because they were, and had been for nearly seven decades, dependent on an outside power, namely the US, for their national defense and very survival.

If the US were to fail, or were to fall into irreversible decline, these states would be dead men walking, sure to fall to an outside hostile power such as Russia or perhaps to a consortium of ISIS and al Qaeda sympathizing combatants. As the fearful implications of the Obama years began to unfold it became obvious to a plurality of Americans that, should the US be unable to lead, a fearful new order would surely descend and the once-great nations of France, Germany, and England would likely be among its casualties.

After the publication of my book, I was fortunate to be invited to appear as a guest on a number of talk radio shows. Many of the hosts were particularly interested in the topic elicited by my subtitle - *Can the US Survive the Current Islamic Threat?* On the air, I was almost always asked variations of the following two questions:

"What is your book about?" (Here the host was usually looking for a short answer to a different question which was - "well, are we doomed?")

To the question - "What's it about?" I developed the following answer: "It's about why great civilizations fail and what that means to us."

To the question, "Are we *doomed?* I came up with the following two short responses, in media parlance, sound bites: "By my reading of history, no nation can have a world-class military and a world-class welfare state. It might have neither but it can't have both."

And I would follow by saying, "Unlike the British Empire, we Americans will not have the luxury of going quietly into the night. We've made too many enemies."

Regarding my reference to "too many enemies," in my radio appearances, I would go on to explain that we have amassed enemies because, since the close of World War II, America was given little choice but to become the world's policeman. But to our credit, despite the protestations of the Left over the past seven decades, the US did not take territory for glory, plunder, and power. Instead we defended the territory of our allies at great expense to us, both in blood and treasure. In just one cold war theater alone, the US lost 33,746 young Americans in order to keep half the Korean peninsula free from Communist rule.

Among the innumerable tasks the US performed in keeping Western Europe free, during the tenure of Ronald Reagan, in 1984, we installed several hundred short-range nuclear missiles inside west Germany, Italy, and Great Britain which threatened the Soviet Union with annihilation should they send their tanks across the Warsaw Pact line.

But by the middle of President Obama's second term it had become obvious he had dropped all pretense of using American military to protect the free world, its vital interests and its trade routes. In 2015, several members of the senior US military testified before Congress that Putin's revanchist Russia and its rogue-state allies, Syria, Iran and Iran's stateless terrorist allies posed an existential threat to America. As a result, on Obama's watch, a *new even more dangerous cold war had commenced.*

The Dangers Facing Donald Trump and Those He Would Govern

This book was completed shortly after what was for many, especially in the mainstream media, the shocking election of Donald Trump to become the 45th President of the United States. He inherited a much more dangerous world than the one Barack Obama inherited eight years previously. Despite the fact that Obama had pledged to end America's wars, the US was waging three active wars: Iraq/Syria, Afghanistan, and a worldwide fight against jihadis that ranged from the tribal regions of Pakistan, to Libya, to within our own borders.

The dangers to the US and its western allies, which had to be confronted by the new president, were hardly limited to America's active wars. Obama's agreement with Iranian Mullahs had released to them over $100 billion, emboldening the world's leading state sponsor of terrorism to step up its drive to dominate the Persian Gulf. Obama's hapless inability to deal with Russia's Putin had offered the revanchist dictator a green light to bully Eastern Europe in his quest to reconstitute the old Soviet Union. On Obama's watch, Putin also had actively allied with Iran, selling it anti-aircraft weapons systems designed to take out US and Israeli jets should war commence. On his watch, North Korea had also allied with Iran, sharing with it nuclear weapons and ballistic missile technology, while closing fast on its own acquisition of long-range missiles able to reach the US.

This is the second volume of a work that grew out of my response to 9/11. Along the way, I met many people from both sides of the political spectrum who believe that the "war on terror" can't really be won. Islamic-inspired terrorism was something to be managed and that we would simply need to live with it. This two-volume set is a warning to the West which lays out the case that if we succumb to complacency and/or bad decision-making, we can be destroyed by a consortium of resurgent militant Islam and its allies. To quote the late, great Tony Blankley, "We've lost the margin for error."

By November of 2016, Iraqi military forces, combined with American Special Forces and airpower, were poised to retake Mosul, the largest city in Northern Iraq, from ISIS. Its fall would mean that ISIS would no longer control any major population centers in Iraq and greatly damage its claim that it was the new Islamic Caliphate. Yet, it is important to note that a defeat of ISIS in Iraq would be achieved only by Obama greatly reneging on his promise that all would be well if he just ended George Bush's wars in Iraq and Afghanistan and pulled our troops out.

At the same time, there were 4,460 Combat Brigade troops on the ground in Iraq and presumably a nearly equal number of aviators. This buildup, which began in 2014, was done with no fanfare because it was hardly what Obama promised and what his voters thought they had purchased. Nevertheless, as ISIS was about to be expelled from Iraq, it would be denied sanctuary and the revenues commensurate with controlling the populous there. This would be a defeat both militarily and psychologically for resurgent militant Islam; a win for Obama and the West. Instead, Obama allowed the most vicious terrorist organization ever conceived two years to recruit and train thousands of terrorists, some of whom were deployed to Western Europe and the US. In this sense, it was something of a defeat for the West.

With respect to Afghanistan, as Obama was preparing to leave office he was managing to lose a war that George Bush's military had already won a decade earlier. Six of Afghanistan's 34 provinces were in danger of falling to the Taliban. As in Iraq, Obama's decision to draw down our troop strength too rapidly, despite the protests of his military advisors, had created the vacuum that was rapidly being filled by our Islamist mortal enemies.

As ISIS was losing territory in Iraq, it had metastasized and migrated to many other countries, including in the West. Obama's slow, incremental approach, combined with his infantile desire show the world he could take our troops out of theaters they had fought so hard to win, had made the world much more dangerous as Donald Trump prepared to occupy the White House.

What Are the Immutable Principles Governing the Fall of Great Civilizations?

On the morning of September 12, 2001, the day after the attacks which killed more people than were lost at Pearl Harbor, I was on my rather long commute to my job in California's "Silicon Valley" when it suddenly dawned on me - we're at war! (By that time, albeit only 24 hours after the first aircraft struck the Tower 1 of the World Trade Center, it was already known that the attackers were alien Muslims and that they had, in all probability, been commissioned by Osama bin Laden.) I next wondered how many other bands of Muslim terrorists there were in our midst poised to launch even more dramatic attacks. How many follow-on attacks would there be and how rapidly would they follow? How many millions of radical Muslims might be plotting our demise and could they use WMD's to do so?

Like many Americans, I presume, I took the 9/11 attacks personally. Seeing my fellow American men and women leap from those 100-story burning buildings caused me to begin a decade-long journey to find out why Muslims attacked us, danced in the streets at seeing the coverage, and what were the underpinnings of their rage. More specifically, because all great civilizations one-day fail, I wanted to find out if, and how, they might destroy us.

This began a ten-year odyssey writing *Lessons from Fallen Civilizations,* where I attempted to discover causation in history, more specifically, the subset of causes which contribute to the

World Trade Center Towers in Lower Manhattan, September 11, 2001

fall of civilizations. I studied and chronicled the fall of five great civilizations, the Greek Polis, Carthage, Rome (in the West), Byzantium (which I refer to as the fall of the Christian Middle East) and the Ottoman Empire. This portion of *Lessons from Fallen Civilizations* begins at the battle of Marathon in 490 BC and ends in 1918 at the end of World War II. The main character, or protagonist, is Western Civilization. With the fall of Byzantium/the Christian Middle East, I chronicle also the rise of militant Islam. And with the Ottomans, I give you the fall of the last great Islamic caliphate. In the final third of the book, I chronicle the rise of what I call *Resurgent Militant Islam*, culminating with 9/11, the war in Afghanistan and what we must do to avoid defeat by the Islamists.

In my research, I emphasized original sources including two men, both ancient Greeks, who are credited with having invented the craft of modern history writing, Herodotus and Thucydides. With respect to Herodotus, he is the first westerner to seek to find causation in human events. From Thucydides, we get the admonition - *those who don't know history are doomed to repeat it*. While I don't disagree with the substance of this bit of conventional wisdom, it is not exactly what Thucydides held. Instead he wrote that history does repeat because human nature changes little, generation over generation. And to demonstrate this phenomenon, he developed a set of Immutable principles which govern the affairs of men. For example, from him we get the indisputable notions:

Weakness invites the domination of the stronger
Power always seeks to increase itself
Necessity is the engine of history

As Thucydides was my mentor, I developed the following set of Immutables which from my research both govern the fall of great civilizations and can be seen to repeat over the millennia. Please note that for each of the following Immutables there is a reference to my original book and a modern corollary.

Note to my reader: The following descriptions of my Immutables appear in the *Introduction* of *Lessons from Fallen Civilizations*. I am adding them here for the benefit of the reader who has not yet read the first book.

Immutable Law # 1

No nation has ever survived once its citizenry
ceased to believe its culture worth saving.

In Professor Victor Davis Hanson's essay, *War Will Be War*, which became the genesis for this book and was the inspiration for this Immutable Law, he wrote, "Themistocles' Athens beat back hundreds of thousands of Persians; yet little more than a century later Demosthenes addressed an Athens that had become far wealthier - and could not marshal a far larger population to repulse a few thousand Macedonians."

Hanson goes on to make reference to the fact that the allied armies of less than 30 Greek city-states defeated the Persian Empire, repelling an army 10 times their size in 479 BC. Yet 140 years later, after losing only one battle to Philip II of Macedon at Chaeronea, in 338 BC, the same Greek city-states ceded their magnificently innovative culture and its associated freedoms to their new Macedonian overlords. In so doing, the Greeks remained a subjugated people for the next 2,400 years.

Modern Corollary

In October 2001, American Special Forces troops, mounted on horseback during a pitched battle with the Taliban in Northern Afghanistan, reported seeing enemy fighters running toward them with their hands in the air and, in the next instant, falling forward, dead in the dirt. They were native Afghan men who had been shot in the back by their foreign Taliban commanders from Pakistan, Chechnya, and Saudi Arabia. The Taliban had conscripted the Afghans with the threat they would kill their families if they did not join the army. The Afghan farmers, shopkeepers, and teachers who had once welcomed the Taliban as their liberators from the Russians now dreaded them.

Immutable Law # 2

In battle, free men almost always defeat slaves.

In 450 BC, Herodotus completed his *Histories* of the great war between the Greeks and the Persians. (It is from his work that we know the details surrounding the battle of Thermopylae popularized in the film *300*). Herodotus, considered the first Western historian, attempted to understand how an army and navy of only 100,000 Greeks were able to defeat an invading army of 1,000,000 men. Herodotus tells us that Pythius, a Greek-speaking subject of the Persian Empire, received an audience with the king. He explained that he had five sons and had sent four of them into the Persian army that was on its way to Greece. Pythius then presented his youngest son to Xerxes and asked if he could keep him. He begged the king to spare his youngest boy from service in the campaign. In a rage, Xerxes had the boy cut in two and each half of the body dumped on either side of the road so that it would send a message to the army as they marched past.

Herodotus spent many years wandering the Mediterranean and recording interviews with soldiers who had fought in the war or who were eye witnesses. He determined why the Greeks defeated the vastly larger army of Persians who were forced to fight and were treated like slaves. The Greeks won the great war because they were free men fighting to retain their freedom. The men who fought for Xerxes were slaves.

Modern Corollary

In 2003, some months after the fall of Baghdad, Paul Bremer, the US interim Governor of Iraq, wrote an op-ed for the *Wall Street Journal*. He stated that Saddam Hussein's army collapsed in a matter of weeks because his Sunni-dominated regime commanded an army of mostly Shiite conscripts who, seeing the US forces moving toward them, deserted and went home. The Shiites, along with the Kurds, comprised the vast majority in Iraq, and hated the ruling Sunni Baathist regime. Once they believed that the US was finally about to liberate their country, they saw no reason to fight and die for their slave masters who lived in gaudy and heavily armed palaces. Saddam

Hussein's army, when confronted with the Western forces, stripped off their uniforms and ran away. They too were slaves and were unwilling to fight for the "Butcher of Baghdad."

Immutable Law # 3

Appeasement of a ruthless outside power always invites aggression.
Treaties made with ruthless despots are always fruitless & dangerous.

Prior to the ultimate conquest of the Greek mainland in 338, Greek allies Thebes and Athens negotiated the *Peace of Philocrates* with Philip II of Macedon. This gave him their acquiescence to the capture and of his invading armies. The principle wrapped inside the Athenians' *Peace of Philocrates* has an immutability and colossal significance that cannot be overstated for twenty-first century West. The attempt by a civilization at appeasement of a ruthless enemy committed to its conquest will accomplish the opposite of the appeaser's wishes. It will always invite attack. Further, the attempt at appeasement will signal that the time to strike is now.

Modern Corollary

For Athens and its allies to allow Macedon to absorb two small buffer states without so much as a diplomatic protest was tantamount to Neville Chamberlain's letter to Adolf Hitler. It forfeited the Western Allies' alliance with Czechoslovakia and freed Hitler to absorb a nearly defenseless neighbor without retaliation.

It was tantamount to Bill Clinton's transfer of nuclear weapons technology to China and tantamount to Bill Clinton's and Madeline Albright's gift of uranium-fueled power plants to North Korea. All are examples of the principle of appeasement, a civilization-threatening tactic.

Immutable Law # 4

If a people cannot avoid continuous internal warfare,
they will have a new order imposed from within.

As the fifth century wore on, leading to the final disappearance of Roman governance in Western Europe, Roman armies continued their long suffering tradition of proclaiming their generals Emperor. While vast portions of Europe and North Africa were being overrun by Germanic invaders, Roman armies continued to fight civil wars headed by challengers to the throne; "usurpers" who would be Emperor. By contrast, the Greek speaking Roman Empire of the East, based in Constantinople, enjoyed an orderly succession of Emperors and managed to survive for nearly a millennium longer than did the West.

Modern Corollary

Soon after President Obama was inaugurated, while the US was conducting conventional war in two theaters, Iraq and Afghanistan, and countless other clashes by American clandestine services, he directed his Attorney General to open criminal investigations against members of the previous administration. These investigations were aimed at senior officials within the Bush (GW) administration who had been tasked with drawing up the guidelines for the interrogation of captured terrorists. The launch of these investigations did not result in actual civil war. Yet, it was unprecedented for an American president to signal, during wartime, that he was prepared to criminalize his domestic political enemies and at the same time offer up a propaganda bonanza to the country's real enemy, resurgent militant Islam.

Immutable Law # 5

When a free people, through taxation, is deprived of
its ability to acquire wealth and property, collapse is presaged.

Crushing taxation imposed upon the middle and lower class Romans contributed to the loss of the Roman provinces of Gaul, Iberia, and North Africa to the German invaders of the fifth century. In the second and first century BC, the Roman Empire had a great expansion when its armies ultimately gained control of lands from Southern Scotland to the Euphrates River. Each spring, at the beginning of the campaigning season, Roman farmers and merchants patriotically sent their sons to serve in the legions. Most of the soldiers' fathers were men of modest means and loyal citizens who could pay their taxes with the produce of as few as two days a month. By the fourth century AD the beleaguered ordinary citizen was ruined by his tax burden, forced to give up most of his produce to the state. Loyalty to the government, composed of wealthy bureaucrats who resided in distant Rome, disappeared. Roman provincials sided with the local German warlord as a method to escape the Roman tax collector.

Modern Corollary

Today, one in seven Americans is unable to adequately feed his family and is forced to collect food stamps. Due to burdensome regulations and taxation, more and more American private enterprises, from shoe manufacturers to technology call centers, continue to move their operations out of the United States. This has made it more and more difficult for US citizens to find gainful employment within the borders of the world's lone superpower. As it was in the last days of the Western Roman Empire, wealthy bureaucrats are provided risk-free cushy employment and lavish retirements by out-of-work citizens who are losing their homes to foreclosure. If this situation is allowed to persist, patriotism and a willingness to defend the country will surely be replaced by a wide-spread *refusal to defend* the central government.

Immutable Law # 6

To hold territory, a state must be populated by those loyal to the central authority. When immigration overwhelms assimilation, the fall is predicted.

In the summer of AD 376, the Roman Emperor, Valens, agreed to allow a very large tribe of Goths to settle in Thrace. He could not have imagined that this decision would set in motion events which led to the Empire's total defeat at Adrianople and, ultimately, the sack of Rome. It was in Thrace, an Eastern province, where the Goths first settled. After they migrated into Italy and sacked Rome, it was the West that granted this very same band of brigands a homeland in southern Gaul, proving to the barbarian world that rebellion would be rewarded.

In the East, the disastrous policy of settling whole tribes inside imperial borders was abandoned. Moreover, the East never lost its devotion to the realm. The citizens of Constantinople proudly proclaimed themselves Romans until the last day of their empire in 1453. During the second, third, and fourth decades of the fifth century the West continued to admit vast numbers of Germans into the Western Empire under the terms of formal treaties while they fecklessly allowed Roman localities to be plundered and, ultimately, subjugated by these same new arrivals. Consequently, in large swaths of the West, Romanization and a commensurate loyalty to the central government continued to disintegrate. The result was that often whole Western regiments failed to report for battle while others even defected to the German side.

Modern Corollary

Today, all across Europe, in Britain, Sweden, the Netherlands, Belgium, and France, there are huge numbers of "no go" zones (over 180 in France alone). These zones are inhabited by unassimilated Muslims where the police will not enter; where Sharia courts, not Euro common law, are increasingly the legal authority; and where homegrown terrorists are cultivated and attacks are planned. In 2008, British Intelligence services were following 2,000 potential terrorists, 200 radical Islamic networks, and 30 active terrorist plots.

Immutable Law # 7

*With the loss of fiscal solvency
comes a loss of sovereignty.*

After the fall of the Roman Empire of the West in AD 476, the Emperor Justinian came to power in Constantinople, the capital of the still existent Roman Empire of the East. With the help of some able generals, Justinian was able to reclaim portions of North Africa and Italy previously lost to the Germanic invasions. His wars of early sixth century AD devastated the Eastern Roman population with crushing taxation. While Roman armies of the East reclaimed portions of the former Western Empire, they were unable to establish a tax base, and the core Greek-speaking population in Constantinople and Anatolia had no more to give. Justinian's hold on his reclaimed territories was tenuous and short lived. The Romans, never again a dominant power, were a people in decline.

Modern Corollary

By 2011, under Barack Obama, the federal budget ballooned to $3.5 trillion dollars with projected revenues of only $2 trillion. Mid-year 2011, US creditors China and Japan began to signal that they had no more desire to invest in our debt. Moreover, American entitlements (Medicare, Medicaid, and Social Security) were projected to be equal to the entire revenue collected from taxes. This meant America would need to borrow or create $1.5 trillion in fiat money before it could pay one soldier's salary or fuel one fighter jet. Spring 2011, the midpoint of Obama's first term in office, polls indicated that 70% of Americans believed that the country was "headed in the wrong direction," a euphemism for decline. That's right - *seven in ten Americans believed the country was in decline!*

Immutable Law # 8

Debasing the currency always
destabilizes the governing authority.

During the late second century and early third centuries AD several Roman Emperors attempted to inflate the Empire's wealth. They recalled some of the outstanding gold coinage, secretly melted it down, and reissued it with leaden cores. In each case, this tactic was nearly catastrophic. The secret became instantly common knowledge among the Roman citizenry who reacted by refusing to accept the Empire's coinage in exchange for goods and services. This, in turn, meant the Emperor could not pay or provision his own armies. Each time the Roman debasement was attempted, all bogus coinage was again recalled and reissued with the lead removed.

Modern Corollary

Since the United States abandoned the gold standard in 1971, the buying power of the dollar has plunged by 96 percent. In 1971 an ounce of gold sold for $35. By 2011 an ounce of gold sells for $1,500. Instead of melting our coinage and adding lead, the US debased its currency by issuing trillions of new dollars. During the Bush (GW) years, 2000-2008, the entire US economy grew in real terms from $10 trillion annually to $14 trillion. This increase was roughly the size of the entire economy of China. Yet, due to trillions of fiat spending and the wholesale debasement of the US economy during the post-Bush years, the International Monetary Fund predicted in 2011 that the size of the Chinese economy will eclipse that of the American economy by 2016.

Immutable Law # 9

When a civilization accepts the propaganda
of its enemy as truth, it has reached the far side
of appeasement and capitulation is nigh.

In 340 BC, the Athenian ambassadors to Macedon, who had negotiated the *Peace of Philocrates*, returned to Athens and addressed the Assembly. They extolled the virtues and peaceful intentions of the warlord to the north, King Philip II. "He has no intentions of conquering Athens and he will be an important ally in deterring Persia from returning to make war on the Greeks," they said. Only Demosthenes stood to warn the men of Athens that they would one day lose their freedom to Macedon. Just two years later, in 338 BC at Chironea, 20,000 Athenians and Thebans were killed by the pikes of the Macedonian phalanxes and by the cavalrymen led by Philip's son, the future Alexander the Great. With that appalling loss of life, all organized resistance to Philip on the Greek mainland of Attica ceased.

Modern Corollary

In the so-called "Arab Spring," revolutions overthrew Muslim dictators with many of the newly liberated Muslims bristling for another war with Israel. In May 2011, coordinated attacks on Israel's northern border by Syria and Hezbollah were joined by calls from the new ruling elites in Egypt to bring the whole of the Arab world against Israel. With the chaos reining across the Middle East, the Iranian regime, who continued to vow to wipe Israel off the map, was emboldened and gained influence across the region. While the storm gathered around our only reliable ally in the Middle East, the president of the Free World took the side of the Muslims. He pretended to be outraged by Israel building some new houses in Jerusalem, its ancestral capital of 2,500 years. He failed to observe that no other country in human history, continuously attacked by its surrounding enemies, could survive if it operated its capital city and foreign policy according to the dictates of those same enemies. The fact that our president made the case that Israel, one of America's most important allies, should do so, represented the far side of appeasement.

Immutable Law # 10

Declining civilizations will always face superior firepower from ascending civilizations because sovereignty is only temporarily uncontested.

In the First Punic War, during the late 240's BC, the Carthaginians grew weary of the long war with Rome and made the decision to decommission much of their fleet and to release from their employ many of their mercenary sailors. This proved to be an extraordinarily ill-fated decision. They voluntarily ceded to Rome, their mortal enemy, naval superiority and mastery of the seas.

Although it would be another 100 years before the fall of Carthage, over this period Rome continued to consolidate its naval superiority and mastery of the Western Mediterranean. This would prove decisive in preventing Hannibal from being provisioned and supplied with new weaponry, especially siege equipment. The Carthaginians' decision to cede military control of the seas made them, a naval trading power, vulnerable to Rome. It was a fatefully bad decision which set in motion the events which led to a huge military advantage for Rome and to the ultimate destruction of Carthage.

Modern Corollary

By 2008, Barack Obama's election year, America had enjoyed air superiority since World War II and it had been 60 years since a single American soldier had lost his life on the ground due to an attack from the air. During the Bush (GW) presidency, the country had proven that it could build a missile defense system capable of mindboggling technological precision and capable of "hitting a speeding bullet with a bullet." Obama stated numerous times during his campaign that he "would not weaponize space" and that he would not deploy a "costly, unproven" missile defense system. Incomprehensibly, in 2009, President Obama cancelled the F-22 Raptor jet fighter, an act which threatened Americans' air superiority. As the eminent military historian, Mark Helprin, apocalyptically put it, "Cancelling the F-22, the most capable fighter plane ever produced, is yet another act in the tragedy of a nation that, bankrupting itself, (is) losing its will to prevail."

The Eleventh Immutable

Immediately after my first book appeared the spring of 2012, I began writing columns about the ongoing war with resurgent militant Islam; a war which I contend we are losing. In my research for those columns, and for this second edition, I've come to believe that my list would be incomplete without the eleventh Immutable below. Like its ten other siblings, it also echoes one of the West's most iconic poems:

Ozymandias

". . . Two vast and trunkless legs of stone
Stand in the desert . . .
. . . And on the pedestal these words appear:
'My name is Ozymandias, King of kings:
Look on my works, ye Mighty, and despair!'
Nothing beside remains. Round the decay
Of that colossal wreck, boundless and bare
The lone and level sands stretch far away."

The poem by the English poet, Shelley, powerfully speaks to the inevitability of the fall of all great civilizations. Having spent over ten years researching why great civilizations fail, it has become abundantly clear to me that remaining a great world power is fraught with perils; seeing there are limitless ways to fail given, as Thucydides warned, the hubristic nature of men. In that regard, with the monumental events which have taken place in the Middle East since the publication of *Lessons from Fallen Civilizations* in the spring of 2012, I have added an eleventh Immutable to the list of those destabilizing factors governing the fall of great peoples. It is a factor which can be seen to threaten the US now and which can be seen to repeat throughout the past several millennia.

Immutable Law # 11

If a great nation fails to prepare and execute a sound military response, it can be destroyed by a much smaller adversary sworn to its destruction.

In *Lessons from Fallen Civilizations* I wrote:

The Roman Emperor, Honorius, cowered in Ravenna, whose defenses amounted to disease-ridden swamps and marshes that surrounded the city. There he was able to make only the feeble gesture of sending a small contingent, some 4,000 troops, to aid in manning Rome's walls. Some sources tell us these troops were ambushed and massacred on their way. But it may very well be that they deserted. No one knows. What is clear is they didn't show up.

Our sources are frustratingly imprecise in what happened in the spring AD 410. What is known is that Roman army regiments located in Italy, many of which were all-Barbarian units loyal to Stilicho, simply disappeared. Certainly some defected to Alaric while other non-Barbarian regiments presumably went home. Meanwhile the Gothic hoards under Alaric continued to grow in size, taking on defectors, runaway slaves, and the displaced farmers and craftsmen unable to earn a living in the collapsing economy…In the summer of AD 410 the city of Rome was sacked for the first time in 800 years. When the news reached the masses, the civilized world was profoundly shocked.

Modern Corollary

At the beginning of his presidency, President Obama, hoping to achieve a rapprochement with Russia, cancelled missile-defense deployments in Eastern Europe which were the result of long and difficult negotiations between the George W. Bush Administration and the governments of Czechoslovakia and Poland. The cancellation set US relations with Eastern Europe on a dismal track because it made their leaders look like fools in front of their own electorates.

As a thank you to Obama for cancelling the missile defense systems, Russia's Putin, in 2015, slapped Obama in the face by selling its S-300 anti-aircraft systems to Iran. These systems would be used to take out Israeli and American aircrafts in a preemptive strike on Iran's nuclear sites.

By 2015, the Obama presidency had come to represent, for the first time in history, an enabler of the proliferation of weapons of mass destruction and the moment in time when the leading military power on the planet could be destroyed by a third-rate military power. In short, through the election of this one man, America had forfeited its margin for error.

Did Obama Waste the American Lives Lost in Iraq & Afghanistan?

Due to Obama's failure to negotiate a sound, workable status of forces agreement with Iraq, and his subsequent pullout of all troops in 2011, he inadvertently allowed the largely beaten remnants of Al Qaeda in Iraq to metastasize into an even more barbaric entity, ISIS. By the fall of 2015, it controlled 30,000 square miles of territory in Iraq and Syria. In October of 2015, a Rasmussen poll found that 46% of US respondents felt the West was losing the war on terrorism.[9] Also in that month, despite the fact that he spent the first 7 years of his presidency declaring that he would be remembered as the one who had ended wars (as opposed to winning them), President Obama declared that he would not be removing all US troops from Afghanistan as he did in Iraq. For all but those of his loyal acolytes, this was a stunning admission that his policies of endless negotiation, appeasement and retreat had been a spectacular failure. It was an admission that in order to prevent future historians from writing that he had lost both wars he would leave some beleaguered US troops in Afghanistan to hopefully maintain the status quo.

But instead of rebuilding troop strength to 20,000 in Afghanistan, as his senior military advisors had recommended, he would reduce their numbers from 10,000 to roughly 5,500 by 2017, when he would leave office. Meanwhile, in 2016, due to both Taliban and ISIS incursions, fighting had broken out in a third of Afghanistan's 34 provinces, with the terrorists threatening Ghazni, a city a short distance from the capital, Kabul.

On March 22, 2016, CNN reported, "Since declaring its caliphate in June 2014, the self-proclaimed Islamic State has conducted or inspired nearly 75 terrorist attacks in 20 countries other than Iraq and Syria, where its carnage has taken a much deadlier toll; those attacks outside Iraq and Syria have killed at least 1,280 people and injured more than 1,770 others."[10]

Note to my Readers

The Building Islamic Reformation: In my first book, published in the spring 2012, I posited that one of the elements necessary for the West to ultimately prevail over resurgent militant Islam would be a massive reformation movement within Islam. Four years later, in 2016, I'm proud to say that in the *Way Forward* section of this book I report there were some powerful forces within Islam calling for, and moving toward, its reformation. The movement had definitively begun.

The Iranian Government Was a Co-Coonspirator in the 9/11 Attacks:
In Lessons from Fallen Civilizations I wrote,

...on July 26, 2001, in a backwater US Embassy in Baku Azerbaijan, a high-level Iranian security official, Hamid Reza Zakeri, walked in. He told the receptionist that he wanted to speak to the CIA because he had information related to the security of the United States. He explained to the station chief, "Joan," that in his capacity as a high-level security officer at Iran's Ministry of Information and Security (MOIS) headquarters, he observed "Arabs" training pilots and briefing them on their appointed targets. He even described models that were on the table in the meeting room—the World Trade Center, the White House, the Pentagon, and Camp David. He told her that the attack was coming from the air that Arab pilots had already left for America and the date for the attack was 9/11/01. Joan called for backup. Several days later a senior CIA officer, "George," arrived from headquarters to debrief the "Baku walk in." He immediately decided that Zakeri was peddling lies, paid him $200, and told him to get out. The information that could have saved 3,000 lives was never passed up the chain-of-command.

On the fifteenth anniversary of 9/11, Joe Lieberman, former senator from Connecticut and Chairman of United Against Nuclear Iran, vindicated me. The *Wall Street Journal* published his article entitled, *Remember Iran's Role in 9/11*. In it he wrote,

Newly declassified letters captured in the May 2011 raid that killed Osama bin Laden reveal how crucial Iran has been to al Qaeda. In a 2007 letter, bin Laden directed al Qaeda not to target Iran because Iran is our main artery for funds, personnel and communication.

Lieberman also reminded his readers that the 9/11 Commission found that "there was strong evidence that Iran facilitated the transit of al Qaeda members into and out of Afghanistan before 9/11 and that some of these were future 9/11 hijackers." Lieberman concludes by wondering why the US-led collaborators, known as the P5+1 countries, could possibly think that giving Iran access to billions of formerly frozen funds, and a clear pathway to deliverable nuclear weapons, was a good idea given its "unyielding desire to destroy our country" and its continuous acts of war perpetrated against us.[11]

Obama's War: What follows here in *Section One* is a selection of published essays that I have written since the publication of *Lessons from Fallen Civilizations*. They are commentaries on Obama's prosecution of our war with resurgent militant Islam over his eight years in office. These essays are not assembled in chronological order but rather thematically; that is, by the Immutable Law which they isolate. They are also not meant to form a comprehensive history of the war prosecuted by Obama. Rather, they are meant to be snap shots of how that war was so terribly mismanaged during the Obama presidency.[12]

If legitimate history is still being written 100 years from now, historians will no doubt marvel at how President Obama single-handedly managed to not only grievously weaken America's military capabilities through economic malaise but also weaken its very resolve to survive. As I wrote in the first book: great civilizations are often destroyed militarily *after* they suffer cultural, moral, and economic decay. Those same future historians will no doubt debate the question - was Obama the "Manchurian Candidate?"

Section One

Published Essays

Published Essays

Immutable Law #11

If a great nation fails to prepare and execute a sound military response, it can be destroyed by a much smaller adversary sworn to its destruction.

Based on the events surrounding our failing war with resurgent militant Islam during the Obama years, I felt compelled to add this new Immutable Law to the original ten which appeared in *Lessons from Fallen Civilizations*. It is a law well understood by Churchill, one he so brilliantly elucidated:

Statue of Sir Winston Churchill

If you will not fight for right when you can easily win without bloodshed; if you will not fight when your victory is sure and not too costly; you may come to the moment when you will have to fight with all the odds against you and only a precarious chance of survival. There may even be a worse case. You may have to fight when there is no hope of victory, because it is better to perish than to live as slaves.

- Winston Churchill

In April of 2016, Jeffrey Goldberg published a major retrospective for the *Atlantic* entitled *The Obama Doctrine*. In it he asked Obama to describe the threats he most worried about in the waning months of his presidency.

His first response was as follows, "As I survey the next 20 years, climate change worries me profoundly because of the effects that it has on all the other problems we face."

This president had it profoundly wrong. The greatest and most immediate threat this country faced in 2016 was an EMP[13] attack.

As you will read in this piece, *Blackout*, a cover story in *The Blaze* magazine, the rogue state of North Korea and the world's leading sponsor of terrorism, Iran, were close allies in the development of nuclear weapons arsenals and long-range delivery systems and also an EMP weapon that could destroy the US with the detonation of one single device.

On April 26, 2016, President Obama told Charlie Rose of *CBS* that he was "setting up a shield that could at least block the relatively low-level threats that North Korea is posing now."[14]

The host, Rose, was either too ill-informed or too inadequate to ask, "But Mr. President, how is it wise to build out our missile defenses now when you cancelled, in 2009, missile defense installations negotiated by President Bush and scheduled to be installed in the Czech Republic and Poland? And why rush to build the shield now when your administration, over the past seven years, cut billions from missile defense development?"

THE BLAZE

SECOND AMENDMENT — The Top 10 Pro-Gun Rights Debate Who Might Surprise You

PROGRESSIVES — The Clinton Machine Is on an Anti-Free Speech Crusade Against Hillary Bios

MIDDLE EAST — Critics of Israel: Younger, Less Educated, Less Informed, More Democratic

TREY GOWDY — Get to Know the Man Tapped to Find the Truth About Benghazi

TRUTH LIVES HERE. | SEPTEMBER 2014

BLACKOUT

WWW.THEBLAZE.COM   VOL. 4, NO.

Our most lethal enemies have the means to knock us out with an EMP weapon and have even conducted test runs. Throw in a new caliphate that's willing to play along, and the threat to the U.S. grows exponentially.

---

13. An EMP, or electromagnetic pulse, is a short burst of electromagnetic energy. This burst is disruptive to electronics and electrical systems.

BLACKOUT
Published in *The Blaze*, September of 2014

When France fell to Nazi's in June of 1940, the Soviet Premier, Molotov, cabled the Nazi Foreign Minister, Ribbentrop, congratulating him on "the splendid victory of the Wehrmacht." In the dark days of 1940, President Roosevelt watched the defeat and evacuation of the British at Dunkirk and the capitulation of the French to the Nazi war machine and confided to his staff that he worried the vast populations of Europe, Eurasia, and the Far East would soon coalesce into one vast global enemy able to "hold a gun to America's head."

The New Axis of Evil

A new consortium composed of America's most maniacal and most powerful enemies, Iran, North Korea, Russia, China, are in the final stages of developing an electromagnetic pulse (EMP) weapon and a clandestine delivery system capable of destroying the US in the blink of an eye. Moreover, there is unmistakable evidence that they have already conducted a dry run of the attack.

In early May of this year Peter Vincent Pry, a member of the Congressional EMP Commission and the Executive Director of the Task Force on National Homeland Security, issued some dire warnings in his testimony before Congress. He stated that a single EMP nuclear weapon, if detonated between 25 and 300 miles over

THE NEW AXIS OF EVIL

RUSSIA

NORTH KOREA

CHINA

IRAN

PUBLISHED ESSAY BY LARRY KELLEY

the lower 48 states, would act like 10,000 lightning bolts and permanently knock out the nation's entire electrical grid. Airplanes would fall from the sky; most cars would be inoperable. Water, sewer and electrical devices would fail simultaneously. Systems of banking, energy, transportation, food production, water, emergency services and even cyber space would collapse. Nine out of ten Americans would die due to starvation, disease, and societal collapse.

Both Russia and China already have advanced EMP weapons, have close trade partnerships and, more importantly, interlocking alliances with the rabid rogue states of North Korea and Iran. China is not only a patron of North Korea but is its agent in Pyongyang's nuclear weapon sales and proliferation. Recently, in the *Wall Street Journal*, Claudia Rosett reported,

> In April the US government offered a $5 million reward for help in apprehending Li Fangwei, accusing him of running a sanctions-violating international procurement network out of China that has sold Iran (North Korean-made) missile and nuclear-related materials. The US has asked China to shut down the network since at least 2006, to no avail.

Additionally, Russia is a patron of the Assad regime in Syria which is Alawite, a sect of Shiite Islam, and is closely allied with Iran. North Korea was quietly helping Syria build a reactor at a remote area, Al Kibar, on the Euphrates River. Nearing completion, the Israelis destroyed it in September 2007. Iran has tested scud missiles fired from freighters on the Caspian Sea. Whenever North Korea tests a nuclear weapon, Iranian nuclear scientists are present for the launch. North Korean nuclear scientists are frequent visitors to nuclear facilities in Iran. And Iran and North Korea have mutual defense treaties. Both Putin and Iran's Khamenei have a common strategic objective - ejecting America from the region. Various Iranian senior officials have stated publicly, "We can see a time when there is no more America." They don't say - no more New York City or D.C. but "no more America."

Thinking the Unthinkable – An Interview with Peter Pry

I asked Pry, "How is it, we can't detect an EMP attack coming at us and probably wouldn't be able to trace its source should we be attacked?"

Pry: "For those of us on the Congressional EMP Commission, our nightmare scenario is a nuclear armed scud missile launched from an unmarked freighter near our shores because it wouldn't give us enough time to detect it with missile defenses. It could come from a direction where we are completely blind like the Gulf of Mexico. And we wouldn't know which nation launched it because it's coming off an anonymous freighter. And because it detonates high in the atmosphere, there's no bomb debris so you can't do forensic analysis the way you would do in a city with glass, steel, and concrete debris to determine where the bomb originated. Essentially, there are no fingerprints."

LK: "You were quoted as stating that North Korea made preparations for a future attack on the US. Can you elaborate?"

PP: "North Korea was likely experimenting with that same scenario I just described to see what it could get away with. Last July there was a tramp freighter they sent into the Gulf of Mexico. On board were two SA-2 nuclear-capable missiles on their launchers. They weren't equipped with nuclear warheads but they were the exact kind of missile you would need to do a short-range, high-altitude EMP attack to take out the US grid.

The only reason we found out about it was because, once they saw that they could bring the missiles in close to the US (off our southern coast), they decided to see if they could get them through the Panama Canal. And that's where we caught them. We found the two launchers under a few thousand bags of sugar."

I asked, "And am I correct that was not the only time that North Korea and its allies tested their capabilities to attack the US with an EMP weapon?"

Pry went on to explain that both North Korea and Iran have extensively tested long-range missiles that were originally designed to launch space satellites but which can easily be adapted to carry and detonate an EMP weapon. Unlike a military ICBM, these space-launch vehicles have a different trajectory. Therefore, NORAD (North American Aerospace Defense Command) ignores them because they look like a missile designed for a peaceful space mission.

Moreover, to further disguise its real objectives, last year North Korea launched such a missile away from the direction of the US and toward the South Pole but then directed it toward us from the South, where they know we have no missile

PUBLISHED ESSAY BY LARRY KELLEY

defenses. It continued to make low-earth passes above us at just the right altitude for an EMP detonation which would blanket the lower forty-eight states with electromagnetic pulses, permanently crashing the grid.

Several months later, in April of 2013, with their satellite, the KSM-3, still making low-earth passes right above us, the US entered into its worst ever nuclear crisis with North Korea. That week, the Iranian regime made numerous threats to destroy the US. Obama responded by flying B-2 bombers (capable of dropping nuclear weapons) over the demilitarized zone and brought Aegis missile defense ships in close to the Korean Peninsula. On April 16, 2013, on the same day the North Korean satellite (with a possible nuclear warhead onboard) was passing directly over Washington D.C., a terrorist attack was mounted on the Metcalf substation outside San Jose, California which provides electricity to the country's high tech capital, Silicon Valley.

Pry said, "This seems to fit in perfectly with the all-out cyber warfare doctrine as defined by the Chinese, Russians, North Koreans and Iranians where they see an operation as not just limited to computer viruses and hacking, but as a combined arms operation where you also use physical sabotage, snipers attacking substations and nuclear EMP attack as all part of the mix."

For a rogue nation, the all-out cyber-attack is therefore the blue-print for defeating a super power, "…hitting us in our Achilles' heel and throwing in the kitchen sink," as Pry puts it.

"So you think April 16, 2013 was a dress rehearsal for just such an all-out cyber-attack?"

Pry answered the question in a measured way you'd expect of a CIA analyst, "The North Koreans and Iranians have a treaty. They're strategic allies. The reason the Iranians were able to launch three of these (low-earth orbit, simulated-warhead) satellites is because they were helped by the North Koreans. The Iranian missile development program is all based on North Korean technology. Are you familiar with the use of the Stuxnet worm which was used to try to disrupt Iran's nuclear program?"

"Yes, but I thought it was an Israeli operation," I answered.

PP: "It was a joint US/Israeli program. Typical of this White House, it took credit. And it's true, we developed the virus but they (the Israelis) inserted it because they have the human connections. The Iranian Revolutionary Guard vowed to take revenge. Given the White House descriptions, it became obvious that the worm was developed in the Silicon Valley. And we know that the Iranians have lots of (sleeper) terrorist cells here inside the US so there are many connections you can easily make."

Hardening Reality – An Interview with Congressman Trent Franks (R-AZ)

The Roman Emperor Theodosius, upon moving his permanent residence and court to the Empire's eastern Capital, Constantinople, ordered a massive expansion of its fortification, expanding its four miles of moat and two concentric inner walls of 20 and 50 feet tall. It proved to be perhaps the most decisive defensive measure in human history. The last vestige of the Roman Empire of the West disappeared in AD 476. Yet the Eastern capital city survived for nearly another millennium, surviving numerous sieges by the armies of Allah, some lasting four years, until it was finally destroyed by Ottomans in AD 1453.

Congressman Trent Franks (Republican, AZ) is the co-sponsor of two bills, the Critical Infrastructure Protection Act and the Shield Act. They are aimed at providing the needed funding and specifications necessary to harden the US electrical grid so as to prevent it from destruction by either a geomagnetic solar storm or an EMP attack from a terrorist state. To borrow a phrase made famous by Dan Ackroyd in the now classic film, *Animal House*, "he's on a mission from God."

I spoke to Representative Franks and began by asking him, "Whether it be by natural causes, such as a solar storm, or a terrorist attack: how is it that we have allowed ourselves to become so vulnerable to a catastrophic collapse of our infrastructure?"

"We have become a society profoundly dependent upon electricity and the grid which supplies it. And consequently, we've engineered ourselves into a place of great vulnerability," he said.

Congressman Franks went on to reiterate Pry's admonition - a successful EMP

PUBLISHED ESSAY BY LARRY KELLEY

attack would be "a worst-case scenario that would certainly threaten American life as we know it." But as he sees it, the good news is that we know how to harden our grid to make it impervious to an attack by the sun or a Muslim rogue state. In fact, we've spent the past several decades hardening our defense-critical assets like the missile defense apparatus and our nuclear triad from an EMP attack. Yet he adds a critical "but…"

"…But we've done almost nothing to harden our civilian grid which our military relies upon for 99% of its electricity needs and without which it cannot affect its mission."

Congressman Franks went on to tell me that he was confident that both houses of Congress would pass some version of his bills; one which will provide the funding, the other the specifications for hardening and protecting the grid from attack. But when I asked him if he thought we'd see passage and that this president would sign them before the end of this year, he replied, "That would be a miracle, given this president's proclivity to avoid reality."

I then asked him, "How long from the passage of your bills would you expect it to take to complete the task of hardening the grid?"

Franks replied, "That's the right question," and went on to say that, although the cost would only add about 20 cents a year to the average rate payer's bill, it would likely take three to four years to complete the hardening of the main components of our grid.

Reflecting upon what Peter Pry had told me a few days prior, I said, "Congressman, I don't think we have four years. Don't you think that, once our enemies see us pass this legislation and begin preparations to harden our grid, it will signal them that the time to attack is now?"

"Ironically, the reverse is also true," he said. "You would think that when we see terrorists (and terrorist sponsoring states) actively threatening the US with nuclear weapons, and Iran's inexorable drive to acquire the bomb, and Pakistan's existing (and vulnerable) nuclear arsenal, this administration would have begun hardening the grid four or five years ago."

Franks explained that the Congress has commissioned 11 major government studies on the EMP threat; from the Department of Defense, to the National Academy of Sciences, to the Energy Regulatory Commission, to Pry's Task Force, all of which reached the exact same conclusion, all were forwarded to the White House in order to alert this president as to the urgency and catastrophic nature of the problem, all to no avail. "He's been completely asleep at the wheel!" he said to me with a tone of utter exasperation.

Might the US Follow the Egyptian Model?

My last question to Congressman Franks was, "Would it surprise you to learn that there were secret discussions inside some senior inner sanctum of the Pentagon regarding the need for a US military coup?"

I followed up my question with explaining to him that I had recently written a four-part series of articles entitled, *Why Will the US Not Go Egypt?* In these stories I reasoned that coming events might cause us to follow the Egyptian model, with one variation. Instead of the US military backing the millions of American protestors filling the streets of Washington D.C. amid massive protests and rioting in D.C., senior Pentagon officials receive actionable intelligence showing that Iran has loaded, onto an unmarked freighter, a launcher and scud missile that is likely nuclear equipped. Moreover, the freighter has left the Persian Gulf and is sailing west. The Pentagon Chiefs then go to the distraught, confused and conflicted Commander in Chief asking for the command to preempt the coming attack. As he did on the night of Benghazi, he fails to give the order and retires to his private quarters. Hours later the Pentagon Chiefs remove the president, order the freighter destroyed, the Iranian and North Korean satellites blown out of the sky and the surgical bombing of Iran's nuclear sites to begin. The following morning, in their initial press conference, the Chairman of the Joint Chiefs of Staff tells the world that they have done this to, "save the lives of 300 million Americans."

Congressman Franks answered my query and long preamble by saying, "I know our senior Pentagon officials are deeply committed to civilian command structure authorized by the Constitution." And, although he said he would be surprised to learn of a secret plan to remove the president even in such a dire circumstance, he said, "almost any scenario seems plausible due to this president's prodigious ability to get nearly everything related to foreign policy and national security wrong."

PUBLISHED ESSAY BY LARRY KELLEY

"Dangerously wrong," I would add.

News from the Front

Since the 2012 publication of my book, *Lessons from Fallen Civilizations*, I've been writing a column, *News from the Front*. It is an on-going chronicle of the war which Norm Podhoretz has dubbed World War IV: the war declared by resurgent militant Islam against the West. Just recently, Nigeria, the Sudan, Malaysia, Saudi Arabia, China, Lebanon, Central African Republic, Libya and Syria have all seen terrorist attacks. What is stunning to consider is that there is a portion of the planet stretching from Indonesia across the Middle East and North Africa to the Atlantic Ocean and, in nearly every one of the countries resident in this vast arc of lands, there are Islamist fighters building their armies and on the attack. Despite this president's now absurd assertion that he had "al Qaeda on a path to defeat," the Rand Corporation recently released a study that found there are now twice as many jihadist fighters worldwide as there were in 2010. The trend is appalling. Researchers who chronicle Muslim atrocities globally for the *Religion of Peace* website posted on July 4th - Muslims have mounted 23,324 deadly attacks since 9/11/2001.

But by far the greatest tectonic shift in this war since the fall of Saddam Hussein's government in 2003 has been the victories won by ISIS in Northeastern Syria and Iraq. Their ranks have grown from the 1,300 fighters who took Mosul to 10,000-15,000. They don't just attack and run, they hold territory. They are well-equipped and well-funded. In defeating Iraqi military contingents, many of whom are Sunni and consequently switched sides, ISIS (which now wants to be called the Islamic State) has captured American Humvees, armored vehicles, even by some reports Black Hawk helicopters. Unlike other terror groups, ISIS is not in hiding. Instead it distributes recruitment videos on YouTube, Twitter, and Facebook. It actively encourages Western would-be jihadists to message them privately and is actively recruiting Europeans and Americans. They are the best funded terrorist state in the modern rise of militant Islam because they have been able to clean out the Iraqi banks in the territory they now control. ISIS means to take Baghdad and move on from there.

The Meaning and Allure of Baghdad

In order to effectively fight this war, it is critical that the West first know our enemies' motivations and understand that the average Muslim derives his identity by reveling in Islam's glorious, albeit distant, past. Most Muslims have been taught that by 749, or a little over 100 years after the death of Mohammad, the first Muslim Caliphate was based in Damascus and ruled the Levant, North Africa, Spain, (what had been two-thirds of Western Christendom), Central Asia and the Indus Valley. But in that year a great revolution occurred. Rebel armies swept across the empire and destroyed the Caliphate, which had lost the loyalty of its subjects due to its failure to conquer Constantinople in two sieges of AD 674-678 and in AD 717-718.

In 762, the new Caliph commissioned the construction of a new capital in Baghdad. It was many years in the making and the result of over 100,000 laborers. In command of East and West trade routes, it was the capital city ruling an enormous land mass until its destruction by the Mongol hoards in 1258. Nevertheless, it was a glorious 500-year reign, a great empire for which the average Muslim yearns for its return. It is not an exaggeration to state that practically every Muslim understands that it is his sacred duty to reestablish the great Caliphate in order to ultimately gain dominion over the unbeliever.

Therefore, the Enemy of My Enemy is Still My Enemy

In 2009, upon his release from Camp Bucca, Iraq, Abu Bakr al-Baghdadi, the sultan of Islam's newest terrorist state, said to his American captors, "I'll see you guys in New York City."

Despite the fact that the Sunni-led ISIS is at war with the Shiite dominated Iraqi army, the fact remains that the Middle East is now swarming with terrorists, some with European and American passports, operating freely and openly inside the new terrorist Caliphate, but also in Libya, Yemen and elsewhere. Why would this president and American military planners assume that the Axis of Evil will not outsource an EMP attack on the US? Why wouldn't the Axis simply hire a stateless, anonymous terrorist cell, Sunni or Shiite, provide it with an unmarked barge armed with a nuclear tipped missile and launcher, sail the barge into the Caribbean, and mount the attack? Wouldn't the current lawlessness of the Muslim

PUBLISHED ESSAY BY LARRY KELLEY

world present a perfect opportunity for a "false flag" operation, where the Axis of Evil would assume plausible deniability, abetted by the full weight of the Chinese and Russian nuclear arsenals?

An argument against the likelihood of such an attack is that the disappearance of the United States would instantly destroy 25% of World GDP, thus causing mass starvation of millions inside China, Russia, Iran and North Korea as well as the third world. But what if the Axis is fine with that? What if its calculation is that a thinning of its own populations would make the imposition of tyranny over its peoples more manageable? In summary, due to so many Americans' inability to vote in their own self- interest, they have lost their collective instinct for survival and are lurching toward this moment in history when America's fate, and that of millions outside its shores, is now in the hands of evil madmen.

H.G. Wells said, "History has always been a race between knowledge and catastrophe."

[End of Essay]

PUBLISHED ESSAY BY LARRY KELLEY

Immutable Law # 1

No nation has ever survived once its citizenry ceased to believe its culture worth saving.

The following is a five-part series I wrote in the aftermath of the two back-to-back Egyptian revolutions. In February of 2011, the world watched the culmination of millions of people flooding into the streets of Cairo and shutting down the operations of their hated government. As mentioned in my *Introduction*, for the first time in their 4,000-year history, the Egyptian people rose up and got rid of their pharaoh named Mubarak and elected a man named Morsi in a free and fair election. Thirteen months later the Egyptians performed the act a second time. Again millions flooded into the capital and, when the military was called out by the hated ruler, the military sided with the people and brought Morsi down. In short, the modern Egyptians showed the world that their culture, which was dominated by oppressive, incompetent government, was not worth saving.

Egyptian President,
Hosni Mubarak

My series of essays entitled, *Why Will the US Not Go Egypt?* was not meant as advocacy but rather was a thought experiment. In it I muse as to what might cause Americans to fill the streets of Washington D.C. and cause the US military to side with the protestors. What might motivate Americans to want take a pause in living within what had become an incompetent, oppressive, formerly-representative republic?

PUBLISHED ESSAY BY LARRY KELLEY

Why Will the US Not Go Egypt?
Part One of a Series of Articles Published by *Freedom Outpost*, July - September 2013

In the Spring of 47 BC, Cleopatra's rivals to the Egyptian throne, her brothers Ptolemy XIII, Pothimus and Achillas, were all dead. The Emperor, Julius Caesar, successfully intervened in the civil war occasioned by her father's death and made Cleopatra the sole heir to the throne; Egypt a vassal state of Roman Empire and her his willing concubine. In so doing, he discovered that Cleopatra was, in many respects, similar to her country: a shame to lose, a risk to conquer and a headache to govern.

On July 10, 2013, Egypt lurched closer to full-blown civil war. As a crowd of Morsi supporters finished their dawn-time prayers, they gathered near the site where their leader was held under house arrest.

Thoughts on July 4th

<u>Thoughts on July 4th</u>

At the declaration, 237 years ago, our founders made it abundantly clear that citizens of a new America would obtain the rights to life, liberty and the pursuit of happiness and that those rights were inalienable; that is, not granted by the state but by God. Moreover, if at any time their government became destructive of those rights, it was not their *right* but their *obligation* to abolish it.

In researching my book, *Lessons from Fallen Civilizations*, I found that not only did the ancient Greeks invent the philosophy of governance we call democracy, but no other civilization untouched by the Greeks ever came up with the notion that "the many should rule the few."

<u>Are We Becoming Greece or Egypt?</u>

A bit earlier in this era of Obama-led western decline, Americans saw the financial unraveling of the insolvent EU PIGS (Portugal, Italy, Greece, and Spain). We watched the televised riots of outraged government pensioners burning businesses and throwing rocks at police on their capital city streets. We learned that they were rioting because their governments couldn't meet its obligations to them and because the German taxpayers were cutting them off. It was the complete vindication of what Margaret Thatcher had so memorably predicted: *The problem for socialists is that eventually they run out of other peoples' money.* Sadly for the Greeks, the people who invented democracy, it became a cliché among the American punditocracy who looked at Obama's soaring debt and America's potential financial collapse, and asked, "Are we Greece?"

Now, given the riots in Egypt, Tunisia, Turkey and Brazil, another much more ominous marker has been laid down, an even more dangerous precedent has been set. This is because these insurrections are massive in size. In Brazil and Egypt, they number in the millions. They also differ because they are made up of a few people who cannot collect on their pensions but they are mostly made up of young people who just hate their corrupt, inept governments.

Through massive marches, demonstrations, civil disobedience, some violence, and with the tacit approval of their military, Egyptians have now deposed their second president in the space of a little over two years.

But perhaps the even bigger story is that they are hardly alone. Insurrections are brewing all over the world. Some of these are the more conventional armed rebellions. The Sunnis are attacking the ruling Shiite majority in Iraq. The civil war in Syria, which has claimed over 100,000 lives, has grown into a proxy war between Iran, Russia, Hezbollah and the Assad regime on one side versus Syrian rebels backed by Saudi Arabia, other Sunni Emirates, and belatedly, the US. (As Senator McCain put it on last week's Sunday political shows, "Our offer to supply the rebels with small arms won't do much against tanks.")

But other insurrections around the world are following more closely the Egyptian model. Over the last several weeks, marches numbering into the hundreds of thousands have spontaneously occurred in Turkey, Tunisia, and, most notably, Brazil. And while these latter three rebellions have some unique defining aspects, they have a common central theme. They are populated by mostly young, middle-class citizens, or students who are potentially middle-class, who are fed up with lousy government that imposes massive and coercive regulations, confiscatory taxation, poor services and presides over general economic misery.

Francis Fukuyama writes in his recent column, *The Middle Class Revolution*:

> In Turkey Brazil, Tunisia and Egypt, political protest has been led not by the poor but by young people with higher-than-average education and income. They are tech-savvy and use social [media] to broadcast information and organize demonstrations. Even though they live in countries that hold regular democratic elections, they feel alienated from the ruling elite.

Fukuyama makes the case that insurrection is going to become common as corrupt, poorly-managed governments fail to meet the expectations of the newly prosperous, technologically equipped middle-class. And he issues this warning: "No politician in the US or Europe should think it can't happen here."

[End of Essay]

PUBLISHED ESSAY BY LARRY KELLEY

Why Will the US Not Go Egypt?
Part Two of a Series of Articles Published by *Freedom Outpost*,
July - September 2013

Toward the end of his second term as America's first president, there were many Americans, some in high places, who beseeched George Washington to remain in office and to essentially become king. Having led the country through seven years of rebellion and eight years of its first freely-elected presidency, he would hear none of a Washington monarchy and quietly and gratefully repaired to his farm at Mount Vernon on the sumptuous banks of the Potomac.

How is Egypt Nearly Ungovernable?

Even in the best of times, Egypt is nearly ungovernable because it is so polarized. Approximately 30-40% of Egyptians are secularists who would like to drag the country more thoroughly into modernity and be governed by a pluralistic western-styled democratic system. Most of this group are well-educated and/or have private-sector business interests. Another 30-40% are mostly less-educated and want to return Egypt to its purer Muslim roots and, as the Muslim Brotherhood advocates, be governed by an Egyptian version of Sharia law. Most of them were Morsi supporters.

Another faction within this faction is the al Nour tribe who are Salafists (radical Islamists who wish to wage violent jihad against Israel and the West). Another 10% are the highly-persecuted Coptic Christians and Shia Muslims. Forty percent of the country is desperately poor and lives on about $2 a day. The educated middle-class expects the government to provide subsidies for virtually everything from bread to fuel (staples they can't afford on their low salaries which they receive from their life-time public sector jobs) and they expect the government to provide for them once they've graduated from college.

Still another faction is the 450,000-man armed forces who comprise a cadre of Egypt's elite but who surprisingly enjoy 94% approval rating in a recent poll. They are seen as the one Egyptian institution that is honest and competent and therefore is entrusted to be the impartial arbiter of popular will. Paradoxically, the military, along with tens of thousands of its retired officers, enjoy a privileged

PUBLISHED ESSAY BY LARRY KELLEY

control of state and private businesses from oil production to the operation of the Suez Canal. And of course, with this month's coup, US aid is once again controlled by the military.

To say that these factions have unsustainable warring interests would be a gross understatement. Jumping into this toxic brew was the newly elected, hapless Morsi/Brotherhood administration. They proved that playing the victim of persecution has nothing to do with attempting to govern an arguably ungovernable country. After just nine months in power, had the Morsi government not received a 48-billion-dollar bailout from Qatar and the Arab Emirates, the country would have gone bankrupt and been plunged into chaos. Morsi's removal from office after just one year in power must be a record in the annals of governmental malfeasance.

Might Phase One of the American Revolution 2.0 Follow the Egyptian Model?

Rational observers of the Middle East would have preferred Egypt, the most populous Arab country, to have made its transition to democracy more smoothly, without mob rule. And it is worrisome to note that other countries, Tunisia, Turkey and even Brazil, are beginning to mimic the Egyptian model where, instead of the electoral process, huge mobs in the street drive regime change. Yet it's not difficult to imagine how regime change loosely following the Egyptian model *might* occur in the US and in the near term.

Consider that a microcosm of it has already played out in the US. Several years ago an investigative reporter published a story about the mayor, city manager, and a few cronies running a small burg, Bell, of Southern California. The story exposed the fact that they were paying themselves high-six-figure salaries with sumptuous benefits while the city fell into Detroit-like decline. Learning of this, the mostly Spanish-speaking citizens of the pot-hole-ridden town stormed the city hall shouting, "Fuera!" (Out!) And it worked. The mayor and his cronies resigned and were summarily run out of town.

Moreover, we can imagine that with the coming implementation of his health care act, Obama's ability to distance himself from the devastating effects of his policies will come to an end. The veil over the eyes of the young Obama voters (24 to 34 year olds) may be lifted. They will feel conned and angry. And because they can't find gainful employment but are still forced to buy a healthcare policy that they don't want and can't afford, this will be the unveiling. As in Egypt, perhaps they will respond by the millions to the Twitter and Facebook driven call to come to Washington and to shut the government down. The goal will not be to make their presence felt but, like the Egyptians, to stay and disrupt the nation's capital until Obama, Biden, Reid and Boehner are forced to resign.

It's not hard to imagine how the movement would spawn millions of 2.0 revolutionaries. They could easily emerge in large numbers from all across the political spectrum. Their ranks would be swollen by thousands of:

- Young underemployed college graduates, working only 29 hours a week at places like Wal-Mart, infuriated at being mandated to buy government-sanctioned healthcare
- Young Obama voters who've lost their company health plans and who believed him when he promised, "If you like your healthcare plan, you can keep it."
- Young doctors who've stopped practicing medicine because they can't charge enough to pay off their college loans
- Young veterans, many of whom lost friends in Iraq and in Afghanistan and are mad as hell at this president for squandering all that they sacrificed
- Social media addicts and fans who are pissed off that their government is collecting and snooping into their communications
- Tea Party members who hold Obama accountable for targeting conservative groups, appalled by his multiple violations of his constitutional authority and oath of office
- Coal miners put out of work by Obama's war on coal
- Pipeline workers unable to apply for work for the Keystone Pipeline
- Out of work union and non-union construction workers who've been replaced by lower-cost illegal aliens
- SEIU and other public and private-sector union members who see Obamacare as a "give back" from the gold-plated health plans they formerly had before the passage of the law
- Misfits and anarchists who like "f___ing with the one-per-centers" and who join the march as a means to have good time trashing DC
- And thousands of others

How Might the US Military Follow the Egyptian Model?

On TV and various other media, the world would witness scenes in DC like those in Cairo where millions of protestors fill the streets surrounding the White House and Congress carrying signs and shouting "Obama, Biden, Go Home! Reid, Boehner, Go Home!" And while the everyday business of DC, law making, back-room deal making, and lobbying grinds to a halt, we can easily imagine our enemies in Tehran and their allies are so emboldened that they not only "cross the red line," but make preparations to threaten the American heartland. Amid the chaos swirling around him, and while watching the wreck of his presidency, it is not difficult to imagine that when this president is briefed about an impending new Cuban Missile Crisis, this time an Iranian Missile Crisis, he fails to act.

On the following day, from an undisclosed bunker, the Chairman of the Joint Chiefs of Staff, flanked by the heads of the other military services makes the following statement,

> We would like to announce to the nation, to the protestors in our Capital, and our allies around the world, that the Obama family is in a safe comfortable compound. They will not be receiving or making phone calls until new elections have been concluded but their children are with them. In short, the US military will attend to their every need until new elections are held and a constitutional government restored.

> Additionally, based on unmistakable intelligence reports, we have determined that an attack on the US homeland was in its final planning stages, that it was operational and imminent. As I speak, the American Air Force in conjunction with our other armed services and allies are conducting bombing raids over Iran and North Korea. All non-essential governmental personnel outside the Pentagon and our intelligences services are, as of now, on furlough until further notice...

[End of Essay]

Why Will the US Not Go Egypt?
Part Three of a Series of Articles Published by *Freedom Outpost*,
July - September 2013

<u>A Tunisian Fruit Vendor and How the Arab Spring Became the Arab Firestorm</u>

Mohamed Bouazizi was a 26-year-old fruit vendor in a rural village of central Tunisia. His father had died when he was three and from the age of 10 he had worked for less than $100 a month to support his mother and siblings. He hoped to save enough to replace his push cart with a motorized van.

His customers loved him. He would even give free fruit to very poor families. But he was daily bullied by corrupt police who demanded bribes and confiscated his produce when he couldn't pay. On December 17, 2010, the police approached him and demanded his vendor's permit when no such permit is required in Tunisia. He had no money to pay the shakedown and in fact had borrowed the money for this day's offering.

Shortly thereafter an even more corrupt city official, Faida Hamdi, confronted him. She spat in his face, insulted his dead father, and told him he would be fined. Then she overturned his cart, ruining his fruit. With no way to repay the loan or pay the fine, Mohamed believed his life was over. So he went to the steps of the governor's office, doused himself with gasoline and shouted, "How do you expect me to make a living?!" then lit a match and set himself ablaze.

Over 5,000 people attended Mohamed's funeral. In the days and weeks that followed, millions of Tunisians formed up into massive, somewhat-permanent and immovable demonstrations that were so wide spread that in the space of only one month Tunisian president Ben Ali and his family fled to Saudi Arabia. But the rage against corrupt governance was just beginning.

Over the next 30 months (from January 2011 through July of 2013) massive demonstrations or outright armed rebellions broke out in Libya, Morocco, Bahrain, Egypt, Yemen, Syria, Turkey and, surprisingly, even Brazil. Initially, from the insurrectionists' point of view, their tactics were working well. To use a baseball analogy, they were batting a very respectable 375. The insurrectionists

PUBLISHED ESSAY BY LARRY KELLEY

had achieved total regime change in three out of eight countries. In fact, the Egyptian mobs affected regime change twice in that period, surely a speed record in the annals of modern revolutionary movements. Yet nothing is settled in Egypt and disastrous scenarios impend.

Broadly, there is a sense of gloom descending over much of the Middle East. During the weekend of July 23 and 24, 80 unarmed protestors were shot and killed by Egyptian military forces. In Iraq, Sunni versus Shiite violence results in the commonplace bombing of Mosques, police stations, and schools. Jordan, a staunch American ally, is in danger of being destabilized. And in Syria, over 100,000 rebels, civilians, and loyalists have been killed with no good end to the civil war in sight. Beginning with the self-immolation of Mohammad Bouazizi, over the lands where many in the naïve Western press saw a budding Arab Spring, an Arab firestorm is raging.

Why Wouldn't the Rage of the Fruit Vendor Come to America?

The mainstream press and their allies who inhabit the unholy alliance comprised of utterly corrupt politicians, a vast unelected governmental bureaucracy, public and private sector unions, and the enormous and growing dependent class are seemingly incapable of imagining that insurrectionist movements similar to those in Tunisia, Libya and Egypt would ever come ashore in the US. But the probability of this occurring depends on the level of rage experienced by our American fruit vendors, the young 20-to-30-something citizens who are soon to realize just how badly they've been conned. They will doubtlessly remember that when Obama was peddling Obamacare he promised to "bend the cost curve down" and "if you like your healthcare plan, you can keep it."

There are now 21 million under-employed 20-to-34-year-old Americans living with their parents. It is not difficult to imagine that the sticker shock associated with next year's implementation of Obamacare could be the catalyst, the tipping point that will drive millions of them to follow the example of Tunisia and Egypt. It's easy to imagine them leaving their parents' basements to march on Washington when they learn that that they were not only conned but that their shameful government will now force them to buy expensive health insurance that they don't want and can't afford. Imagine their reaction when they learn that Obama has, unconstitutionally, granted big business a one-year exemption from his own onerous law while they, the young under-employed, will be forced to comply.

This President as Pusher

Support for his awful law is even now collapsing. So, in a desperate attempt to get as many Americans hooked on tax-payer subsidized healthcare as quickly as is possible, Obama has brazenly and unconstitutionally not only suspended the employer mandate for one year, but also the income verification bureaus (Both are impeachable offenses. The president does not have the authority to selectively enforce existing laws). These bureaus will eventually be manned by the same hated IRS that will be in charge of determining whether an American earns little enough to get free healthcare or earns too much and thus will be forced to buy a government sanctioned policy.

Next year, one can easily see that among the young under-employed there will be massive non-compliance with, and defrauding of, the Obamacare individual mandates. It seems likely that huge numbers of our young will simply claim to be under the requisite income in order to get free healthcare and therefore will avoid having to buy a government health policy or pay the fine.

The Obama/Saul Alinsky Corollary

The irony here is rich. Before Obama entered politics, he was a Saul Alinsky community organizer. In the 1940's, Alinsky was a Chicago-based radical organizer who preached that the way to gain power was to overwhelm and bankrupt capitalism by, among other means, flooding the system with strikes, phony welfare recipients and fake voters. Hillary wrote her master's thesis about him, extolling him as one of America's great statesmen. Alinsky is given credit by those who study the history of the American Left as having unified all its disparate elements, the Maoists, Trotskyites, Leninists, communists, fascists and anarchists by telling them not to worry about what system comes next. Simply be about "destroying capitalism and taking power."

The Alinsky method could easily come full circle on Obama. For America's young and underemployed, their honeymoon with Obama's emerging police state will likely come crashing down, perhaps as early as next year. Due to massive non-compliance, the overwhelmed system will be starved for cash. And with our

PUBLISHED ESSAY BY LARRY KELLEY

Orwellian government's enormous data collection capability in the hands of its unelected, unaccountable bureaucrats, the young, struggling-to-be-middle class, will soon realize it is they who are the target to be fleeced, and it is they who will be forced to pay for the healthcare of Obama's favored constituencies. Over their social media, stories will abound of non-compliant young Americans who are quickly found, fined or jailed. Their collective rage could be uncontainable.

Meanwhile, the targeted young will also find out that various Obama-privileged groups, such as Congressional staffers and even the new foot soldiers of American oppression, the IRS, will be exempted from the healthcare mandates and fines. This will further enflame their rage. Due to the huge non-compliance by the young and the need to shift pension-guaranteed healthcare costs from bankrupt cities like Detroit to US taxpayers, it's also easy to foresee that the mandate costs and fines will necessarily skyrocket. The need to use the Obamacare law as a mechanism to bail out failed Democrat fiefdoms, that is, bankrupt cities and even whole states, will put the Alinsky method on steroids. And with it, the rage of the American fruit vendor could easily be at hand.

[End of Essay]

The American Revolution 2.0 - A Thought Experiment
Part Four of the Series *Why Will the US Not Go Egypt*,
Published by *Freedom Outpost*, July - September 2013

Last September 11, 2012, al-Qaeda affiliated jihadists attacked our consulate in Benghazi, killing our ambassador and three others who disobeyed orders to stand down and died trying to defend him and his staff. Yet on the night of the attack, Obama failed to order a rescue mission, went to bed, and when he awoke flew off to Las Vegas for a campaign stop as if nothing out of the ordinary had happened. The attack had been an act of war. The president's actions were very likely a dereliction of duty, an impeachable offense, and had the effect of making elements of his own military begin to conspire against him.

Obama won reelection six weeks later by constantly bragging, in every campaign speech, that "bin Laden was dead" and "al Qaeda was decimated and on the run." But by mid-July of 2013, based on intercepted communications between al Zawahiri (al Qaeda's new leader) in Pakistan and the Yemeni leaders of al Qaeda in the Arabian Peninsula (AQAP), Obama ordered 21 embassies in the Middle East be shut down and evacuated for a week. The members of Congress who were briefed on the impending attacks would not reveal what they were: airline bombs, a dirty bomb, etc. A senior US official anonymously and ominously told *ABC*

US President, Barack Obama, speaking at the Chicago Hilton

PUBLISHED ESSAY BY LARRY KELLEY

News, "Al-Qaeda jihadists are planning a calamitous attack, one that is going to be big and *strategically* significant."

In the Cold War, when national security experts spoke of *strategic* as opposed to tactical nuclear weapons, the word carried huge weight. In the case of a weapon, it refers to one *designed to destroy the military potential of an enemy.*

The Egyptian Model and Regime Change in the US

On August 31st the *AP* reported from Cairo:

> Reeling from a fierce security crackdown, the Muslim Brotherhood brought out mostly scattered, small crowds Friday in its latest protests of Egypt's military coup. While the remnants of the Brotherhood's leadership are still able to exhibit strong coordination from underground, the arrests of thousands of its supporters and members - and the fear of more bloodshed - have weakened its ability to mobilize the streets.

> On that same day, the largest single Cairo demonstration, numbered 10,000 people, amassed outside the presidential palace. However, the majority of protests Friday were smaller than in the past, consisting of several hundred protesters or fewer around the country.

Egyptian mobs in Tahrir Square, Cairo

In short, the Egyptian Revolution 2.0 appears to be holding. In a stunning series of events, Egyptians by the millions flooded the country's central squares and, in 2001, brought about the abdication of their Dictator for Life, Hosni Mubarak. Next, the first freely elected leader in Egypt's 6,000-year history, Muhammad Morsi, assumed office. But in less than 24 months millions of Egyptians returned to the streets and, with the help of the military, deposed the hapless Morsi regime.

The role of the Egyptian military is paramount. Egypt is rife with corruption. Virtually every Egyptian knows this. But the military has a 90% approval rating. Therefore, because the Egyptian military intervened on the side of the marchers in the removal of Mubarak and Morsi, both regimes fell with relatively little loss of life.[15]

The Egyptian model for regime change involves two elements:
1. millions of angry disaffected citizens flooding and staying in the citadels of power, demanding that the regime leave office and,
2. a military which sides with them

Given the stunning success of the Egyptians, two regime changes in 24 months, I would ask - now that we have seen insurrections by disaffected youth in Greece, Turkey, Tunisia, Egypt, Brazil and Chile, why won't the Egyptian model come ashore in the US? All the underpinning elements are present here.

Going Egypt in Chile

You undoubtedly didn't hear about the recent youth insurrections in Chile. Due to social media, youth insurrection is becoming a global phenomenon. A month ago my eldest son and I had an eight-hour layover in the Santiago airport on our way back to the States. On overhead television monitors in our airport restaurant we watched live television coverage of pitched battles between riot police and angry throngs of students fighting in the capital's streets. While neither side was firing guns, they each were armed with clubs and truncheons and the fighting was desperate and intense. We saw dramatic footage of large throngs of students beating back outnumbered police and individual footraces ending in a policeman tackling a student, clubbing him mercilessly and dragging him off to the waiting

---

15. There were human rights abuses committed by the military against his Muslim Brotherhood supporters in Morsi's deposition. But relative to what has occurred in Syria and even our own revolution, the loss of life was comparatively small.

PUBLISHED ESSAY BY LARRY KELLEY

paddy wagon.

I asked our waiter why the students were rioting. "They say that the education is too expensive and it is useless because there are no jobs," he told us.

The American Tipping Point

It's impossible to know what might be the tipping point that would send millions of Americans into DC, committing massive civil disobedience, blocking the entrances to the Capital and the White House, shouting "Obama, Biden, Reed, Boehner go home!"

But the fact remains, young Americans are suffering a similar situation as their counterparts in Chile or Egypt. Young American college graduates, most of who voted for this president, have every right to feel betrayed. Due to lousy government policies and the impending implementation of Obamacare, the real unemployment rate among young Americans under 25 is over 20%, if you count those who are so discouraged that they have stopped looking for work. But it's much worse than that. Due to the perverse incentives of Obamacare and our regulatory state now on steroids, over 70% of the jobs created during the last 12 months are part-time jobs. This negates the American dream for millions of our young.

So let's do this thought experiment: Imagine a recent college graduate, Bob, who feels that he's worked hard and mostly played by the rules but finds that, in order to pay off his student loans and to afford a crappy studio apartment, he's got to work two part-time jobs at Wal-Mart and Taco Bell. Now imagine that Bob finds out that Obamacare is going to force him to buy a healthcare policy he doesn't want or he will be forced to pay a fine. Bob thought, based on all that Obama said, his healthcare was going to be free! On top of that, he learns that there is no global warming but his government has made gasoline prices so high he can't afford to drive or own a car.

Now let's imagine Obamacare is fully implemented and Bob gets a call from an IRS agent letting him know that his pay will be garnished if he doesn't pay the over-due fine he owes for not buying a government-sanctioned healthcare policy. And let's also imagine that Bob realizes that the threatening IRS agent, along with his Marxist college professors who taught him to hate his own country, earn much more money than he does while working far fewer hours and will retire with gold-plated pensions that Bob has no hope of acquiring. If millions of young Americans come to realize the enormity of their betrayal, won't that be the tipping point?

<u>So How Might the Military Side with the Millions of Insurrectionists?</u>

In July of this year, at the Panama Canal, Panamanian drug agents boarded a North Korean cargo ship returning to Korea from Cuba. On board they discovered Cuban SA-2 surface to air missiles. While his crew desperately fought the boarding agents, the North Korean captain committed suicide.

Passenger aircraft flights between Tehran and Caracas Venezuela continued to increase. Once the Iranian aircrafts are on the ground, satellite photos reveal that the aircrafts contain no passengers. Instead, they are met by forklift trucks which off-load vast numbers of unmarked containers onto awaiting government trucks and are driven deep into the interior.

If we see millions of disaffected Americans flooding the streets of DC, we can also imagine two other existing phenomena that could cause the American military to intervene in the protestors' behalf.

The first is, as I wrote in my previous column: Obama is losing his ability to be the Commander in Chief. Major General Robert Scales, former commandant of the Army War College, recently wrote a scathing article for the *Washington Post* in which he describes the growing discontent among military leaders regarding Obama's reckless combination of dithering and bravado. And his abject failure to order a rescue mission in Benghazi.

Add to that, in order to inflict maximum pain during the government shutdown, the administration ordered the National Park Service to fence off the World War II Memorial and other public monuments in the nation's capital, threatening those who entered with arrest. This closure meant World War II veterans who had traveled great distances were initially denied access to the memorial. Many in the military were certainly outraged.

PUBLISHED ESSAY BY LARRY KELLEY

PUBLISHED ESSAY BY LARRY KELLEY

With his loss of authority over his own military as a backdrop, we can imagine the consortium of Russia, Iran, North Korea and Cuba watching the chaos swirling around this president and deciding this was the time to act. And it is this that initiates a bloodless but necessary coup.

*Egyptian General,
Abdul el-Sisi*

As did Egypt's General Abdul el-Sisi, we can imagine that Chairman of the Joint Chiefs of Staff would inform Americans and the world there would be an interim executive branch and acting president appointed to rule until the Congressional and presidential elections were held and concluded. Moreover, every member of Congress would need to stand for reelection whereas the fate of the current president and his vice president would necessarily need to remain vague. And with that announcement the millions of protestors gather up their camping gear, pick up the trash around their capital city and go home. And with that, the enormity of what they had done would only begin to sink in.

[End of Essay]

Operation Free Persia
Part Five of the Series *Why Will the US Not Go Egypt*,
Published by *Freedom Outpost*, July - September 2013

In the same week the nation watched the Obamacare rollout, crash and burn, American supremacy in the Middle East continued to implode. Our allies signaled they had had enough of this president's relentless propensity to court enemies while snubbing friends. Among this administration's myriad of foreign policy blunders, the Syrian debacle continued to degrade our ability to defend our national interests and influence world events.

The Saudi's Dump Us

Last month Prince Turki al Faisal, former Saudi Ambassador to the US, told the London press, "The current charade of international control over Bashar's chemical arsenal would be funny if it were not so blatantly perfidious and designed not only to give Mr. Obama an opportunity to back down, but also to help Assad butcher his people."

This week, the Saudi Intelligence Chief, Prince Bandar, decided to limit his ties with the CIA in training Syrian rebels because he preferred to work more closely with the Jordanians and the French. It truly is a sad day for America when one of our supposed Middle Eastern allies finds the French socialists more battle-ready than are we. Even more importantly, our lack of influence in Syria can have real catastrophic repercussions because it will mean that Saudi's will not be constrained by us to keep surface-to-air missiles out of the hands of the Sunni rebels, their allies. In an increasingly dangerous world, this failure can lead to catastrophes; to terrorists bringing down civilian aircraft as they did with TWA 800 over Long Island in 1996.[16]

The Saudi's have come to learn the consequences of America electing a Marxist president. They have been pressing him even harder than the Israelis for the US to take out the Iranian nuclear sites. But, as the Editorial Board of *Wall Street Journal*

---

16. Amazingly, like Benghazi, the downing of TWA 800 was an act of war carried out by terrorists, using a surface-to-air missile, a couple months before a presidential election and covered up by a sitting president.

PUBLISHED ESSAY BY LARRY KELLEY

puts it, "Now Riyadh is realizing that Mr. Obama's diplomacy is a journey with no destination, that there are no red lines, and that any foreign adversary can call his bluff."

American and Iranian Regime Change after the Bombing

As described in my previous articles in this series, it seems plausible, or at least a possibility, that our betrayed youth, those who mostly voted for Obama and who can't find a job but who will be forced to buy an over-priced healthcare policy will, at some point, come to Washington and, following the Egyptian model, attempt to close down the government. And it seems also plausible that the worldwide coverage of millions in the streets of DC might signal to the consortium of our enemies, Russia, North Korea, Venezuela and Iran, that the time to strike is now.

As we have witnessed in Egypt, the Egyptian military sided with crowds in the streets and twice removed a head of state in the space of 24 months! So, if America was confronted with mortal danger and Obama was too paralyzed to act, might the Egyptian model not be operative for the next American Revolution 2.0? Might not the military step in?

What follows here is an excerpt from my book, *Lessons from Fallen Civilizations*. It is a conjectural look into the future, where the new interim president, appointed by the American military, realizes that although Iran has lost most of its weapon making capacity after the bombing, the regime is still a mortal threat to both Israel and the US.

Operation Free Persia - An Excerpt from *Lessons from Fallen Civilizations*

…It will be the first time any power has ever attempted to conquer a rogue state armed with nuclear weapons. Yet, he judges the prospect of doing nothing as even more dangerous. In preparation for the launch of Operation Free Persia, the new president and a very small group of his closest advisors have been meeting and communicating in total secrecy with Iranian/American expatriates' former diplomats from the Iranian Foreign Service. Each member of the president's team of Iranian expatriate advisors is in constant touch with his or her network of resistance leaders poised to begin the fighting inside Iran.

The US Navy has begun to selectively blockade Iranian shipping by searching ships for prohibited materials destined for Iranian ports. Through intense diplomatic pressure, the US has greatly slowed the regime's ability to import refined petroleum. All known shipments from North Korea are being interdicted. The US and European allies have seized and shut down nearly all Iranian front groups. Dubai and the Arab Emirates have frozen many of the Mullahs' foreign bank accounts. Most US allies have liquidated their Iranian investments.

While the world holds its collective breath, few nations, even in the Middle East, have condemned the US and its allies for their actions against the regime. Meanwhile the Iranian economy is collapsing. Over 50% of the population is unemployed. Many of the elite Iranian Revolutionary Guard (IRG) are secretly communicating with Iranian resistance groups inside the country and letting their contacts know that when the fighting begins, they will switch sides. Police protection is collapsing. There is widespread looting.

The new president's plan to aid the Iranian revolution is built around the fact that the center of Iran is ringed by disaffected, mostly Sunni, minority provinces: the Kurds in the northwest, the Azeri's in the north, the Arabs in the southwest province of Khuzestan, and the Baluchis in the southeast.

Political map of Iran and surrounding countries

PUBLISHED ESSAY BY LARRY KELLEY

For many months, rogue elements within the US Intelligence and Special Forces, based in Afghanistan to the east, in Iraq to the west, and even from Turkmenistan to the north, have been supplying revolutionary commando brigades with ultra-secure satellite phones, weapons, ammunition, money and rations.

In turn they are mounting incessant attacks on government targets and escaping back across the border. Iranian Kurds entering from the northwest have launched the most attacks. But in the lawless southeast province of Baluchistan, the attacks have been the most lethal and dramatic. They even attacked Iranian President's motorcade, killing one of his bodyguards, and waged an all-out gun battle with Iranian security forces in the center of the Baluchi capital city of Zahedan.

Twenty-three-year-old Abdol Maleck Rigi has emerged as the commander of the Baluchi revolutionaries. The CIA arranged for him to be interviewed by *Voice of America* that was transmitted into Iran in Persian. The program introduced him as the "leader of the Iranian resistance movement."

One morning, when the new president arrives at the Oval office to meet with his national security advisors, he is handed a report with alarming news from his CIA Director. The Iranian missiles, photographed by satellite as they were loaded onto huge trailers and moved south by military truck transport toward the southern Iranian port of Bandar-e-Abbas, are now missing. Although the new president has greatly improved intelligence gathering operations inside Iran, the administration is still only guessing if the missiles, seen in transit, are nuclear armed and if they will be assembled as part of an impending new EMP attack. At the end of the meeting the new president tells his advisors to launch Operation Free Persia the next night.

The plan is to send in units comprised of US armed Iranian commandos who have formed camps inside Turkmenistan, Afghanistan and Iraq. They will lead fellow Farsi-speaking expatriates, from Europe and the US, and join with Special Forces and CIA paramilitary officers disguised as Iranian revolutionaries. The Americans have been ordered not to be taken prisoner under any circumstances - this is a do or die mission.

As the first units cross into the country from the north, east and west, a signal is sent via secure satellite phones to other teams of commandos and civilian revolutionaries inside Tehran and other key Iranian cities. It is time to attack government installations, fire smuggled rockets into weapons depots and blow up bridges and key roads leading away from military installations to disrupt troop movements. Additionally, they send out the call to encourage every citizen to join in the revolution and come out into the streets to fight the Basiji (the regime's thug force) with rocks, bottles, and any other homemade weapons they can fashion. Their call-to-arms is to create chaos, set fires on military and government buildings, disrupt military movements and overwhelm the regime.

Under the cover of darkness, the first units coming in from the outside, wearing Chinese-made night vision goggles, will attack weapons depots and other military storage facilities where Iranian Revolutionary Guard (IRG) units are billeted in border towns. Before engaging in combat they will attempt to make contact in Farsi and convince the Iranian soldiers to surrender and switch sides. Once those border installations have been taken or neutralized, mobilized units of armored hummers will cross and begin moving a second wave of reinforcements, men and material, inland.

The plan contains numerous layers of contingency plans. The president knows that the Mullahs, seeing the regime in its death throws, may elect to launch their nuclear missiles at Europe, Israel or even at the East Coast of the United States. For missile defense, the Navy has strategically stationed every available Aegis (ship-based) interceptor vessel in the US arsenal. Roughly half the Aegis ships are in the Eastern Mediterranean to defend Israel and Europe with the balance arrayed in the Atlantic to defend the Eastern Seaboard of the US.

In the Persian Gulf, a carrier group is ready to engage the Iranians should the regime begin to turn its airpower upon its own citizens. Massive American air and naval powers stand ready to launch several hundred aircraft and cruise missiles at military targets. Bombers with tactical "bunker buster" nuclear weapons are poised to take out hardened underground nuclear weapons centers.

The president's plan provides the means for the Iranians to conduct the overthrow of their own county in a manner that allows the world to see it as legitimately their revolution. The plan is conceived to prevent the conflict from escalating to include Russia, China, Pakistan or India. In his final consultations with Pentagon officials regarding the US missile defense systems, he repeatedly asks, "Is the

PUBLISHED ESSAY BY LARRY KELLEY

system fail safe?" To which he receives the answer, "We hope so."

Four days later, having slept very little, the bleary-eyed new president stands before the television monitors inside the war room in the basement of the White House. Tech-savvy Iranians have posted to YouTube scenes of unimaginable jubilation in the streets of Tehran. He looks up to see choppy footage shot by Iranian hand-helds of just released prisoners streaming out of the notorious Evin prison into the arms of their tearful families.

Next, there is footage of the first NATO troops arriving to aid in securing the military installations. Iranian women are singing and dancing in the streets and there is not a head covering to be seen anywhere in the crowds.

The new president's thoughts turn to President Kennedy on that Sunday morning October 28, 1962, the day Khrushchev agreed to remove the Soviet missiles from Cuba. On the following day, hundreds of thousands of Iranians return to the streets of Tehran. Singing ancient Persian nationalist hymns, they march solemnly toward the city's central mosque and watch as it is consumed in flames. Fourteen centuries of Arab/Islamic rule over Persia has come to an end.

[End of Essay]

Immutable Law # 2

In battle, free men almost always defeat slaves. (Herodotus' law)

As I wrote in my *Introduction,* in the fifth century BC, Herodotus, who is considered the father of western historiography, asked the question: How was it that a disunified collection of Greek city states, which could only muster an army of 100,000, defeated an invading Persian army of 1,000,000? His answer - free men, fighting to

Statue of philosopher Herodotus in Vienna

protect their homeland, will almost always defeat slaves.

By the spring of 2016, the Kurds, fighting to protect their native homeland in northern Iraq, had showed they could defend their lands and even take territory from a much larger and better armed ISIS invading force. And while the ISIS invaders were not exactly slaves (but deserters were summarily crucified or beheaded), their desire for booty and sex slaves was no match for the Kurdish fighters who were fighting to protect their homes, their neighbors and families.

In this series, I proposed that the US, having lost its influence in Iraq, should not only request military basing rights in Iraqi Kurdistan, but recognize a free and independent Kurdistan should the Kurds grant Israel's right to exist. This, combined with the Kurds' current embrace of full women's' rights, could make a major contribution in the effort to bring about the coming Islamic reformation. And finally, a fully supported free Kurdistan could begin the process of destabilizing the Iranian regime next door.

PUBLISHED ESSAY BY LARRY KELLEY

Create a New Kurdistan & Destabilize Iran

Part One of a Series of Articles Published by *Townhall.com*, August 2014 - January 2015

In 627, Mohammad's earliest biographer, Ibn Ishaq, records that his army held off a 25-day siege by Mecca's ruling tribe, the Quraysh, at his redoubt near Medina. When the prophet learned that the Meccan army included some of the city's Jews, he ordered the attack of a nearby, largely defenseless, Jewish settlement and tribe, the Banu Qurayza. While the prophet was overseeing the decapitations, "He caught a glimpse of Rihanna, a beautiful Jewish woman, whose husband and father were beheaded before her eyes just hours earlier. Muhammad asked her to become his wife. She refused. So he took her as his unwilling slave and concubine.

The Horror that is ISIS

As the world is horrified to learn that innocent Iraqis, even little girls, are being beheaded and women are being captured as sexual booty by ISIS, one could easily ask, "What inspires such cruelty?" The answer is - the Prophet, Mohammad. As I explain in my book, *Lessons from Fallen Civilizations*, every Muslim learns from childhood that there is nothing about the life of the Prophet that can be judged. Rather his is the life by which all others are judged.

ISIS is now a far more brutal and, in every category, capable terrorist organization than was bin Laden's al Qaeda when it mounted the 9/11 attacks. It controls a land mass the size of New England, has emptied banks, has control of commerce including oil production, has captured American-made sophisticated weaponry including 30 M1 tanks and howitzers and has absorbed Iraqi military leaders including Sunni generals who commanded Baathist troops under Saddam Hussein. It has even gotten control of uranium which could be used to construct "dirty bombs."

ISIS is also openly threatening to attack the US. Its mercurial leader, Abu Bakr al Baghdadi, upon his 2009 release from the Camp Bucca prison in Iraq, said, "I'll see you guys in New York City." What worries defense planners most is the fact that ISIS is not just recruiting wannabe jihadists from all over the Muslim world but from Europe and the US also. The nightmare scenario is that hardened

ISIS fighters, traveling on European and American passports, will return to their adoptive countries armed with the ingredients for, and the knowledge to, detonate crude WMD's.

Meanwhile, America's Commander in Chief is playing golf and James O'Keefe dressed up as Osama bin Laden walks across the Rio Grande and into the Texas interior without ever even seeing a border control agent. It seems that what needs to happen now is that a coalition of leaders from the Defense Department, Homeland Security and our intelligence agencies must lay out a concise doomsday scenario which will scare the hell out of Obama and scare him out of his faculty-lounge, capitulationist pacifism. It needs to be delivered in private and in person to the president. Perhaps Joint Chiefs Chairman Martin Dempsey would be a good messenger as he has finally begun to speak openly of a strategy to "initially contain, eventually disrupt and finally defeat ISIS over time."

The Kurdistan Grand Strategy

The advance of ISIS, and the chaos engulfing the Iraqi government, dramatically showcase this administration's disastrous foreign policies; but, strangely, offer the US the chance to once again seize the initiative while, at the same time, capture the minds and hearts of a significant portion of the Muslim world - the Kurds.

Kurdish soldiers search a house in Arbil City, Iraq

PUBLISHED ESSAY BY LARRY KELLEY

The Kurds were the first indigenous population to be attacked with chemical weapons by their own government. Ever since President Bush the Elder installed the no-fly zone over Northern Iraq after the cessation of hostilities in the first Gulf War, the Kurds have been extremely trustworthy and grateful allies of the US (They also have active trade and warm relations with Israel).

This president and his leftist lap-dog media must first quit this stupid talk of "war weariness." How wearying will it be if we wake up one morning to learn that WMD's have been simultaneously detonated in numerous American cities? America needs a reliable, permanent base in the Middle East for nearly the same reason we still have bases in South Korea. Even if we can gain the collective resolve to defeat ISIS, there will be, for the foreseeable future, unremitting new threats emanating from the region. Therefore, America needs a major military presence in the Middle East because, as we observed in the second Iraq war, it is far better to be battling the jihadists in Fallujah than in New York City. In short, an intelligent approach to national security would dictate that we need to be gathering intelligence on the ground in the heart of the Middle East, partnering with friendly allies and have the ability to respond quickly to destroy growing terrorist cells. Good intelligence and overwhelming military capability are what is needed to stamp out terrorism, not passivity and talk.

The rise of ISIS has been a huge distraction from the even bigger threat from resurgent militant Islam: Iran. The theocracy ruling Iran has been at war with the US since it overran our embassy in 1979. It is the world's leading state sponsor of terrorism and is responsible for a great deal of our soldiers' loss of life in the Iraq war. It was even a co-conspirator in the 9/11 attacks. Now that Iran has become a nuclear-weapons capable state, the regime must be toppled.

For all these reasons, the US must change course and forge an alliance with the Kurds, offering them all the military support necessary to defeat ISIS as well as our unconditional recognition of Kurdish statehood when they choose to declare themselves an independent state. Every US president since Jimmy Carter has sought a two-state solution for the Palestinians. Why should we and every other nation who's sought Palestinian independence over the last 50 years deny the Muslim Kurds their own homeland? We should be wise enough to turn this endless rhetoric around in favor of the Kurdish homeland. In return, we should ask for American military basing rights in Kurdistan and, even more importantly, that the Kurds put the Muslim militants and their Western apologists back on their heels by formally decreeing that Israel has the right to exist and that it be free to defend its territory.

We've Crossed the Rubicon

In 49 BC Julius Caesar and his army, having conquered all of Gaul, crossed the Alps and were approaching a small creek, the Rubicon. Based on an ancient Roman law, a general returning to Italy by this route was to disband his army before crossing into what was considered Italy proper or he was guilty of treason. Caesar had received word that leaders of the corrupt republic in Rome would kill him if he was to return without his army. He was too popular and too powerful. When he crossed the stream, he famously stated, "The die is cast." Rome would be plunged into civil war and the republic lost.

Over the last few days, Obama has ordered bombing raids against ISIS convoys in and around the City of Irbil and the trapped Yazidis on the Sinjar Mountains. This is war, Mr. President. You've killed ISIS members and their brethren are now more determined to come for you and for us. You must now forget about appeasement. Only total victory is going to gain us safety. The die is cast.

[End of Essay]

PUBLISHED ESSAY BY LARRY KELLEY

Create a New Kurdistan & Destabilize Iran
Part Two of a Series of Articles Published by *Townhall.com*, August 2014 - January 2015

By 207 BC, Rome and its allies on the Italian peninsula had lost approximately 100,000 soldiers to the invading armies of the great Carthaginian general, Hannibal. To make matters more desperate, the Carthaginians were in the final stages of securing massive reinforcements from Phillip V of Macedon. That year the Roman Senate sent a secret group of provocateurs to Northern Greece who started violent insurrections among Phillip's disaffected subject peoples to his south. The Macedonian armies never sailed and for the next 600 years the course of Western Civilization would be charted by Rome.

Special Forces Will Again Change the World

As I write in *Lessons from Fallen Civilizations*, "Since the mythical era of Achilles, ascendant civilizations have always produced small cadres of elite warriors. Their prodigious skills and audacity, combined with the element of surprise, have continuously, throughout the history of warfare, produced an astonishing means of martial leverage."

Over two millennia after the Roman provocateurs destabilized Macedon, in the immediate aftermath of 9/11, President Bush ordered one of the most audacious operations ever attempted in the history of special forces warfare. By early October, just weeks after the attacks, CIA paramilitary units were lifted out of Uzbekistan into Northern Afghanistan, testing the altitude limits of their helicopters. Their orders were to link up with the beleaguered Afghan Northern Alliance guerillas, a collection of tribes which the CIA supported in exchange for intelligence but who were losing the war to free their country from its foreign Taliban overlords. Like their Roman forbearers, their mission was to befriend, recruit, equip, advise, and lead the Northern Alliance fighters in attacks against Taliban and al Qaeda positions. The Americans were both soldier and diplomat.

Additionally, they were to provide the necessary on-the-ground GPS/laser coordination for precision air strikes. In Doug Stanton's *Horse Soldiers*, he describes a battle that saw the first American cavalry charge since the 19th century.

"Ahead our horsemen charged the middle of the line about 600 yards ahead. The men on foot trotted behind. Nelson looked up just as the Taliban line exploded. Next, another bomb from the jet overhead smashed one of the tanks…Up ahead; Nelson could see the Taliban line breaking in places, here and there, like a sand wall crumbling."

By December 7, 2001, only two months later, the Taliban had abandoned Kabul, all of Kandahar province and were attempting to hold on to their mountain redoubt in Tora Bora. The war to defeat al Qaeda in Afghanistan was essentially over.

The combination of ancient specialized guerilla tactics with high-tech laser guided air attacks are already, once again, at work in the war against ISIS in northern Iraq. This week Kurdish Peshmerga fighters, the PKK (a Kurdish separatist group designated by the US as a terrorist organization) and US F-18 and F-16 jets have combined to win several victories after an unbroken series of defeats and a massive loss of territory to the terror army, ISIS.

The new, unlikely allies opened a corridor on mount Sinjar, allowing the trapped Yazidi families there to escape and avert a humanitarian catastrophe. They captured some small towns to the west of Erbil, giving the capital of Iraqi Kurdistan a larger buffer zone of protection from ISIS weaponry. And, most importantly, they retook the Mosul Damn. Assuming the allies can hold the damn, this first victory was of critical strategic importance because it provides most of the electricity to Iraq. The allies' fear was that even if ISIS could eventually be driven out of the country and back into Syria; on their way out they could blow up the damn, sending a 60-foot wall of water down the Tigris Valley, destroying whole cities and towns, inundating Baghdad, and turning the lights out over most of the country. The damn needed to be retaken immediately.

Remembering James Foley

ISIS retaliated by publicly beheading American journalist, James Foley. For ISIS, which by some estimates has ballooned into an army of up to 80,000, this was both its first terrorist attack against the US and a declaration of war.

James Foley

War Accelerates History

It was for maximum effect that the ISIS executioner of James Foley spoke on film to the world in a perfect English accent. The message was clear - if the US does not stop the bombing, we have English-speaking Muslims who will be coming to kill you. As the military historian, Victor Davis Hansen, has observed, major conflicts always have the effect of greatly accelerating historic events. And in this regard, the brutal invasion and ethnic cleansing by ISIS presents the US and its western allies with a chance to press the "reset button" in the Middle East after six-years of a disastrous capitulationist foreign policy. Rather than fighting to a draw and then leaving, the ISIS invasion presents the US with a chance to chart a positive course toward actually winning the on-going war between the West and resurgent militant Islam. One important key to victory will be forging a close alliance with the Kurds. The Kurdish diaspora forms a vast arc of lands stretching from Eastern Turkey, Eastern Syria, Northern Iraq and, most importantly, *Northwestern Iran.*

Within this region there are an estimated 40,000,000 Kurds. They are one of the world's largest stateless groups. If the US were to become not just their partner in the destruction of ISIS but also their champion in securing a sovereign homeland, it would have the potential to change the Middle Eastern chess board in the favor of the West and its Arab allies.

Kurdish all-female Peshmerga fighters

Although Obama has had to reiterate his campaign pledge to never put boots back on the ground in Iraq, we can be assured there are not just hundreds but probably several thousand American "advisors" already in Iraqi Kurdistan training, overseeing weapons shipments and directing laser-guided air strikes.

To destroy ISIS, in addition to airpower, it seems likely that the US will ultimately require, at the least, 10,000 – 20,000 soldiers and Special Forces personnel to partner with Iraqi, Kurdish and Free-Syrian soldiers. Ironically this was the number of soldiers that Obama's military advisors had told him was the bare minimum we needed to remain in Iraq in order to maintain the peace George Bush had left him. But when Obama only offered 2,000 to 3,000 advisory personnel, Maliki told him to pound sand and decided to go with the Iranians who would offer him a better personal security arrangement.

The huge loss of life in this new round of fighting in Iraq is the direct result of Obama's abysmally flawed politicized war planning. But Obama's place in history is his problem. Early in the Bush administration, America proved that the combination of highly skilled clandestine Special Forces combined with determined indigenous people fighting for their homeland can be very decisive. We have no choice but to act decisively again. We simply need a president with the will to lead and win.

[End of Essay]

PUBLISHED ESSAY BY LARRY KELLEY

PUBLISHED ESSAY BY LARRY KELLEY

Create a New Kurdistan & Destabilize Iran
Part Three of a Series of Articles Published by *Townhall.com*, August 2014 - January 2015

The US now needs a free and stable ally in Kurdistan which can supply basing rights, intelligence, logistical support and trained military personnel to successfully prosecute this new phase in the West's war with militant Islam. Secretary of Defense, Chuck Hagel, and Chairman of the Joint Chiefs of Staff, Martin Dempsey, recently held a Pentagon briefing regarding the threat posed by ISIS, a threat once dismissed by Obama as "junior varsity." "This is an organization that has an apocalyptic, end-of-days, strategic vision which will eventually have to be defeated," Dempsey said.

Hagel characterized the Islamic State as "beyond just a terrorist group." "They marry ideology, a sophistication of strategic and tactical military prowess. They are tremendously well-funded. This is beyond anything that we've seen. So we must prepare for everything,"

In the *Washington Times*, Monica Crowley reports, "…the jihadists' stunning success includes conquering wide swaths of territory across Syria and Iraq, seizure of US and Russian-made weapons, including possibly surface-to-air missiles, and control of oil fields generating an estimated $2 million per day in revenue…"

And while it is a hopeful sign that some officials in his inner circle seem to instinctively know that all-out victory is what must be done to stop this building threat from ISIS, every American should be worried that this president will revert to type and try to find an "off-ramp" to disengagement or a way "to lead from behind."

The War Between ISIS and the West Has Only Just Begun

Given that the US has already attacked ISIS from the air, some adults in this administration need to somehow convince this president that half-measures are now off the table. Any appeasement will surely embolden the largest, best-funded, most ruthless terrorist organization ever faced by the West. Moreover, as the thirteenth anniversary of 9/11 approaches, various media outlets are reporting that "chatter" emanating from known terrorist-linked sources speak of an "imminent attack."

High-level federal law enforcement, intelligence and other sources have confirmed to *Judicial Watch* that Islamic terrorist groups are operating in the Mexican border city of Ciudad Juarez and are planning to attack the United States with car bombs or other vehicle born improvised explosive devices (VBIED). A warning bulletin for an imminent terrorist attack on the border has been issued. Agents across a number of Homeland Security, Justice and Defense agencies have all been placed on alert.

Even the Saudi King, Abdullah, seemed to know something he wants Obama to hear. "If we ignore the Islamic State, I am sure they will reach Europe in a month and America in another month," he said at a welcoming ceremony for new ambassadors, including a new US envoy to the Kingdom.

Create a Free Kurdistan to Save Obama's Legacy

Perhaps Dempsey, Hagel and other adults around this president can appeal to Obama's arrogant, self-absorbed nature and make him know that appeasement now may well result in a real catastrophe. Instead, they could let him believe that waging anti-jihad will build for him a legacy and that it's all about him.

They could start by explaining that the Kurdish diaspora contains an estimated 40 million Kurds and forms a vast arc of lands stretching from Eastern Turkey, Eastern Syria, Northern Iraq, and most importantly, *Northwestern Iran*. Over the last century, the Kurds have struggled, sometimes violently, to gain their own homeland. But unlike the Palestinians, they are a distinct people and retain their own culture and language. They occupy a semi-autonomous region of Northern Iraq which contains an estimated 45 billion barrels of oil, the world's sixth largest reserve. They continue to carefully invest their oil revenues and create a broad-based prosperity. Moreover, the Iraqi Kurds have demonstrated themselves to be not only a loyal and trustworthy ally of the United States but of Israel as well. The significance of this latter fact cannot be overestimated.

This June, Israeli Prime Minister, Netanyahu, declared that he supported Iraqi Kurds "aspirations for independence."

PUBLISHED ESSAY BY LARRY KELLEY

Positive relations began in the 1960's when Iraqi Kurdish rebels sent emissaries to Israel to plead for help fighting their mutual enemy - the Arab government in Baghdad. Eliezer Tsafrir, a Mossad agent, headed Israel's covert operations in Kurdistan from 1965 to 1975. His special-op's command supplied the Peshmerga (Kurdish freedom fighters) with weapons and training. The Kurdish military heroically reciprocated during the 1967 Arab-Israeli war by launching an offensive against the Iraqi army, tying down troops that would otherwise have been attacking the Jewish military. Tsafrir has stated he is certain that an independent Kurdistan would be an ally of Israel.

If Obama could be convinced to offer the Kurds not just all necessary military support but also US recognition when they choose to declare their independence, it seems probable that he could negotiate a robust status of forces agreement in free Kurdistan. In this way, the allies, the US, Israelis, the Kurds and others (possibly some moderate Sunni States, the Jordanians and Saudis, etc.) could achieve numerous historic geopolitical victories that have completely eluded this president during the first six years of his failed foreign policy.

The first is a historic military victory. If Obama can be convinced that it is in his interest to totally destroy ISIS (not just contain it), the US and allies based in the Kurdish North of Iraq could begin by starving ISIS's forward armies, cutting off their supply lines into central Iraq and end with the total destruction of the ISIS command and control structure in both Iraq and Syria. It seems that even this faculty-lounge Marxist should be able to figure out that a military victory that liberates terrorized foreign populations is good for his place in history.

Then there is the "Obama-as-humanitarian" victory. Obama could take credit for stopping genocide and the destruction of an enemy which beheads little children.

Then for Obama there is the potential of a "hearts-and-minds" PR victory. The destruction of ISIS with *Jewish and Muslim* allies offers this president a chance to finally demolish the tired, worn-out paradigm which holds that it is the Palestinians' plight that creates the hatreds and myriad crises embroiling the Middle East. Instead, in defeating the evil Islamic State, the US, under Obama's leadership, can demonstrate that he is a historic broker of peaceful relations between Muslims, Americans and American allies, even the Jews.

Soundly defeating ISIS, while simultaneously creating a free Kurdistan, allows Obama to take credit for creating a great cultural awakening in the Muslim world, something that he so clearly hoped would be part of his legacy. Certainly some people around this president can help him grasp the benefit of securing a new sovereign homeland for an oppressed and threatened Muslim people. Clearly it would have the potential to change the Middle Eastern chess board in a way favorable to the West and its "sometime" Arab allies, while at the same time salvaging Obama's foreign policy legacy.

[End of Essay]

PUBLISHED ESSAY BY LARRY KELLEY

PUBLISHED ESSAY BY LARRY KELLEY

Obama's America Continues to be Mugged by Reality
Part Four of the Series *Create a New Kurdistan & Destabilize Iran,*
Published by *Townhall.com*, August 2014 - January 2015

There is an aphorism which holds that a liberal will undergo a conversion to conservatism on the day after he's been mugged. While most liberals would find this statement to contain more than a whiff of racism, they miss the point. It actually refers to the fact that liberals are often mugged by reality. And in fact, the whole of Obama's worldview is being mugged by the reality of what is now a firestorm in the Middle East. Candidate Obama burst on the scene by announcing that, if America will just reduce George Bush's military footprint, we will be safer because the world will hate us less.

But now Obama and the rest of us Americans watch with horror the beheadings, crucifixions and wholesale-murder of thousands in Syria and Iraq at the hands of a new vicious Muslim Caliphate which has gained control of territory the size of Great Britain. Moreover, we have a sinking feeling that these horrors are now coming to the US homeland. In this sense we've all being mugged by the reality of what Barack Obama has set in motion.

Perhaps the nadir of this failing presidency was Obama's recent *60 Minutes* interview where he blamed the rise of ISIS not on his inability to negotiate a status of forces agreement with Iraq but on *faulty intelligence*. There is a great irony here because he and the whole of his party spent nearly a decade condemning George Bush for liberating Iraq based on bad intelligence. But what happened in response to his blame shifting on *60 Minutes* seems unprecedented in modern times. Both retired and enlisted military and intelligence officials (including James Clapper who the president named as one who failed to see the threat) shot back and stated that they had warned Obama that a US force of about 20,000 was necessary to keep Iraq from devolving into chaos and that ISIS was a threat to the region. In short, the whole of the military intelligence community called their own Commander in Chief a liar.

To make matters even worse for Obama, news resurfaced all across the media that he attends only about 40% of his daily intelligence briefings. It may well come out that he was told repeatedly about the rise of ISIS but just didn't read the memos. And his own former Defense Secretary and CIA Director, Leon Panetta, has written in his new memoir, *Worthy Fights*, this president fumbled the status-of-forces agreement with Iraq which could have prevented the ISIS disaster and did so for political gain. So for Obama, the mugging continued but there are some signs that reality is beginning to sink in and that a conversion is beginning to take shape.

Obama is on His Way to Creating a Free Kurdistan

Despite the fact that this president continues to double-down on his misguided Iraq policies by repeatedly telling ISIS and the world that, under no circumstances, will there be American "boots on the ground," his strategy to protect the Kurds in the north of Iraq is bearing both fruit and promise. Before discussing Obama's fruit and promise, it's important to point out that were he a freshman cadet at West Point and tried to justify to his instructor the wisdom of informing an enemy after hostilities had commenced that he would not use ground troops under any circumstances, we can be fairly assured he'd flunk the class.

But to his credit, our reluctant Commander in Chief has managed to enlist five Arab nations, Saudi Arabia, the United Arab Emirates, Jordan, Bahrain and Qatar, who have now flown coordinated combat aircrafts alongside American planes in attacks on ISIS. For longtime followers of the region this is a startling development. Also, the UK has contributed its airpower to the war on ISIS. It came at the last minute to avert a human catastrophe. Kurdish Regional President, Masoud Barzani, made desperate calls to Vice President Biden's office telling him that ISIS was at the outskirts of Erbil, the capital of Kurdistan, before Obama ordered the air strikes to commence. And the Kurds held.

US-led allied airpower combined with Kurdish militias, the Peshmerga, the PKK (a designated terrorist organization), and even some all-women ground units, combined with very intrepid American "advisors" (actually Special Forces) went on to achieve the first military victories in this new war against ISIS. In addition to recapturing the Mosul Dam and rescuing 5,000 Yazidis trapped on Sinjar Mountain, they have retaken a number of Kurdish cities from ISIS and consolidated control of Erbil, the capital of the region, which also houses a large US embassy. For the past month, the Kurds have held their ground against ISIS across a 600-mile front.

PUBLISHED ESSAY BY LARRY KELLEY

In another rich irony, the *Wall Street Journal* reported that US officials stated our support of the Kurds was based on the "need to protect US personnel in the oil-rich region, home to billions of dollars of US investment." We on the Right remember the never-ending accusations by Left-wing pundits and politicians who *so presciently* averred that President Bush waged their wars in the Middle East in order to enrich their oil-company cronies.

While Obama remains in office the allies will likely not only degrade, but will probably not defeat ISIS because, as he continues to say, "we won't be dragged into a land war." But he may have inadvertently set the stage for his successor to go on the offensive against militant Islam, not just against what remains of ISIS but against the head of the Islamofascist snake - Iran.

In April of 2007, in my article for *Human Events Magazine* entitled, *Iranian Discontent May Well Bring Regime Change*, I reported that the regime in Tehran was fighting, on numerous fronts, its own revolutionaries.

> …Iran is surrounded by its own mostly Sunni minority regions, Kurdistan in the Northwest, Azeris in the North, Arabs in the Southwest province of Khuzestan and the Baluchis in the Southeast. As an indicator of discontent with the Iranian Shiite theocracy, all these regions are now producing revolutionary commando brigades that are ambushing Iranian military and government targets with bombings, riots, ambushes, assassinations and kidnappings… Over the past few years, Iranian Kurds in the Northwest have launched more attacks, but in the lawless Southeast province of Baluchistan the attacks are the most lethal and dramatic…

> …A Baluchi group called Jundallah (God brigade) attacked Iranian President Ahmadinejad's motorcade, killing one bodyguard. On Feb. 14, 2007, the same group killed 11 elite Iranian Revolutionary Guard forces and wounded 31 others in a bus bombing using weapons similar to those the Iranian regime is smuggling into Iraq. Two days later, Jundallah forces waged an all-out gun battle with Iranian security forces right in the Baluchi capital city of Zahedan.

Two years later, shortly after the election of President Obama, millions of Iranians, this time in the Persian heartland, took to the streets of Tehran protesting the fraudulent reelection of Mahmood Ahmadinejad. Many in the crowd were heard to chant, "Obama are you with us?" Sadly, for those Iranians who had grown sick of theocratic rule by a small group of deranged mullahs, Obama would show that he was not with them.

But now, six years later, the entire landscape of the Arab World is being redrawn. The old order created by the victorious powers after World War I has collapsed. Ofir Haivry of the Herzel Institute in Jerusalem writes, "The Arab uprisings that began in 2010 have unseated or threaten to unseat every Muslim government in the region…Where there had always been intransigence now there is pliability." With all this upheaval, there are new opportunities for Obama and his successor.

As I've reported in my three previous articles in this series, the 30 million Kurds who occupy a diaspora inside Turkey, Syria, Iraq and Iran represent the third largest nationality without its own homeland. In the wake of the invasion by ISIS and the collapse of the Iraqi army, Iraqi Kurdistan is now a de facto independent and democratic *Muslim* nation. Similarly, semi-autonomous Kurdish enclaves are being established inside Syria. Shared interests and affinities are causing the Kurds to form an alliance and trading partner with Israel. As far back as 2006 Barzani announced that the Kurds, unlike the Arabs, hold no grievance toward the Jewish State. In march of this year, Zubeyir Aydar, representative of the Kurdistan National Congress to Europe, stated that Israel "has the right to live on its own soil." In June, not only was a Kurdish oil tanker seen unloading its cargo in the Israeli port of Ashkelon, but Prime Minister Netanyahu declared that Kurdistan has every right to gain its independence.

<u>Make the Muslim Reformation Begin</u>

All the above elements of free and independent Kurdistan make for a powerful narrative for a US president who can follow the example of Reagan, an American President who led the West to victory in the cold war. What allowed General Petraeus under President Bush to win the second Iraq war was his ability to get Sunni tribal chieftains to switch sides and join the US in the battle against al Qaeda in Iraq and Iran's Shiite provocateurs. It was called the "awakening." The stage is now set for Obama (but most probably, his successor) to instigate the "great awakening" all across the Muslim world. In partnering with the 30 million Kurds, America can help them to become the spear tip in the defeat ISIS. We can aid them in the liberation of their countrymen inside Iran, and we can recognize the independence of a new Kurdistan. But the West and its allies in the Muslim world will need a visionary US Commander in Chief to help the Kurdish people to begin a Muslim reformation. [End of Essay]

PUBLISHED ESSAY BY LARRY KELLEY

PUBLISHED ESSAY BY LARRY KELLEY

Create a New Kurdistan & Destabilize Iran

Part Five of a Series of Articles Published by *Townhall.com*, August 2014 - January 2015

Winston Churchill surveyed the staggering magnitude of worldwide carnage and destruction at the end of World War II and remarked that there was never a war easier to prevent. When Hitler stationed troops in the Rhineland in 1936, in clear violation of the Treaty of Versailles, the French military alone could have overwhelmed the German Army. But with the horrors of World War I still vividly remembered, the European allies were politically unable to move against Hitler. So they waited and talked. The cost of their inaction was 60 million lives.

In the face of Obama's endless decrees that the war with militant al Qaeda was over and his underlying fervent belief that the world will be safer with the US in retreat, his dangerous delusions are now wreaking vast carnage in ISIS-controlled Syria and all across the Tigris/Euphrates Valley, an area the size of Great Britain. As retired Marine Corps General James Mattis puts it, "No war is over until the enemy says it's over."

Despite the grotesque footage of mass executions, beheadings and crucifixions emanating from what many are calling the new Muslim Caliphate, there are some hopeful signals emanating from the emergence of a free, independent Kurdistan; a new western-friendly Muslim state that can become a beacon of hope for positive change in the extraordinarily troubled Muslim heartland.

<u>News from the Syrian Front</u>

Recently, the focus of the war with ISIS shifted to Syria and the Kurdish city of Kobani, far away from Iraqi Kurdistan, located on the border next to Turkey. Over the past few weeks, in the tradition of the seventh-century armies of Allah, ISIS has besieged the city there hoping that its capture would provide it a recruitment boost and demoralize the Kurds who now make up the only effective ground forces confronting it. Due to desperate pleas and western fears that there would be a huge civilian massacre, the US and its allies launched several hundred bombing raids in and around the city. While ISIS did breach a portion of the city's defenses and living conditions are desperate, the valiant Kurds still hold most of the city.

More significantly, Turkey's President Erdogan has now agreed to allow Kurdish reinforcements to transit through Turkey to reach the city. Reports are that they have arrived. This is an important development because a portion of the Kurdish forces fighting ISIS in Iraq and Syria are members of the PKK, the Kurdistan Workers Party, which has been fighting Turkey for its independence. Over the past three decades, Turkey's civil war with the Turkish Kurds of the PKK has resulted in 40,000 dead. Both the US and Turkey list it as a terrorist organization.

Like most Islamic heads of state, Erdogan is almost always playing a double game, balancing his Western interests with his desire to curry favor with various jihadist elements inside his country or in his neighborhood. For example, Turkey buys oil from ISIS, which it produces from captured Iraqi oil wells, for less than half its market value, providing the new Islamofascist state with $3 million a day to fund its war effort.

Turkey recently encouraged its businesses to invest in ISIS occupied Iraq and it allows ISIS fighters to train and stage attacks on Syria inside Turkey. But perhaps what is more telling: Erdogan has said that his party, the Justice and Development Party, "…is deeply rooted in the Seljuks and Ottomans." By this he is hinting that he wants to see the Assad regime in Syria fall because, as some astute observers have come to believe, he thinks he can manipulate the rise of ISIS to gain control of the lands once controlled for 500 years by the Turkish Ottoman Empire and that he seeks to be the sultan of the new Caliphate. By supplying ISIS and supporting those at war with it, he is playing the ultimate double game.

George Bush once observed that conducting American foreign policy is like playing chess in three dimensions. Nowhere outside of Syria could that observation be more spot on. In Syria there rages a three-sided civil war for control of the country by: those of the Assad regime allied with Iran and Russia, those of ISIS funded by Qatar and influential figures close to the Saudi Royal family and Turkey, and those of the "moderate" FSA (Free Syria Army) of approximately 10,000 rebels which wishes to be funded by the Western powers. The FSA is fighting ISIS *and* the Assad regime. ISIS is also fighting the FSA and the regime. If ever there was a foreign war where American interests were unclear, it's now Syria and its neighborhood. This murderous quagmire also screams a clear admonition to the American electorate - don't elect a foreign-policy-novice to be president!

PUBLISHED ESSAY BY LARRY KELLEY

But the Good News Is…

In my book, *Lessons from Fallen Civilizations*, I record that after the Ottomans lost the battle for Vienna in 1683, European and Russian armies began steadily taking back lands that the armies of Allah had won and held for five centuries. Eventually the lands which form today's Hungary, the Balkans, Rumania, Bulgaria and Greece would be liberated from Muslim rule. The battle for Vienna, *fought on September 11, 1683*[17] would be the turning of the tide.

Throughout the 300-year decline, which culminated in the disillusion of the Ottoman Empire at the end of WWI, the Islamic sages and potentates inside the capital walls of Istanbul continuously grappled with the questions: "Why are we losing battle after battle to the infidel? Isn't Allah on our side?" They continuously came back to the same conclusion: the faithful had fallen away from Muslim purity and they simply needed to be more devout Muslims.

ISIS, Al Qaeda and Militant Muslims Everywhere Are the New Devout

The Egyptian writer Aly Salem, who lives in New York and is an advocate of reforming Islam from within, writes that various polls such as the Pew Research's 2013 poll, *The World's Muslims*, "indicate that in many Muslim countries, the population is overwhelmingly in favor of veiling women, the death penalty for leaving Islam, stoning as punishment for adultery and where rabid anti-Semitism is rampant."

Salem also points out that Sayed Qutb, also an Egyptian, in the late 50's published *In the Shadows of the Quran* which has become the manifesto of today's jihadists. His life and writings created ardent disciples of al Qaeda's Zawahiri and bin Laden. It is not an exaggeration to say that he is to militant Islamism what Marx is to Communism. And just as his 18th and 19th century Ottoman predecessors, his message is: conquer the infidel with a pure Islamic heart.

While Obama constantly reminds us that the barbarity of ISIS and the rising stream of lone-wolf attacks inside the West have nothing to do with Islam, Salem

---

17. Muslims know that September 11, 1683 was the high point of Muslim domination over the Christian infidels and that it is the reason bin Laden selected that day for his attack.

counters, "Saudi Arabia (our putative ally) routinely bedheads women for sorcery and witchcraft."

Enter the Kurds, who are fighting for their survival, who are allied with the West and even Israel and who deserve to live in a free and independent Kurdistan. If we did not have a president who was blinded by his multiculturist dogma, he might realize that we in the West are embroiled in an ideological war with a significant portion of Islam and that no amount of bombing raids can win it. He might therefore go to the podium and champion the valiant, all-female Kurdish fighters who are on the front lines of this war. Theirs is an example of female liberation and respect that the whole world should applaud and emulate, the president could say. The world has already seen their photos. They fight not wearing veils or burkas but in fatigues and with Kalashnikovs.

Perhaps this president will now see the necessity of waging an ideological war against the barbarous wing of Islam. He could go on to praise Kurdistan for its faithful alliance with the Western powers including its recognition of Israel. He could double down by authoring a new US doctrine which would withhold US aid from any country which did not recognize Israel's right to exist. And when the Kurds where ready he could offer to the Kurds, conditioned by a vote from Congress, a recognition of their independence. These are things which the developments in Kurdistan offer the US – a chance to go on offense in the war with militant Islam while at the same time encouraging the much needed Islamic reformation.

[End of Essay]

PUBLISHED ESSAY BY LARRY KELLEY

Free Kurdistan & Destabilize Iran

Part Six of a Series of Articles Published by *Townhall.com*, August 2014 - January 2015

Question 4: Is it permissible to have intercourse with a female captive?

It is permissible to have sexual intercourse with the female captive. Allah the almighty said, "Successful are the believers who guard their chastity, except from their wives or captives and slaves…for then they are free from blame."

- IS (The Islamic State)

As ISIS moved into remote communities of northern Iraq last August, it enslaved thousands of Yazidi, Christian, even some secular Shiite and Sunni women after the men of their villages were lined up, shot one by one, and dumped into mass graves. The above quotation is one of 27 questions answered by a pamphlet entitled, *Questions and Answers on Taking Captives and Slaves*, now being circulated by ISIS in cities they have captured in Iraq and Syria, outlining the Koranic dictates governing female sex slaves.

The pamphlet, which ISIS took no pains to hide from the West, is a ruthless and cunning recruiting tool calculated to attract Muslim low-life's from around the world, inviting them to flock to the new Caliphate with the reward of endlessly raping young girls. Despite Obama's vehement protestations, the actions of ISIS are those of "no religion," the pamphlet offers as its justification the words and actions of the Prophet.

The Kurds Can Be Our Best Ally in the Defeat of ISIS

…If the US were to recognize a free and independent Kurdistan, at a time of the KRG's choosing, numerous benefits could redound to the US. These an enterprising US president could reap despite the murderous chaos engulfing much of the Islamic world:

- Despite the loss of a status-of-forces agreement in Iraq, the US could establish a new important base of military and intelligence operations with a reliable Kurdish partner.

- Given our support, it would be very easy to secure from a new, Islamic-free Kurdistan a formal recognition of Israel. And this, combined with the Kurds' respect for women's rights, a US/Kurdish led Muslim reformation could begin.
- With our Kurdish base on the border of Iran, we could begin the process of destabilizing Iran, an arch-enemy terrorist-sponsoring state which has declared and waged war on the US since 1979 and which will soon have, or already has, nuclear weapons.

<u>The Kurds Continue to Make Strides Toward Independence</u>

Early this month, in addition to holding firm against ISIS along a 300-mile border protecting its semi-autonomous homeland in Northern Iraq, the KRG, based in Erbil, negotiated an agreement with the Iraq government in Baghdad. This agreement allows it to sell and receive <u>all</u> the revenues

Kurdistan flag

from its production of roughly 550,000 barrels a day of its own oil. This will be done through Iraq's oil marketing company, SOMO. It is a huge step toward Kurdish independence. It is an admission that Kurdish oil is owned by the Kurds. Additionally, given the threat posed by ISIS, the agreement calls for joint military operations resembling an agreement between two independent allies.

With more help from US Special Forces, intelligence officers and air forces, the Kurds in the north of Iraq, along with the support from Shiite militias in the south, the allies are poised to retake more ground lost to ISIS. With the proper backing, they can break out, cut off its supply lines, starve it, surround it and kill it. And while the death of ISIS would greatly improve the safety of the West and of large portions of the Middle East, it still leaves the greatest threat, Iran.

Thomas Sowell was recently asked to reveal his current greatest fear. He responded, "If Iran is able to detonate a couple of WMD's inside one or two American cities prior to this president leaving office, I fear Obama will surrender." [End of Essay]

PUBLISHED ESSAY BY LARRY KELLEY

Immutable Law # 3

Appeasement of a ruthless outside power always invites aggression. Treaties made with ruthless despots are always fruitless and dangerous.

As I've discussed in this book and in my first book, the way you can think about these "Immutables" is that they are undermining factors resulting from bad decisions and which contribute to the fall of great civilizations. In my reading of history, I found that this one, Immutable Law #3, which I refer to as my "appeasement Immutable," is one of the most common factors in the fall of empires. While it is not usually the cause of a great civilization's collapse it is indicative of its decline.

In the fifth century BC, Thucydides understood this principal well. Among his many timeless dictums he wrote, "Weakness invites the domination of the stronger."

From the peace of Philocrates, which led to led the conquest of the Greeks by Alexander the Great's Macedonians in 343 BC, to Neville Chamberlain's Munich pact, to Bill Clinton's appeasement of the soon-to-be nuclear-armed North Korea, to Barack Obama's horrific JCPOA (his Iran deal), I found this factor to repeat very often on the way toward the dissolution of great civilizations.

What Does American Decline Look Like

Published by *Freedom Outpost*, November 26, 2013

A Betrayed Generation

In a recent five-part series of columns, I have posed the questions, "Why won't America follow the Egyptian model?... That is, as we saw in Egypt, why won't millions of betrayed, out of work and/or underemployed young Americans flood the streets of DC, committing civil disobedience on a massive and permanent basis?... And why won't the American military side with the young freedom fighters in a military coup?"

In this, and in several other columns to follow, I will focus on why tens of millions of young Americans, many of whom voted for Obama, should feel betrayed and what are the clear harbingers of America's decline. Churchill famously remarked, "Countries don't have friends. They have interests." Under this president, America is in inexorable decline in terms of our economic strength, military strength and our ability to influence events on the world stage. In short, our interests are being squandered by bad decisions and by appallingly bad governance. And the likely net effect of this is civil unrest.

For America, which led the war to defeat the Axis Powers in World War II and went on to win the Cold War, its 21st century decline emanates from its massive insolvency, its inability to pay for the hugely-bloated regulatory and welfare states. When I tell acquaintances that I have written a book entitled *Lessons from Fallen Civilizations* they will invariably pose a version of this question, "Well, are we doomed?" To which I answer, "By my reading of history, you can't have a world-class welfare state and a world-class military. You might have neither; but you can't have both."

I made this observation while appearing on Jim Bohanan's syndicated radio show. He challenged me by replying, "You're not saying that the late Roman Empire was running a welfare state are you?"

I said, "No. By the fifth century AD, the dying Roman Empire of the West was a kleptocracy. But the net effect was the same as to what is happening now. They destroyed their middle class."

If we celebrate our parents' generation, dubbing those who fought and won World War II as our greatest, it seems that there can also be a "worst" generation. That would be my generation, "the boomers," because we will be the first generation to turn the country over to their children in worse shape than when they inherited it. Thus the question - why won't the appalling state of our union precipitate the next American Revolution? Given the current economic decline, amplified by the rapid escalation of tax rates in Obamacare and elsewhere, its arguable that American youth are now being subjected to far worse oppression than our founders faced under 18th century British rule.

A Food Stamp Nation – A Key Indicator Decline is Spiking

The Weekly Standard reported that the number of food stamp recipients in the US had risen from 30.9 million in 2008 (the year Obama was elected) to 44.7 million by June of 2012. This meant 1 in 7 Americans could not feed themselves. This month, *Newsmax Magazine* reported an extremely alarming trend. "The 23,116,928 food-stamp households, an all-time record, was an increase of 46,000 from the previous month. A full 1 in 5 households now depend on food stamps…" Consider the trend, Americans!

How on earth can we expect young Americans to shoulder the cost of all our dependents who now need help feeding themselves, whose numbers exceed Poland, Hungary, and Sweden combined? How can we expect them to fund the $17 trillion in actual debt, the 50 to 100 trillion in unfunded liabilities and the federal, state and local governments with their vast minions of highly paid retirees? The answer is they can't and they shouldn't even be forced to try. Just as the Roman officials stole what little gold came in from their disappearing empire, America's young are being defrauded and betrayed by their ruling class.

New Signs that our Military Could Side with Insurrectionists

Quoting a recent study of Army morale, the *Boston Globe* reported, "only a quarter of the Army's officers and enlisted soldiers believe the nation's largest military branch is headed in the right direction" - a survey response that is the lowest on record and reflects what some in the service call a "crisis in confidence."

PUBLISHED ESSAY BY LARRY KELLEY

But if the enlisted men and women are suffering from low morale, many in the officer core are in full outrage. *Investor's Business Daily* accuses Obama of a military coup. Over the five years of his presidency, across all branches of the armed services, he has fired 197 senior officers. Just this year he fired nine commanding generals, including General Ham, head

Military family reunited

of US Africa Command, who publicly stated that he disagreed with the order not to send a rescue mission into Benghazi on the night of the attacks when our people were pleading for their lives. Retired and active members of our most elite warriors are openly speculating that an Obama purge of its commanders is under way.

Retired Army Major General Paul Vallely puts a fine point on this by stating that this administration will protect its own bureaucrats no matter how flagrant their malfeasance. "The White House protects their own. That's why they stalled on investigations into Fast and Furious, Benghazi and Obamacare. He's intentionally weakening and gutting our military and Pentagon and reducing us as a superpower. Anyone in the ranks who disagrees or speaks out is being purged," he said. Moreover, the sequester, which was designed by Obama and which allocates 50% of all spending cuts to the military, is a perfect vehicle for him to do just that.

Why the Iranians are Playing Obama and Kerry for Fools

In my book, *Lessons from Fallen Civilizations*, I develop a list of ten Immutable Laws governing the fall of great civilizations. My Immutable Law #3 reads:

Appeasement of a ruthless outside power always invites aggression.
Treaties made with ruthless despots are always fruitless and dangerous.

As long as there have been civilizations to prey upon, men of property have attempted to appease outside ruthless predators. When dealing with a ruthless outside power, not only is the attempt at appeasement a foolhardy tactic but an incitement.

Despite the fact that Iranians continue to refer to the US as the Great Satan, have not renounced their vow to destroy Israel or pledged to stop funding terror organizations such as Hezbollah, our secretary of State, and by extension his boss, keep referring to "progress" in nuclear disbarment talks in Geneva. In an ominous twist of fate, Israel is now more closely allied with the Sunni kingdoms of Oman, the Emirates, Bahrain and Saudi Arabia than it is with the US. All five are openly contemptuous of this most recent delusional attempt to get Iran to halt what has been its 30-year quest to get the bomb and to dominate the Middle East. And in a recent poll, even 62% of Americans don't believe the US will be able to use diplomacy to stop Iran from getting nukes.

[End of Essay]

PUBLISHED ESSAY BY LARRY KELLEY

As America Declines, So Goes its Martial Spirit
Published by *theBlaze.com*, December 10, 2013

The Roman historian, Tacitus, records the words of a doleful Briton defeated by the Roman legions who said, "You made a desert and called it peace." Any credible historian will concede that Rome, at its zenith, took on its enemies with overwhelming brute force. But the fact remains, beginning with the end of the reign of Augustus in AD 14, for 250 years those living within the vast expanse of the Empire enjoyed the safety and security of the pax romana.

5ᵗʰ Century Asian Barbarians

In the fifth century AD, as the Roman Empire of the West proceeded toward dissolution, the pitiable Romans were beset by unending invasions of Germanic tribes as well as Attila's hordes of Eurasian Huns. One of the primary signatures of a declining civilization is its unwillingness and or inability to defend its vital interests, allies, and ultimately its homeland.

With the Iran Pact, More American Allies Jump Ship

Reminiscent of John Kerry's famous flip flop, French Foreign minister, Laurent Fabius, called the new pact with Iran a "sucker's deal" before he later signed on to it. Left-wing pundit, Laura Secor of the *New Yorker,* believes the agreement has the potential to be historic. Prime Minister Netanyahu, who views a nuclear-weaponized Iran as an existential threat to his country, condemned the pact as a "historic mistake."

But for this beleaguered administration, perhaps the most humiliating blowback of this pact was that of Iran's Foreign Ministry Spokeswoman, Marziyeh Afkham,

PUBLISHED ESSAY BY LARRY KELLEY

who told the Iranian press on Tuesday, "What has been released by the White House as a fact sheet is a one-sided interpretation of the agreed text in Geneva and some of the explanations and words in the sheet contradict the text of the Joint Comprehensive Plan of Action, and this has unfortunately been translated and released in the name of the Geneva agreement which is not true." Thus the Iranians don't believe they've agreed to the terms Kerry and this administration say they have. Thus, the deal has the potential to attach to Obama as a variation of his promise, "If you like your plan, you can keep it."

With the Iran pact, Israel has become the latest among a long list of former American allies, such as Iraq and Egypt, who are now forging new strategic alliances outside the US security umbrella. Breaking with a US policy that has existed since the formation of Israel in 1948, this US-brokered pact with Iran has pushed Israel to be estranged from the US. Stunningly, now, in the beginning of Obama's second term, Israel is more closely allied with Saudi Arabia and the other Sunni kingdoms, Kuwait, Arab Emirates and Qatar, who are engaged in a proxy war in Syria with Iran and its allies.

Rumors abound that Israel and Saudi Arabia have struck a secret deal to attack Iran's nuclear sites. Israel has recently conducted long-range air refueling exercises and taken the unprecedented step of posting footage of it on the internet. Despite the predictable remonstrances from the mainstream media, most Western defense policy experts see the pact as containing small or unimportant concessions by Iran which garner it significant relief from economic sanctions. The enormous threat contained in the pact stems from the fact that Iran is allowed to keep its reactor grade enriched uranium which it can upgrade to weapons grade in a couple of months.

<u>What if Israel Decides to Act Alone?</u>

I spoke to James Carafano[18], Vice President for Defense Policy at the Heritage Foundation, regarding the crisis facing Israel.

> LK (Larry Kelley): I've read that if Iran develops nuclear weapons, Saudi Arabia has on order numerous finished weapons from Pakistan. Why does Iran need to build their own weapons and not just buy them?

18. Interview with James Carafano, Vice President, Heritage Foundation, December 1, 2013

JC (James Carafano): Because it makes it self-sufficient. It doesn't make them dependent on someone else. Shipping finished weapons are easier to interdict. They'd likely face a Cuban missile crisis scenario. Also, if North Koreans were caught shipping finished weapons, not just components, all hell breaks loose.

LK: Some members of Congress have announced they will try to block the Iran pact. What could they do?

JC: First, it's a joint agreement with European signatories. So, American Congress members can't stop them from lifting their sanctions. Second, even if a bill to block the treaty got through (both houses of Congress) the president would veto it. Whatever they do will be symbolic. In practical terms, they can't stop him (Obama).

LK: With Saudi help, can Israel completely destroy Iran's nuclear programs?

JC: No. There are too many targets, not enough intelligence, and Israel doesn't have enough military power. On the other hand, they (the Israeli's) can send a very strong message. That's actually worked before. In 2003, in the wake of Iraq invasion, Iran froze its nuclear program, fearing that they would be next. There is a possibility Israel could change Iranian behavior. (That same year Kaddafi, in 2003, fearing that he would be next, allowed US inspectors to completely dismantle the Libyan nuclear program and to ship the components to the US.)

LK: Might Israel use an EMP weapon?

JC: Highly unlikely. It's too blunt an instrument.

LK: In the event Israel strikes, what will be the likely counterattacks and can it survive them?

JC: Survive, probably yes. As to what the Iranians would do it's hard to tell. They might not attack directly but through Hamas or Hezbollah. That's why there's such an internal debate inside Israel as to whether or not to do this (attack Iran's nuclear sites). It's not that they care about world opinion. They're not sure what the Iranian response will be. It's simply a very dangerous course of action.

<u>Military Weakness and Appeasement Are the Handmaidens of Decline</u>

It's predictable that, seeing our attempts to back away from sanctions on Iran at precisely the time they appear to be working, the Chinese would brazenly announce that they now govern the South China Sea, naming it their "air defense identification zone" or ADIZ. Two days after China's announcement, America, along with Korea and Japan, sent military aircrafts into the zone without asking for authorization. However, one week later, the US is now quietly asking Japan to file travel plans with China before navigating through or above China's new waters. Yukio Okamoto, a former senior Foreign Ministry official, said in an interview with Japanese press, "I can't think of any case like this in the past where the US took a step that hurt Japan's interests over an issue directly related to Japan's national security in a way visible to the whole world."

So it seems we can now add Japan to the list of our allies seeking new security alliances.

President George Bush, the younger, once remarked, "Conducting American foreign policy is like playing chess in three dimensions." In watching Bush's successor, I agree with William Kristol who wrote, "As Iran moves closer to nuclear weapons, undeterred by the West's leading power, a 21st century tragedy threatens to unfold…It is a strange course of events, heavy with historical irony, that has made the prime minister of Israel the leader of the West."

[End of Essay]

PUBLISHED ESSAY BY LARRY KELLEY

Can Congress Protect Us from the Next Munich Pact?
Published by *Townhall.com*, August 7, 2015

With the Iran deal, the JCPOA (Joint Comprehensive Plan of Action), now being reviewed by Congress, many of us worry that Obama and team will prove to be even worse negotiators than was Neville Chamberlain, the man whose contribution to the 1938 Munich Pact with Hitler's Nazi Germany guaranteed World War II. All Americans must worry that Obama's desperate quest for a legacy may well embolden Iran and its rogue-state allies, Syria, North Korea, and Russia, to begin the march toward the next world war.

News from Iran is ominous. Ali Akar Velayati, a top advisor to the Supreme Leader, Ali Khamenei, on July 31 was interviewed on Al-Jazeera television and stated, "Regardless of how the P5+1 countries interpret the agreement, their entry into our military sites is absolutely forbidden." And it was recently discovered that the Supreme Leader has published his own Mein Kampf, *Palestine*, a 416-page guide to ridding Israel of the Jews.

Secondly, Obama's own State Department's newly released, *Country Report on Terrorism*, found that Iran, even during its final negotiations on this "historic" agreement, had stepped up its aid to Shiite militias in Iraq, to Hezbollah in Lebanon (in direct violation of U.N. Security Council Resolution 1701 which has been in place for over a decade), and increased its aid to the Palestinian terrorist groups, Hamas and Islamic Jihad, and to the Syrian government which has killed over 200,000 of its own people and which continues to use chemical weapons to do so.

Thirdly, Iran is one of the worst violators of human rights on the planet. As Jared Genser of Harvard's Carr Center for Human Rights Policy (hardly a Right-wing group) reports, more than 1,500 politically-based executions have been carried out in Iran since the supposedly "moderate" Mr. Rouhani was elected president in 2013. There are another 900 political prisoners, including one American journalist languishing in the notorious Evin prison where torture is one of the primary tools of state.

Fourth, Kerry's State Department has failed to deliver timely reports, every six months, to Congress on the nuclear proliferation activities of Iran, North Korea, and Syria, as required by law, with delays ranging from 22 months to three years. And in the tradition of Neville Chamberlain, Kerry has proven himself to be a serial cave machine. One of his latest caves was when it was disclosed that the Administration is ready to lift sanctions without a full accounting of Iran's past secretive, military-related nuclear work as required under the interim 2013 deal.

Make the Politicians Defend the Indefensible – A New Form of Journalism

In an effort to craft a new form of activist journalism, I decided to contact a number of my elected representatives here in California to see if any were on board with saving the country from entering into the neo-Munich pact. And I have a specific report regarding my contacts with the Senior Senator from California, Dianne Feinstein. I first logged into her website and wrote her a brief email explaining that I had deep concerns about the terms of the agreement and wished to speak with her.

Ten days later, on July 7, I got a two-page, cut-and-paste letter from her explaining why she was supporting the JCPOA, which Obama and team don't call a treaty so that they can bypass Congress, if the necessary two-thirds vote from the Senate is unavailable. She wrote that she was supporting the agreement not yet signed by the P5+1 countries, US,

US Senator Dianne Feinstein (D-CA)

China, Russia, the U.K., France and Germany, and listed a few bullet points as to why I should be secure in her judgement. For example, she contended that the agreement provides for "…unprecedented International Atomic Energy Agency (IAEA) access to all nuclear facilities, which is unparalleled in its invasiveness"

To which I respectfully wrote back, "Senator, how can that be true when the Iranian parliament recently voted 199 to 14 to *prohibit* U.N. and IAEA inspectors access to military, security, and ***their defined*** non-nuclear sites as well as access to related scientists and documents?"

Another erroneous bullet point stated, "(the agreement provides for) the preservation of all U.N. sanctions related to conventional weapons, terrorism, human rights and ballistic missiles."

To which I asked, "How can that be true? Obama and Kerry have themselves admitted that the agreement has no correlation to Iran's euphemistically termed "bad behavior" or their sponsorship of terrorism or their development of ICBMs capable of hitting the US mainland." (Moreover, the Iranian regime has been killing American soldiers beginning with the 1983 attacks on our embassy and Marine barracks to the present, with over 1,000 soldiers killed by Iranian IED attacks in the Iraq war. Arguably, the US should be at war with Iran, not appeasing it.)

As I was instructed by Feinstein's office, I submitted by email the above questions and a few others to the Senator's press secretary, Dean Lieberman, asking if he would deliver them to her and if he could arrange for me to speak with her regarding my grave concerns. Not receiving even a one-word response to my email, I followed a few days later with a phone call and was able to speak with Mr. Lieberman. But he made it abundantly clear that not only was I not going to speak with the Senator regarding my fears but that no one else in the office was going to speak with me either. He kept repeating "I'm not in a position to respond to that at this time. But I'm happy to pass your questions on."

In addition to my questions, or more accurately put, counters to her false assertions, I wanted to ask Mr. Lieberman, or anyone else in the Senator's inner-circle, how she could be in favor of this agreement where, for the first time in its history, the US is potentially entering into a pact with a country committed to the annihilation of another people - a pact that doesn't even require that the Iranians repudiate their genocidal aims? But I figured it was pointless. He was in full "deflect-and-evade" mode and was "not in a position to respond." So is the sorry state of our current representative republic.

[End of Essay]

The Iran Deal Makes War Inevitable
Published by *theBlaze.com*, September 29, 2015

The theocrats running Iran are very much ruthless despots. The regime has massive American blood on its hands, responsible for the 1983 embassy and Marine barracks bombings and the IED's manufactured and smuggled into Iraq which killed many hundreds of our soldiers. It is also an evil regime which shortly after it deposed the Shah in 1979, summarily executed thousands of its own countrymen whose only crime was that they were former Shah loyalists.

Ruthlessness is the operative concept in my Immutable Law #3 because the ruthless despot, pick any of them, Attila the Hun, Hitler or Mao, is one who says to those whose property he covets, "I will not only kill you in order to take from you what I want, I will risk my own life to do so." Most of us living in the civilized, asset-rich world look down upon the ruthless as insignificant ruffians. Few of us would concede that ruthlessness is a tactic that works.

Obama and Kerry have looked into the eyes of the ruthless theocrats running Iran and have decided not to oppose them but to appease them with their Iran deal. Yet the inevitable outcome will be the exact opposite of what they tell the world they desperately wish to avoid, that being, war. In a recent interview with Prime Minister Benjamin Netanyahu, Steve Forbes asked him, "What happens if Congress doesn't derail this deal?"

He answered, "We always have the right and the duty to protect ourselves against a regime that, while denying the Holocaust, is planning another Holocaust against the 6 million Jews of Israel. That will not happen. We won't let it happen."

This statement is blunt and direct. Netanyahu will not wait for his nation to be destroyed. Moreover, implicit in his response is his admission that this administration's appeasement of Iran emboldens the theocrats and makes war much more likely, not less so.

In the March to War, Can Israel Succeed Alone?

When will Israel strike? And what are the probabilities they will succeed in stopping the Iranian march toward the nuclearization of its terror network? Of all those who are regular media analysts, called upon to comment on national security matters, I would place John Bolton in the top five of those who we can count on to give an accurate assessment, to understand the nuances and the big picture, in short, to get it right.

In his *National Review* piece, *Facing Reality On Iran*, he points out that even if, by some hugely improbable quirk of fate, a Republican bill to reject the Iran deal passes Congress and Obama's veto is overridden, the die is cast. The bazaar is now open. Europe, Russia and China have already lifted sanctions and have their trade representatives in Tehran negotiating contracts. Moreover, Obama has shown, and has already signaled, that he will not enforce laws with which he disagrees. Even if the US does elect a new Republican president by January 2017, he is unlikely to find any country willing to revive sanctions.

To make matters worse, in April of this year, Putin authorized the sale of Russia's S-300 anti-aircraft system to Iran. The sale was consummated by Iran's Quds Force Commander, Qassem Suleimani, in open disdain for the sanctions which supposedly prevented his travel abroad and for the delicate negotiations led by John Kerry.

So the question Bolton poses is - can Israel succeed alone? His answer is, "Not as well as the US could, to be sure, but well enough," and quotes the British statesman, Mick Jagger, "You can't always get what you want, but if you try sometimes, you get what you need."

Bolton goes on, "Israel has the military capability to cause massive damage to key choke points in Iran's nuclear program, notably the Isfahan uranium-conversion plant, the Natanz uranium-enrichment facility, and the Arak reactor and heavy-water production facility."

Both Isfahan and Arak are above ground and would be easy targets for Israeli bombers and jets. Little is publicly known about Isfahan but Bolton intimates that his intelligence contacts have let him know that it is "particularly important and particularly vulnerable."

Natanz is buried and hardened and could be easily destroyed by US air power but

Bolton assures his readers that the Israelis can "do the necessary." Fordow, a newly discovered uranium enrichment facility, poses an even more difficult problem, but that there is little doubt that Jerusalem can close the entrance tunnels, air shafts, and electrical connections to both these facilities and as Bolton puts it, "it's hard for scientists to work when they can't breathe."

<u>What Will Result If Israel Strikes Alone?</u>

Here again, Bolton is definitive. Israel has struck nuclear weapons programs twice (Iraq in 1981 and Syria in 2007). But other than a flurry of activity in the U.N., Israel sustained no long-term consequences. Iran will order rocket attacks from Hezbollah and Hamas aimed at civilian centers but will be unwilling to go so far as to mine the Persian Gulf or attack our deployed forces in the region. Losing their nuclear program would be bad enough. Losing their air force and navy would probably cause the regime to fall. Now, as in 1981 and 2007, they have no choice. The Israelis cannot preserve the world as it is. It is rapidly becoming a world with a nuclear Iran. The die is cast.

In reading his piece, I would love to have known what Bolton thinks the Obama administration's response will be or when he predicts the Israelis will strike (I think if the Israelis have already decided to take out the sites, the strikes might well come just before the delivery of the Russian S-300 anti-aircraft systems.) But in this age of paid liars like Josh Earnest, it is reassuring to know that we have a few commentators like Bolton who can cut through the fog of propaganda designed to mask the sorrowful American capitulation. To quote the minstrels, Simon and Garfunkel, "a nation turns its lonely eyes to you."

[End of Essay]

Immutable Law #7

With the loss of fiscal solvency comes a loss of sovereignty.

According to my reading of history, appeasement of a ruthless despotic regime bent on your destruction is a very common component of the fall of great civilizations. However, I found that the *destruction of the middle class* is the most common feature of failing civilizations and is not a component, or a feature, but a prime cause of failure.

Liberal Policies Can't Help but Destroy the Middle Class
Published by *theBlaze.com*, March 27, 2014

In the mid-fifth century AD, in the waning days of the Roman Empire, the corrupt ruling elite in Rome turned their once revered legions against their citizen provincials in order to exact what had become a crushing tax burden. In my book, *Lessons from Fallen Civilizations*, I observe that one of the most recurring features of failing civilizations is that a corrupt ruling class will inevitably impoverish, and ultimately destroy, its own middle class. In the case of the Romans: the small farmer and merchant.

Janet Yellen Eschews Capitalism

Recently, Federal Reserve Chairwoman, Janet Yellen, when testifying before Congress, was asked by the avowed socialist senator from Vermont, Bernie Sanders, "Are we still a capitalist democracy or have we gone over to an oligarchic form of society run by the billionaire class?"

If Obama's newly appointed Federal Reserve Chairman is confused about her role in protecting American capitalism, aren't we headed toward a form of Marxism which cannot help but destroy the middle class? After all, inspired by Marx, Vladimir Lenin created a new system of governance for the Soviet Union based

PUBLISHED ESSAY BY LARRY KELLEY

on class warfare which targeted and destroyed the "bourgeoisie," the small farmer, merchant and factory owner for its crimes against the workers. While America's middle class is somewhat difficult to define, the American Democratic party cannot abide a thriving middle class precisely because its prime movers know that most Americans who, through their own industriousness, begin to acquire even modest degrees of wealth, soon cease to vote Democrat.

Obama's America is Shutting Down Entry to the Middle Class

President Obama has recently headed up the Democrats' new campaign to resolve the problem of income inequality and stated that it is the "defining challenge of our time." Like so much of what passes for Democrat economic policy, this is a misdirection play; that is, one that is designed to distract their voters, especially the impressionable, from focusing on the real issue - Why Americans, especially the young, can't find work. "The scope of the situation is shocking," said Keith Hall, a former commissioner of the Bureau of Labor Statistics. The Brookings Institute found that the share of teens that held any paid job at any point in the year fell from 55% in 2000 to 28% in 201,1 and that only half of high school graduates not enrolled in college worked at all. A young dental student and an expert on the plight of millennials (Americans age 18-30), Salvator Lamastra, writes, "My generation is losing hope, and fast. In fact, the economy is so debilitating that some 22.6% of us live with our parents."

And the situation is even worse for many new college graduates, that is those who, in previous generations, expected to enter the American Middle Class. Lamastra puts it this way, "Obama has let down the millennials economically in every way possible: high unemployment, sickening health care reform, skyrocketing living and energy costs, staggeringly high student loan debt and a national debt of $52,948 per capita." The entire middle class is shrinking.

As a result of policies put in place by this administration over the past five years, statistics abound which demonstrate that not only is America making it more difficult to enter the middle class but those who were recently counted among its members are increasingly falling into poverty. Examples are:

- One out of seven Americans are on food stamps. The number has grown from 31 million recipients in 2008 to nearly 50 million today, a shocking increase of nearly 50%.

- The country has 91 million men and women over the age of 16 not working and perennially unemployed. This is 10 million above the 80.5 million when Obama took office.
- Jobs are scarce. For the first time since the Carter years, businesses are dying faster than they are being created. Entrepreneurs have greatly pulled back on their plans to expand their businesses or start new ones, citing the huge costs associated with Obamacare, Dodd-Frank and the general uncertainty of the crushing regulatory climate.
- Forty-nine million now live below what the Bureau of Labor Statistics refers to as the poverty level.
- The value of the American dollar, and its commensurate buying power, continues to plummet.

Why are Liberal Policies So Destructive?

If Yellen exposed her ambivalence about capitalism in her recent statements, Obama was famously exposed during a 2008 debate against Hillary Clinton. Charles Gibson asked candidate Obama why he wanted to raise the capital gains tax to 28%, despite the fact that Clinton lowered the rate to 20% and Bush further reduced it to 15%, and in both cases, revenues from capital gains tax greatly increased.

To which he responded, "We saw an article today which showed that the top 50 hedge fund managers made $29 billion last year. $29 billion for 50 individuals. And part of what has happened is that those who are able to work the stock market and amass huge fortunes on capital gains are paying a lower tax rate than their secretaries. That's not fair."

While Obama's facts are highly suspect, his logic is even more specious. If he truly wants to be able to fund more government programs to aid the poor and middle class, why would he enact a higher tax and lower revenues to the treasury just to punish 50 people? The answer lies in the fact that for a true Marxist/progressive, there's no benefit in raising living standards. That's not his real game. Rather, he benefits by having as many as possible dependent on government and/or resentful of others, hence the word "fairness." His income inequality campaign is a thinly veiled class warfare tactic designed to manipulate. It is at the core of Marxist dogma and based on one the most ignoble of human emotions - envy.

PUBLISHED ESSAY BY LARRY KELLEY

Now, six years later, despite this administration's attempt to manipulate and misdirect regarding their appalling economic record, one senses that Obama, along with the liberal establishment, is now experiencing a crisis of confidence given that they've tried nearly everything from their redistributionist playbook - bailouts, vast stimulus spending, $5 trillion in deficit spending, Obamacare, green energy failed investments and tax increases. Yet, based on Census Bureau Data median household income is $4,000 lower than it was in 2008. Adjusted for inflation, this is a catastrophe for the middle class.

Karl Marx

With the recent publication of Thomas Piketty's *New York Times* best-seller and ode to redistribution, *Capital in the Twenty-First Century*, American liberals can also celebrate the near 150-year anniversary of Karl Marx's *Das Kapital*. They can also celebrate the 50th anniversary of Lyndon Johnson's *War on Poverty*. After his landslide victory in the 1964 election he brought about the largest expansion of government in US history. He pushed through 200 new laws which created 40 new federal programs designed to lift people out of poverty.

With nearly 100 million Americans receiving some form of government assistance, his great society has created the great dependency. The size of government, in real terms, is now five times larger than it was in 1964. Its cost will be unbearable for those attempting to join or remain in the middle class.

[End of Essay]

Immutable Law #9

When a civilization accepts the propaganda of its enemy as truth, it has reached the far side of appeasement and capitulation is nigh.

Bernard Lewis, who is the Professor Emeritus of Near Eastern Studies at Princeton University, an advisor to several presidents and who turned 100 on May 31, 2016 wrote:

> In the Muslim perception there has been, since the time of the Prophet, an ongoing struggle between the two world religions, Christendom and Islam, for the privilege and opportunity to bring salvation to the rest of humankind. For a long time, the enemy was seen as being the West, and some Muslims were, naturally enough, willing to accept what help they could get against that enemy. This explains the wide-spread support of the Arab countries for the Third Reich and, after its collapse, the Soviet Union. These were the enemies of the West, and therefore natural allies.

In April of 2016, not only was the United States Congress, but also the much-watched television program *60 Minutes*, shining a bright spotlight on the 28 pages of classified evidence omitted from the original 9/11 Commission's report which implicated senior members of the Saudi Royal family with aiding the 9/11 attacks. Even then-candidate, Hillary Clinton, broke with her former boss, President Obama, in support of the Senate bill, Justice Against Sponsors of Terrorism Act (JASTA), which would have allowed the 9/11 families to sue foreign sponsors of terrorism in federal court. The legislation, which would have also declassified those 28 pages, was passed out of committee with a unanimous bipartisan vote of 19-0.

In response, the House of Saud threatened to dump its $750 billion in US Treasury Bonds if the bill were to become law. The threat of blackmailing their largest customer reflected the Saudi Royal family's fear that their 15-year pass for sponsoring global terrorism was about to be rescinded.

The articles that follow here implicate the leadership of both houses of Islam, Sunni and Shiite, in conspiring to mount the most devastating attack on the US since Pearl Harbor. In my view, the implications could not be more profound for relations between America and the leaders of Islam.

PUBLISHED ESSAY BY LARRY KELLEY

The New Axis of Evils
Published by *theBlaze.com*, June 14, 2013

In my book, *Lessons from Fallen Civilizations*, I write:

By 1500, the Sunni branch of Islam, administered by the Ottomans, ruled lands from Syria and Iraq across the Maghreb to the Atlantic. And on the European mainland, it ruled all of Greece and the Balkans. By 1529, the Ottomans began their first siege of the Hapsburg imperial Christian capital of Vienna and were not successful in taking the city. They lost that battle because the Sultan, Selim "the Grim," was temporarily distracted from his conquest of Europe, feeling obliged to wage wars against his Islamic rivals both in Egypt and in Persia. Selim's armies fought Persia to a stalemate. They were victorious against the Mamluks of Egypt, incorporating within the Turkish Ottoman Empire, Egypt, and the holy citadels of Islam, Medina, and Mecca. Most important for the ultimate survival of Europe, Persia remained an enemy of the Ottomans.

The Syrian, Iranian, Russian Axis – An Update

To date, the two-year long Syrian Civil War has cost 80,000 lives, displaced hundreds of thousands of Syrians into neighboring states, is spilling over the border into Lebanon and may ultimately explode into a full-blown war between the two branches of Islam. For those of us in the West who fear state-sponsored Muslim terrorism, that is, today's Islamic aggression, it's tempting to look at what is going on in Syria and believe it to be a good thing. The thinking goes - among those 80,000 dead are many would-be jihadists who would have otherwise been at work attacking Western targets. Their crimes against humanity are *theirs* not ours. And as Bret Stevens of the *Wall Street Journal* puts it, "If al Qaeda fighters want to murder Hezbollah fighters and Hezbollah fighters want to return the favor, who in their right mind would want to stand in their way?"

Leader of Iran, Ali Khamenei

Syrian President, Bashar Al-Assad

In *Lessons from Fallen Civilizations*, I write, "although history is an imperfect road map for the future, it is the only navigation aid we have." But in the case of Syria, the word "imperfect" is operative. The Pope, the Dodge of Venice, the Holy Roman Emperor of the Hapsburg Empire and the Queen of England of the sixteenth century did not face the specter of the invading Ottomans forming an alliance with a nuclear-armed Russia or a soon-to-be nuclear-armed Persia. Our times are far more hair-trigger. It is tempting to think that if Vladimir Putin or Iran's Ayatollah want to enter the Syrian horror zone, they're welcome to it. But as Stephens puts it, "These guys aren't dupes getting fleeced at a Damascene carpet shop. They are geopolitical entrepreneurs sensing an opportunity in the wake of America's retreat."

What is unfolding in Syria, with its huge death toll and with Assad's ever stronger ties to our mortal enemies, is a microcosm of what the whole world will look like when the US is as fiscally and militarily weak as Europe. While our president issues flaccid warnings of "red lines" regarding the Syrian regime's use of chemical weapons, Iran and Russia are playing to win. The *Economist of London* reports,

> Mr. Assad's allies, Iran and Hezbollah, the Lebanese Shia movement, have backed the regime with more dedication that the Gulf Arab and Western States have helped the opposition…Hezbollah and the Iranian al-Quds force are helping to train a new "national defense force" of 50,000 drawn mainly from Alawite militias. Recent sectarian killings in and near the port of Banias suggest a plan to cleanse some of those areas of Sunnis. Hundreds of them have been killed in what seems to have been premeditated massacres.

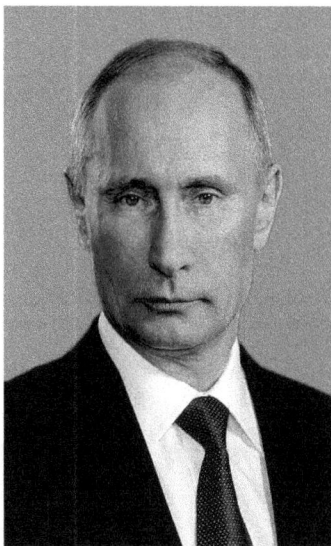

Russian President, Vladimir Putin

PUBLISHED ESSAY BY LARRY KELLEY

This is a snapshot of what Russia and Iran are willing to do to win, what they're willing to do when they occupy an America-free zone. Their ruthless commitment to the war of terror far exceeds our commitment to make war **against terror.**

Iran, Now on the Move in Latin America, Threatens the US Homeland

In 1994, an Iranian operative blew up the AMIA Jewish Community Center in Buenos Aires where 85 people died. Argentines still refer to it as their 9/11. In Mary Anastasia O'Grady's important article, *Uncovering Iran's Latin Networks,* she reports that Iran is running massive terrorist operations in the Western Hemisphere, operations that threaten the US homeland.

Shortly after the bombing, an Argentine prosecutor, Alberto Nisman, began an eight-year study in which he determined that Iran is sowing revolution all over the world and that Latin America is its key base of operations. He is also the author of a just released 500-page report which describes in great detail the Iranian terror network that stretches from the Caribbean to the southern tip of the hemisphere. And its targets are not just in Latin America. Nisman reports that the 2007 foiled plot to blow up JFK airport was an Iranian operation planned in Guyana and in a manner nearly identical to the Buenos Aires attack.

But we have nothing to fear because Obama has just elevated Susan Rice, of post-Benghazi fame, to be his national security advisor, and the activist, Samantha Powers, to be his U.N. Ambassador. Ms. Powers once said, "We need a historical reckoning with crimes committed, sponsored or permitted by the United States." Both Powers and Rice are mirror images of our Commander in Chief. They are capitulationists.

This is a problem for every American no matter what his party affiliation. If world-wide Muslim jihadism is a snake, the regime in Tehran is its head. Almost all Muslim terrorist activity in the world can be traced back to, or will have some connection with, the Mullahs running Iran. They are the new Nazi's.

[End of Essay]

Saudi Royals & Iranian Mullahs Were Co-Conspirators in 9/11

Part One of a series of articles published by *FreedomOutpost.com*,
February 2014 - June 2014

Recent news reports and declassified documents show that both the Mullahs running Iran, and even some Saudi Royals, were not only involved in the planning of 9/11, but both Shiite and Sunni leadership continue to aid and abet America's most lethal enemy, al Qaeda. Documents are surfacing that prove that the Shiite Mullahs running Iran provided safe haven, intelligence assistance, secure communications, training in explosives and training on airline hijacking for the Sunni 9/11 terrorists.

This is the first in a multi-part column which will expose these highly covered-up stories and will attempt to conclude what it means for this administration as it attempts to obfuscate its policy failures while it retreats from a mounting, emboldened Islamic threat. It is the fusion of Sunni and Shiite in Islam's war against the West that is new in the modern era. For the first time in fourteen centuries of Islamic aggression against the West, both the Shiite leadership in Iran, some Sunni leadership in Riyadh and Sunni jihadists not only conspired on 9/11 but continue to plot the destruction of the US. Moreover, with the reelection of this president, both branches of radical Islam are emboldened precisely because they view him as their unwitting partner.

Saudi Secrets

Recently two Congressmen, Walter Jones (R), NC and Stephen Lynch (D), MA, read the redacted 28 pages of the "foreign sponsorship" section of the 9/11 Commission Report. *The Wall Street Journal* reports that the two law makers walked away "absolutely shocked." In response, they have authored a resolution, H.R. 428 urging the president to declassify the report. The families of the 9/11 victims, who have been relentlessly demanding to know who plotted and killed their loved ones, are likely to continue to be disappointed. But some of the redacted information continues to leak out and it points to high-level complicity within the Royal Palaces in Riyadh. Obama will not risk doing any further damage to an already fraying alliance.

PUBLISHED ESSAY BY LARRY KELLEY

Iranian Not-So-Secret Secrets

In March of 2013, the US government announced that Sulaiman Abu Ghaith, Osama bin Laden's son-in-law and spokesman, was arrested in Jordan and is awaiting trial in New York City. While the logic of providing such a high-level terrorist the full protections and benefits of the American legal system escapes military scholars, what has become crystal clear is that al Qaeda's number two man, Abu Ghaith, had been living in Iran for ten years. After the fall of the Taliban in Afghanistan in 2002, he immediately began taking credit for attacks in Tunisia and Kenya, all as Iran's special guest. It will be one more stain on the Obama record and the intelligence services reporting to him as president. His obsession to undo all that was Bush by appeasing Iran, and by trying enemy combatants in US civilian courts, prevents the US from uncovering the next major attack on the West. Potentially thousands of American lives are at stake in order to gratify his ultra-partisan desire to be the non-Bush.

The Secret Files from the bin Laden Raid

Thomas Joscelyn, Senior Fellow at the Foundation for Defense of Democracies, in his recent article, *Partners in Terror: Iran, al Qaeda, and the Secret bin Laden Tapes* writes,

> …hundreds of thousands of documents and files were recovered during the raid that killed bin Laden in May of 2011. The Obama administration has just released 17 of them.

> …The documents released were chosen by the White House officials to push their preferred spin: Osama bin Laden's al Qaeda is on the verge of extinction. Many documents that contradict this politicized narrative remain behind a classified wall.

Evidence that al Qaeda had found safe haven in Iran and had metastasized throughout the Middle East and Africa did not comport with the president's 2012 campaign boast which held that the terrorists who attacked us on 9/11 had been decimated. But this is an administration which cannot shoot straight. In December of 2011, the State Department announced a $10 million reward for Yasin al-Suri who heads up al Qaeda's Iran-based network responsible for a pipeline which funnels operatives and weapons from around the Middle East to

Afghanistan and Pakistan. Operating out of Iran, al-Suri is one of America's most wanted men.

It's Now Clear, Both Branches of Radical Islam Believe They Can Roll the West

While Iran continues to make war on the US through its Sunni proxies, in Geneva this month, the Kerry-led, Neville Chamberlain-like western coalition granted a relaxation of sanctions against Iran in exchange for a miniscule slowdown of its decades-long drive to possess nuclear weapons. Immediately, Iran's President Hasan Rouhani gleefully tweeted, "Our relationship with the world is based on Iranian nation's interest. In Geneva agreement world powers surrendered to Iranian nation's will."

With the ink still drying on the accord, Iran's Foreign Minister, Mohammad Javad Zarif, explained to *CNN*'s Jim Sciutto that, contrary to what Washington claimed, "Iran did not agree to dismantle anything." Next Zarif flew to Nabatiye, Lebanon to lay a wreath at the exhibit of a mass murderer of Americans, Imad Mugniyeh. Like so much of what happens within Muslim citadels, Zarif's selection of the Lebanese terrorist Mugniyeh for special recognition, so soon after the Geneva accord, was meant to send an unambiguous message to the world of terror, both Shiite and Sunni. The message: "We are winning. They are losing."

The Life of Mugniyeh

I write in my book, *Lessons from Fallen Civilizations*, "In February 2008, Imad Mugniyeh was blown into globs of protoplasm by a car bomb on a well-to-do Damascus street in close proximity to the Syrian intelligence offices. His long and storied terrorist career was made possible by the ascendancy of Tehran as the world's headquarters for Muslim Terrorism."

Lebanese born, Mugniyeh was an elite member of the Qods Force, a special branch of the Revolutionary Guards that carried out foreign terrorist operations. Equally comfortable in working with both Sunni and Shiite terrorist cells, he was the mastermind behind the October 23, 1983 simultaneous truck bombings against French paratroopers and the US Marine barracks, attacks which killed 58 French soldiers and 241 Marines.

PUBLISHED ESSAY BY LARRY KELLEY

The United States indicted him for the June 14, 1985 hijacking of TWA Flight 847, which resulted in the death of US Navy diver Robert Stethem. He was also linked to numerous kidnappings of Westerners in Beirut through the 1980s, including Terry Anderson and William Buckley, who was the CIA station chief in Beirut. Some of his targets were later killed; such as Buckley, who was brutally beaten to death. Mugniyeh coordinated the Khobar Towers bombing in 1996, which killed 19 Americans. For 25 years he was the point man for Iran's spectacular attacks against Israel and the US. He is the man responsible for killing more Americans than any other Muslim outside of bin Laden. Iran's Foreign Minister laid a wreath at his grave because perhaps he is the most important modern terrorist in that he was the ambassador which unified both Sunni and Shiite on the 9/11 attacks.

[End of Essay]

Saudi Royals & Iranian Mullahs Were
Co-Conspirators in 9/11
Part Two of a series of articles published by *FreedomOutpost.com*,
February 2014 - June 2014

A High-Level Iranian Defector Warned the CIA that 9/11 Was Coming

In my book, *Lessons from Fallen Civilizations*, I reference Ken Timmerman in his ground breaking best-seller *Countdown to Crisis*:

…On July 26, 2001, at a backwater US Embassy in Baku, Azerbaijan, a high-level Iranian security official, Hamid Reza Zakeri, walked in. He told the receptionist that he wanted to speak to the CIA because he had information related to the security of the United States. He explained to the station chief, "Joan," that in his capacity as a high-level security officer at Iran's Ministry of Information and Security (MOIS) headquarters, he observed "Arabs" training pilots and briefing them on their appointed targets. He even described models that were on the table in the meeting room - the World Trade Center, the White House, the Pentagon and Camp David. He told her that the attack was coming from the air, the Arab pilots had already left for America, and the date for the attack was 9/11/01.

Joan called for backup. Several days later a senior CIA officer, "George," arrived from headquarters to debrief the "Baku walk in." He immediately decided that Zakeri was peddling lies, paid him $200, and told him to get out. The information that could have saved 3,000 lives was never passed up the chain-of-command.

Recovered bin Laden Files Point Straight to Tehran

In August of 2011, based on files recovered from bin Laden's safe house in Pakistan, the Administration released a report indicating that Treasury officials had frozen assets and movements of Atiya Abd al-Rahman. The documents showed that bin Laden had appointed Rahman to serve as al-Qaeda's emissary in Iran and was allowed to move freely to and from Iran. Moreover, he was planning attacks to coincide with the ten-year anniversary of 9/11. The type and scale of the planned attacks remain classified. But the report was remarkable because it was the first

PUBLISHED ESSAY BY LARRY KELLEY

time that the Obama administration admitted that bin Laden, his son Saad, and al-Qaeda's most senior members had been sometimes harbored and financially aided for ten years by the Iranian theocracy.

An Interview with the Author Who Broke the Iranian 9/11 Story - Ken Timmerman

I spoke with Ken Timmerman, who debriefed Zakeri in *Countdown to Crisis* and was the first in the US to directly link the Iranian regime to 9/11. I asked him if anything had changed since his book appeared in 2005 that would make him reevaluate Zakeri's account.

> Yes, there has been significant corroboration since then. In fact, I've learned from my own sources that the Director of National Intelligence, James Clapper, has set up a task force to investigate Iran's ties to 9/11 and to reevaluate the information they already have but that was not included in the (whitewashed) 9/11 Commission Report.

Timmerman went on to explain to me that the reason the CIA and the intel community, for the longest time after 9/11, could not believe that Iran had participated was because it invalidated their decades long analysis which held that Sunni and Shiite jihadists simply would not cooperate. If the Iranian government was a participant, it would further discredit those whose job it was to prevent an attack such as 9/11. As Ken put it, "It's now become an accepted analysis that indeed Iran did play a role in 9/11. Now when you assert this (the intel community) doesn't look at you like you're a kook."

The Saudi Connection

I spoke with Congressmen, Walter Jones (R), NC who, with Stephen Lynch (D), MA, has sponsored a resolution, H.R. 428, which demands that the Obama administration declassify and release a 28-page report which exposes "foreign sources of support for the 9/11 hijackers."

> LK (Larry Kelley): In reading the editorial-page story regarding your resolution, what caught my eye was the *Journal*'s assertion that the report in question, "points back to Riyadh." What can you tell me? Do you feel that members close to, or within, the inner circle of the Saudi royal family played a role in 9/11?

WJ (Rep. Walter Jones): I would answer you this way. That is certainly one of the concerns that needs to be addressed. How does a republic like America remain strong when the government decides what its citizens can and cannot know? If you don't declassify this information, the public will never know the truth. That's why we feel so passionately that the families (who lost loved ones on 9/11) have every right to read this report.

Congressman Walters did concede that there are questions about the relationship between the hijackers (15 of which were Saudi nationals) and the Saudi royals. He told me also, this March, that he and Congressman Lynch would be holding a press conference on the steps of the Capital, along with the family members, attempting to pressure the administration to release the report. And finally, he directed me to seek out former Governor and Senator from Florida, Bob Graham, who, as the former Co-Chair of the 9/11 Commission, has filed law suits in a Federal Court to declassify this report.

Even before leaving the Senate, Graham began working tirelessly on this issue, writing two books on the subject; one non-fiction, which was highly censored, the other a novel. I found a number of live interviews that he has given on the Saudi involvement in 9/11. What follows is a sampling of the assertions that Graham has made in various media interviews:

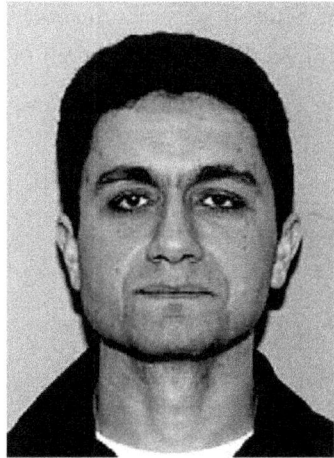

9/11 Chief, Mohamed Atta

- In Sarasota, Florida, near where the leaders of the plot took their flight training, a few days before the attacks a very wealthy Saudi couple fled the US to Saudi Arabia, leaving their house and all their possession including three cars. Phone records showed that they had been in touch with Mohammad Atta, the 9/11 leader.
- In Southern California, a Saudi consulate official Fahad al-Thumairy arranged for an advance team to receive two of the Saudi hijackers, Khalid al-Mihdhar and Nawaf al-Hazmi, when they arrived late in 2000. Omar al-Bayoumi, a suspected Saudi intelligence agent, left the Saudi LA consulate to meet the hijackers at a local restaurant. Bayoumi and another suspected Saudi agent, Osama Bassnan, set up an operating base in San Diego for

the hijackers after leaving LA. They were provided rooms, rent and phones, as well as private meetings with an American al Qaeda cleric, the notorious Anwar al-Awlaki, who was later killed by an American drone strike in Yemen.

On December 15, 2013, in the *New York Post*, Paul Sperry, author of *Infiltration*, wrote:

> The Saudis deny any role in 9/11, but the CIA in one memo reportedly found "incontrovertible evidence" that Saudi government officials - not just wealthy Saudi hardliners, but high-level diplomats and intelligence officers employed by the kingdom - helped the hijackers both financially and logistically. The intelligence files cited in the report directly implicate the Saudi embassy in Washington and consulate in Los Angeles in the attacks, making 9/11 not just an act of terrorism, but an act of war.

Whereas Iran provided planning, training and logistics support prior to the attacks, what seems to be emerging is the fact that agents closely associated with the Saudi Royals met the attackers once they arrived in the US and gave support prior to the commencement of the attacks.

[End of Essay]

Saudi Royals & Iranian Mullahs Were Co-Conspirators in 9/11

Part Three of a series of articles published by *FreedomOutpost.com*,
February 2014 - June 2014

Today, the Iranian government's role in 9/11 has finally become common knowledge within the US intelligence community. Given that both houses of Islam, Shiite and Sunni, actively supported bin Laden's terrorists in the 9/11 attacks, the purpose of this article is to explore the reasons behind this and what the policy implications are relative to our national security.

<u>Why Would the Leaders of Both Branches of Islam Work Together on 9/11?</u>

Iran: The leadership at the CIA had long been wedded to their belief that the distrust between Shiite and Sunni would have prevented the Iranian Mullahs from supporting the Sunni jihadists. And it's only been recently and with near secrecy that senior members of the Agency now concede the Iranians did support the 9/11 terrorists and still do provide safe haven and support for al Qaeda.

The Iranian leadership's motives for wanting to cause harm to the US, which they still refer to as the "Great Satan," are numerous. But their motives can all be boiled down to their knowledge that only the US has the power to stand in the theocracy's way of achieving its long-held dream of becoming nuclear-armed and thereby establishing a dominant Shiite super state stretching from the Indus River arcing north through Iraq, Syria and Lebanon to the Mediterranean Sea.

Saudi Arabia: Bob Graham, in various media interviews, has hypothesized why the Saudi's, or at least some of the royals close to King Abdullah, aided in the attacks against the US, the kingdom's largest customer. In bin Laden's fatwa he names the Saudi Royal Family as the illegitimate steward of Islam's holiest sites in Mecca and Medina. Its crime, among others, was allowing US and other infidel forces to be stationed on the sands of the Arabian Peninsula in the first Gulf War.

Graham theorizes that at least some in the house of Saud feared bin Laden's threat to start an insurrection similar to that which swept the Shah from power in Iran and therefore secretly lent the hijackers support out of a desire for self-preservation.

PUBLISHED ESSAY BY LARRY KELLEY

For the US and Our Allies, What Are the Implications?

The website, *Religion of Peace*, which catalogues Muslim violence around the world, has exhaustively documented over 22,500 attacks by Muslims worldwide since 9/11. Other than blowing up a barracks, this number does not count combat operations in war zones such as Iraq and Afghanistan. *Time Magazine* recently published a 2012 State Department map[19] which shows where militant Islamists are not only operating freely and openly, but collectively hold thousands of square miles of territory. Unlike 2001, when there was one al-Qaeda headquarters domiciled in Afghanistan, now there are many. Beyond Waziristan on the Paki/ Afghan border where remnants of bin Laden's al Qaeda are based, there is Al-Shabaab of Somalia; and al Qaeda in the Islamic Maghreb (AQIM), operating out of Algeria, Mali, Mauritania, and Niger; and al Qaeda in the Arabian Peninsula (AQAP), operating in Yemen and Saudi Arabia; and the largest and most powerful, Islamic State of Iraq and Syria (ISIS).

Islam's New Warrior Prince

In his role very reminiscent of the prophet Mohammad, ISIS is run by the shadowy enigmatic warrior prince, Abu Baker al-Baghdadi (his nom de guerre). Jihadist websites are filled with his battlefield exploits. Born to a religious family in Samarra, Iraq in 1971, he earned a Ph. D. in Islamic Studies from the Islamic University of Baghdad. He joined al Qaeda with the US invasion of Iraq and began reporting to the infamous Lebanese terrorist, Abu Mousab al-Zarqawi, who went on to found al Qaeda in Iraq (AQI). The 42-year-old terrorist has moved into the top post (renaming it ISIS) after Zarqawi and two of his successors were killed.

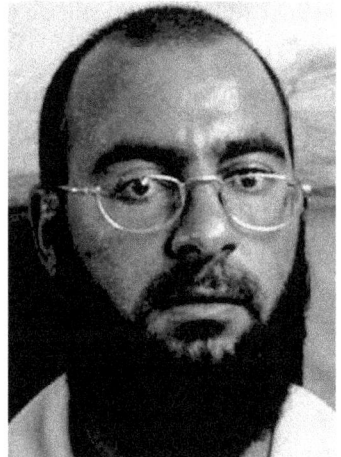

*ISIS Leader,
Abu Bakr al-Baghdadi*

Last July he led 50 ISIS fighters armed with machine guns and stormed Iraq's most fortified Abu Ghraib prison, breaching its huge walls, freeing 500 al Qaeda militants. On January 4th, his army defeated Iraqi regulars in a battle for Fallujah,

19. *Country Report on Terrorism*, 2012

PUBLISHED ESSAY BY LARRY KELLEY

the town which saw an angry mob pull four Blackwater USA employees out of their cars, drag them through the streets and hang their bodies from a bridge over the Euphrates. Beside moderate and radical Sunni forces in Syria, fighting Assad's Alawite and mainstream Shiite forces allied with Hezbollah and Iran. The US State Department has placed a $10-million-dollar bounty on his head.

Baghdadi doesn't only fight. He holds territory. He has taken several frontier outposts on the Syrian side of the border next to Turkey. In the north of Iraq, in the oil rich city of Mosul of two million, ISIS is so strong that it collects taxes which allow it to arm and equip 6,000 to 10,000 fighters with sophisticated weaponry. He and his followers long to recreate the 8th century Abbasid caliphate, the first Islamic empire. Baghdadi is quoted as saying, "We are the real jihadis and are closer to having a caliphate than any other al Qaeda group before."

What Are the Policy Implications?

While it is true that the two houses of Islam are at war with each other in Syria for control of the heartland, the fact of the matter is that they are each fielding armies which are multiplying and gaining strength. And if we come to grips with the idea that the leadership of both branches of Islam came together to launch the bloodiest attack on our shores since Pearl Harbor, it means that the size and scope of the threat posed by resurgent militant Islam is far greater than any current spokesperson from our government has been willing to admit publicly, far greater than at any time in the modern era. It also means that potential attacks can emanate from any of the 57 Islamic-majority countries. Future presidents need to understand that potential attackers now emanate from every corner of the Islamic world.

Even if members very close to the royal family are proven to be complicit in 9/11, no senior member at the Pentagon will likely suggest that we go to war with Saudi Arabia. But at the very least, we should add this revelation to the list of reasons why America should move to become energy independent. It must stop subsidizing such a duplicitous regime. Moreover, some the guilty Saudi's need to be named as co-conspirators so that families who lost loved ones on 9/11, and the American people, can know the truth and chose their representatives accordingly. Since it took over our embassy in 1979, Iran has been relentlessly waging war against the US and killing our soldiers and citizens, including the 1983 attacks

PUBLISHED ESSAY BY LARRY KELLEY

in Lebanon on our embassy and Marine barracks, the Khobar Towers and 9/11. Additionally, our government has publicly admitted that it was well aware that Iran has been very active in both the Afghan and Iraqi theaters, supplying weapons, IED's, training and non-uniformed fighters.

Just last week, in a Red Sea raid, Israeli commandos captured a Panamanian-flagged freighter carrying a shipment of Syrian-made M-302 rockets bound for Hezbollah in Lebanon. With a 125-mile range, the rockets would allow Hamas to reach every major city in Israel. Despite official Iranian denials, the 500-ton shipment was buried beneath bags of cement labeled "Made in Iran." In the case of Iran, as the only responsible super power, it is long past the time when we need to counter attack and remove a regime that continues to kill our citizens and allies and which threatens to start a nuclear World War III.

The fact the leadership of both houses of Islam participated in 9/11 reminds us that, if the US is to survive the modern Islamic threat, we must elect presidents who fully understand that Islam's war against the West has been a historic pattern and a religiously inspired act. Now that the emboldened combatants who populate the modern Islamic threat are growing in numbers and strength, it is imperative that the next president heed the warning issued by the late, great Tony Blankley who wrote, "We've lost our margin for error."

[End of Essay]

Immutable Law # 10

Declining civilizations will always face superior firepower from ascending civilizations because sovereignty is only temporarily uncontested.

Despite the fact that President Obama spent his two terms attempting to discount and alter America's military superiority, the country's technology sector continued to hand him the tools necessary to effectively mount counter attacks on remote terrorist enclaves a half a world away. The great irony is that Obama ran for president decrying George Bush's enhanced interrogation techniques while as president he killed ten times the number of suspected terrorists, including their families, with flying killer robots. And while the West was in decline, the Islamic world suffered from greater firepower because it was still a civilization which could not produce the cell phones on which its jihadists plot to kill us. Resurgent militant Islam was still a failed civilization.

The Flying Killer Robots & Psychological Warfare
Published by *Townhall.com*, May 23, 2016

The recent killing of the Taliban Chieftain, Mullah Akhtar Mansour, by a drone inside the Pakistan province of Baluchistan, is a striking reminder that we have entered a futuristic world where war is waged by flying killer robots and that we have witnessed a massive leap forward in the history of human conflict. Given that war accelerates history and the Islamic world is incapable of producing the cell phones on which its Islamists plot to kill us, the mullah's death by drone reminds us that:

> *Declining civilizations will always face superior firepower from ascending civilizations because sovereignty is only temporarily uncontested.*

The US agency that conducts drone warfare worldwide, the Joint Special Operations Command (JSOC), was constituted in 2002 and has grown ten-fold since its inception. Staffed by both the CIA and military, it now operates in super-secret locations across the globe. For the first ten years of its existence, JSOC conducted operations which were largely under-reported and therefore garnered very little public scrutiny. That changed with the 2011 killing of a very high-profile, American-born, al Qaeda terrorist, Anwar al Awlaki, another American terrorist, Samir Khan, and three others, obliterated in their car as they drove along a desert road in Yemen.

Awlaki was notorious both for his internet-based recruitment of jihadis world-wide and for being a key planner in no-less-than four plots against the US including the underwear bomber (a plot which very nearly downed an airliner over a densely populated area of Detroit and could have killed as many Americans as on 9/11). Khan was the creative force behind the jihadist online magazine, *Inspire*, which posted articles on how to build home-made dirty bombs as well as how to pick "soft" American targets. Oddly enough, the *New York Times* reported,

> Eighteen months later, despite the Obama administration's effort to keep it cloaked in secrecy, the decision to hunt and kill Mr. Awlaki has become the subject of new public scrutiny and debate, touched off by the nomination of John O. Brennan, Mr. Obama's counterterrorism adviser, to be head of the C.I.A.

It was odd because when the attack went public, the *Times* and others in the

Hexascopter drone

mainstream press, wrote worrisome columns wondering in print if the Obama administration was acting outside the law, murdering Americans on foreign soil without due process. But because they are nothing if not faithful Obama supporters, their worry quickly subsided.

The details surrounding the kill of Mullah Mansour reads a bit like a futuristic Tom Clancy thriller. Tips from intelligence assets inside Pakistan had made it possible to track his movements by picking up signatures from the communication devices he used. The members of JSOC already knew he had traveled from his mountain hideout in tribal Waziristan (Northwestern Pakistan) south through Baluchistan and across the Iranian border to visit his family in Iran. (Wait a minute! Why would the Iranians, our supposed new allies, our partners in nuclear non-proliferation, allow a terrorist leader at war with the US to enter their country? And why is his family allowed to live there?)

On his return trip, the drones flew into Pakistani airspace, and flew very low through mountainous ravines to avoid radar detection, on their way to kill him as he travelled, this time north, through the wide-open Baluchi bad lands. They watched as the vehicle carrying Mansour and four other terrorists pulled over near unidentified buildings. They waited and hovered above until the terrorists were back on the road, then launched two hell-fire missiles obliterating the car. They then hovered overhead to see if there were any survivors and then headed back to Afghanistan.

Over the balance of his presidency, Obama has conducted drone strikes at a rate *ten times* that of his predecessor, Bush. And not one in the sycophantantic press core saw the rich irony in the fact that candidate Obama spent much of his political capital condemning George Bush for the use of "enhanced interrogation techniques" when only a few years later, his own drone strikes would often not only kill terrorists but whole families including women and children. Such are the vagaries of being a member of the Leftist press.

Given the hardships soldiers have always faced traveling to distant lands and attempting to survive in devastatingly hostile environments, it boggles the mind to consider the new robot commander. He is seated at his desk in the complete safety of an air-conditioned office, perhaps on the other side of the planet, able to kill the head of the Taliban traveling in *Baluchistan*.

PUBLISHED ESSAY BY LARRY KELLEY

PUBLISHED ESSAY BY LARRY KELLEY

Psychological Warfare and the Defeat of Jihadism

What jihadi leaders like Mullah Mansour or al-Baghdadi of ISIS are peddling is that theirs is a messianic cause, that Allah will bless and protect jihadists in their great religious struggle. But what does it do to that narrative when the godless infidel can build and send mysterious hidden flying machines to kill their leaders and do so without the loss of a single infidel life? It smashes it. Apparently, even Obama gets this. But drone warfare is only one weaponized piece of the great psychological warfare that needs to be ratcheted up against resurgent militant Islam.

While Trump has recently somewhat backed off his earlier stated position that the US should have a temporary moratorium on Muslim immigration, he is essentially saying what most Americans already know - *not all Muslims are terrorists but nearly all terrorists are Muslim*. It would be stunningly brilliant act of psychological warfare if a President Trump were to modify his position to say that he would not ban all Muslims from entering this country but would set up a litmus test, and limit entry to those who would, for example, disavow the belief that a Muslim should be killed if he or she wishes to leave the faith.[20] He could extend that litmus test to include the vow to obey all American laws even if they violate Sharia law. The applicant could also formally proclaim that America's close ally, Israel, has a right to exist. Finally, a President Trump could welcome all qualified Muslim men and women recruited overseas who are joining our military intelligence services and who will be going to the front lines in the war on terror.

Perhaps Donald Trump will figure out the way to defeat a destructive, cruel ideology is with a sound, compassionate ideology.

[End of Essay]

---

20. Currently there are nearly no experts on Islamic jurisprudence who disagree that under Sharia law, apostasy is punishable by death.

Section Two

The Way Forward

The Way Forward

Part One - Understand We Are Losing the War & Losing the Country

How Obama Wasted the American Lives Lost in the Liberation of Iraq

On June 10, 2014, militants overran Mosul, a city of 1.7 million Iraqis on the Tigris River. The speed of the offensive, as well as the numerical disparity between attackers and defenders, caused a dropping of jaws among the Iraqi leadership in Baghdad and military experts around the world. In a single day, a small force belonging to the Islamic State of Iraq and the Levant, numbering perhaps one thousand men, captured a city garrisoned by 52,000 policemen and 12,000 soldiers. Bewildered Americans wondered how Iraqi forces that had received so much American largess could fold so quickly.... Some ISIL leaders were themselves former Iraqi Army officers who had defected out of disillusionment with the Baghdad government.

Mark Moyar, *Strategic Failure*[21]

What the George Bush and Barack Obama administrations could not have predicted was that a plurality of Shiite voters in Iraq, given the chance, would vote to elect such an extreme Shiite partisan as the Prime Minister, Nouri al-Maliki. In the two years immediately after the US withdrawal from Iraq in 2011, he purged from the Iraqi military all of the competent Sunni officers in favor of Shiite regime loyalists. What resulted was the evisceration of Iraq by ISIS. His was a classic violation of:

Immutable Law #6
To hold territory, a state must be populated by those loyal to the central authority. When immigration overwhelms assimilation, the fall is predicted.

When President Obama and his surrogates, Vice President Biden and Sec. State Hillary Clinton, failed to negotiate an adequate status of forces agreement with the then-Prime Minister, Maliki, he demanded that all US troops leave the country, which they did by October of 2011. For Obama, this was actually a positive outcome, given the strange reality in which he lived. He had campaigned on his intention to end the "dumb war" in Iraq. America's ignominious withdrawal from Iraq was payback to all his constituents who wanted the US to lose in Iraq, due to the fact it was George Bush's war and a Republican project.

Shortly after the complete troop withdrawal, thousands of Sunni al Qaeda forces fighting in Syria to overthrow the Assad regime saw a grand opportunity to the south to take vast undefended territory in Iraq. They swarmed south and erased the border between Syria and Iraq, joined up with al Qaeda in Iraq (AQI) and renamed themselves ISIS (Islamic State in Syria and later IS, Islamic State). This was not unbridled immigration, as referenced by my Immutable Law above, but rather it was a massive invasion. The net effect was exactly the same. The central authority governing a vast portion of northern and central Iraq collapsed overnight. The Sunni military of Iraq joined up with the invading Sunni forces of ISIS.

With the fall of Mosul in the North of Iraq, ISIS freed 3,000 prisoners from its prisons, most of whom were fellow Sunni jihadists. They confiscated cash reserves from the city banks, heavy weaponry and armored vehicles from military bases, a huge cash of ammunition and took over large functioning oil fields. One day later, ISIS captured Tikrit, Saddam Hussein's home town and Samarra, only 70 miles from Baghdad. News of these victories caused other Iraqi units to disappear.

Michael Knights, one of the world's leading experts on Iraq, reported on June 17, 2014, "around 60 of the 243 Iraqi army combat battalions could not be accounted for, and all their equipment was lost."[22] Iraqi soldiers in Baghdad were showing up with civilian clothes under their uniforms so that they could quickly strip off their uniforms and slip into the crowds if ISIS began to take the city. Suddenly, ISIS was the richest terrorist organization ever, and one that controlled a land mass the size of Great Britain.

With the sudden departure of the US military from Iraq, not only was the country turned into a sectarian war zone, invading Sunni ISIS fighters were killing Iraqi

Shiite government officials and militia. The mounting violence descended into tribal warfare as well. As Anand Gopal of *The Atlantic* wrote in *The Hell After ISIS*,

For a while, a tenuous alliance of Sunni tribes, ISIS, and other revolutionary groups held together. But ISIS began murdering its allies in order to dominate the movement, and at the same time, the Iraqi government increased its repression - in Fallujah, indiscriminant army shelling killed hundreds of civilians. The Sunni alliance crumbled, forcing some sheikhs to flee and others to join ISIS for protection.[23]

Only a few years earlier, in the late phase of the Iraq war, during what was called "the surge" in Anbar province, General Petraeus had turned the tribal leaders there against the murderous al Qaeda in Iraq. In siding with the Americans, Sunni tribesman helped to defeat the insurgency and aided in essentially winning the Iraq war. This victory had been a great victory for mankind, proving that a Muslim enemy could be convinced to join the West and turn his guns

ISAF Commander, General David Petraeus

toward Muslim jihadism. Obama was able to lose all of these gains by the middle of the year, 2014. Many of the Sunni tribes, which had once been America's greatest allies, joined the Islamic State, mostly out of fear for their lives.

By late 2015, the vast majority of US intelligence experts agreed that ISIS had become a far greater threat to the United States than were its precursors (al Qaeda and affiliates) when Obama took office. While many Americans became apprehensive by the growth of ISIS, the Israelis were becoming terrified by Obama's Iran deal which gave the leading state sponsor of terror a clear pathway to acquiring nuclear weapons.

Obama's Delusional Iran Deal Was a Signal of America's Decline

President Obama's Joint Comprehensive Plan of Action (JCPOA, aka Obama's Iran deal), concluded in July of 2015, was never intended to be a treaty precisely because, if it were, it would have needed to be ratified by Congress. And Obama knew that the Congress, the peoples' representatives, would never ratify the deal. This deal was a unilateral agreement made between Obama, his fellow defeatist Democrats and the Mullahs running Iran. It not only gave Iran a clear pathway to acquiring nuclear weapons, it allowed the regime to develop intercontinental ballistic missiles capable of hitting the US, allowed the regime to inspect its own nuclear development sites and released over $100 billion in frozen assets, a significant portion of which, could be used to underwrite its various terrorist clients around the world.

Obama's Iran deal had yet another very sinister intent. Because a number of the US allies, such as Britain and France, were coerced into endorsing the deal, it made it much more perilous for Israel to attack the Iranian nuclear sites. In effect, the deal created an alliance between the West and Iran which was an alliance *against* Israel.

While ISIS was beheading, crucifying and generally committing genocide against the Christians, Yazidi's and other less-radicalized Muslims in Syria and Iraq, on November 19, 2015, Julia Frifield, the State Department's assistant secretary for legislative affairs, wrote, "The JCPOA is not a treaty or an executive agreement, and is not a signed document."

Frifield wrote the letter in response to a letter Rep. Mike Pompeo, R-KS sent Secretary of State John Kerry, in which he observed that the version of Obama's Iran deal the president had submitted to Congress was unsigned and wondered if the administration had given lawmakers the final agreement. Frifield's response confirmed that Congress did receive the final version of the deal. She wrote, "The success of the JCPOA will depend not on whether it is legally binding or signed, but rather on the extensive verification measures we have put in place, as well as Iran's understanding that we have the capacity to re-impose - and ramp up - our sanctions if Iran does not meet its commitments."[24]

Yet by late 2015, nearly everyone knew, even Obama's compliant mainstream press corps, that sanctions against Iran would likely never be "ramped up" again because once all the participants to the deal, principally the Western European nations, lined up in front of their nations' flags and announced to the world that the deal was done, their commerce secretaries and business executives from all over Europe rushed to the Iranian bazaar. Moreover, everyone knew, except for perhaps Obama's inner circle of sycophants, that Iran had no intention of suspending its nuclear development program. It would cheat as it had been cheating all along.

Iran's Plot to Bomb D.C.

Israeli Ambassador to the US, Michael Oren, in his 2015 book, *Ally*, exposed President Obama's delusional motivations which brought him to be the chief salesman of the one-sided and terribly dangerous Iran pact that put the American people in danger of a preemptive nuclear strike.

Oren reported that on October 11, 2011, Netanyahu informed him by phone of an Iranian foiled plot to bomb the Israeli Embassy in Washington D.C. Simultaneously, the Iranian terrorists had also targeted Saudi Arabia's ambassador, Abdel al Jubeir, and planned to murder him with a bomb while dining at his favorite restaurant, Café Milano. In a scene that could have been plucked from a Tom Clancy thriller, a US undercover agent penetrated the ring and posed as a member of a Mexican drug cartel who the Iranian Government thought it was hiring to carry out the

Israeli Prime Minister Benjamin Netanyahu

attacks. The intrepid agent asked the ringleader, Iranian-American Manssor Arbabsiar, if he cared about the innocent patrons who would also be killed at the Georgetown popular bistro, "They want the guy done," Arbabsiar said, "and if a hundred (Americans) go with him, fuck 'em."[25]

The "they" Arbabsiar was referring to was Iran's most elite terrorist force, al Qods, which was in charge of the Iran's "overseas operations" and was widely known to report directly to the Supreme Leader. The $1.5 million payment for the attacks was to be passed from the regime to an Iranian-American used car salesman, Arbabsiar, and on to the Mexican hitmen working for the drug cartel.

Fortunately, the plot was foiled just before it was to commence and Arbabsiar and another Iranian accomplice arrested. Eventually they pled guilty. Incredibly, the incident (which should have been history-changing) is such common knowledge that much of the above information can be found on *Wikipedia*.

Oren added some additional little known-facts: Iran was selling drugs internationally, partnering with drug cartels, laundering the profits through Iranian-sponsored used-car dealerships and, by late 2011, had financed terrorist attacks in twenty-five cities around the world...including America's capital. As he puts it, "Such brazen aggression should have precipitated an instant military response."[26]

Instead, President Obama called the Saudi King, not the Prime Minister of Israel, Netanyahu, to tell him, "This plot represents a flagrant violation of fundamental international norms, ethics and law."[27]

As backdrop to this attempted attack, it's also important to note that acts of war had been continuously committed against the US by Iran since 1979, when it took over our embassy in Tehran. These acts of war included 1983 bombings of the US embassy and marine barracks in Beirut, the 1996 bombing of the Khobar Towers in Saudi Arabia which killed 19 Americans, and the hundreds of Americans killed in Iraq by Iranian-supplied IEDs.

Given his reaction to the thwarted attacks aimed at *blowing up whole buildings* in America's capital, Oren asked the question - if Obama would not go to war with Iran over a foiled attack a few blocks from the White House, would he deliver a knockout blow on the Iranian nuclear sites, 6,000 miles away? Obviously, the answer was no.

So what was Obama's delusional thinking which led him to steadfastly want to make his nuclear deal with Iran, a treaty which threatened Israel's existence and the American homeland with new, more spectacular, attacks and/or nuclear blackmail? In speaking with administration insiders, Oren was able to learn that Obama had decided to settle for capping Iran's ability to make a nuclear weapon *down to one year*.

In his grossly irresponsible quest to disengage the US from any and all military involvements in the region, Obama regarded Iran as the ascendant power, unlike the disunited Arabs and the "trouble-making Israelis." And he believed that the ascendant Iranians could assist America in resolving regional conflicts. Further, he believed Iran's radical brand of Islam could be mitigated with "sufficient American goodwill."

Obama told Jeffrey Goldberg, his go-to journalist on issues of Jewish concern, "the Iranians have their worldview, and they see their interests, and they respond to cost and benefits. They are not North Korea."[28]

Obama's reference to North Korea was particularly damning because Wendy Sherman, Obama's Under Secretary of State, steadfastly assured Oren and his team that the Obama Administration had "Israel's back" and that it had a "constant squeeze on Iran's major economic artery."

Oren added, "Sherman presided over the 1994 Framework Agreement on North Korea's nuclear program. That "good deal" as President Clinton called it, "…was based on nuclear inspections, and made the world safer."[29] Eight years later, North Korea exploded its first nuclear weapon.

In 2015, North Korea continued to threaten the West Coast of the United States with a nuclear attack. As Lee Smith of the *Weekly Standard* put it, "The problem, as always with Obama, is the world doesn't work the way he thinks it does... His grand theory exposed to reality shatters on contact."[30]

It was clear to all but Obama's sycophants that he was not only losing the Middle East to resurgent militant Islam but he was losing Americans' respect for the rule of law.

Americans Had Come to Fear
& Loath Their Own Government

By the spring of 2016, the bombastic, iconoclastic billionaire, Donald Trump, was the presumptive Republican nominee for the presidency. During the Republican primaries, his success and domination of the other establishment candidates such as Jeb Bush, whose father and brother had both been presidents, confounded the country's political punditry both on the Left and Right.

Forgetting What It Was Like to Live in a Free Country
Published by *Townhall.com*, January 12, 2016

A new Gallup poll concludes that Americans hate their government much more than they did when Obama first took office. In 2009, the burden of government was ranked 4th on the list of problems faced by Americans. At that time, 7% of those surveyed ranked burdensome government as the worst problem they faced. At the end of 2014, that percentage stood at 16%. More importantly, government was the most often cited concern above all others. At his inauguration, Ronald Reagan said, "In this present crisis, government is not the solution to our problem. It is the problem." If we Americans didn't believe Reagan then, after seven years of Obama, seemingly a lot more of us do now.

From Obamacare, to Dodd-Frank, to an out-of-control EPA, to myriad executive orders and tax increases, Americans are increasingly appalled by Obama's massive expansion of government, the size of which has not been seen since the depression in the early days of FDR. At the same time, Americans continue to witness a nearly jobless recovery, soaring health care costs, civil unrest, rising domestic terrorism, a government that continuously lies, governmental intrusion into nearly every aspect of their lives, and a complete lack of accountability when all problems, foreign and domestic, are growing worse.

Recently, more and more conservative pundits are begrudgingly joining the ranks of those who have concluded that the bombastic Republican front runner, Donald Trump, has brilliantly made himself the leader of those who still love their country but hate their government. He's both a presidential candidate and a symptom of their hatred. And while he appears to be greatly enjoying the adulation, there is a

PUBLISHED ESSAY BY LARRY KELLEY

serious danger resulting from his fomenting an even greater disgust and contempt for the agencies of the American government.

An article by Victor Davison Hanson entitled, *War Will Be War*, appeared a few months after 9/11. In it he wrote, "War is not merely a material struggle, but more often a referendum on the spirit. No nation has ever survived once its citizenry ceased to believe its culture worth saving."

Hanson's piece referred to the battle of Chaeronea in 338 BC where the Greek city states, as the result of one lost battle, gave up their magnificently innovative culture and its associated freedoms to their new Macedonian overlords. In so doing, the Greeks remained a subjugated people for the next 2,400 years.

This essay by Hanson was the inspiration for my book, *Lessons from Fallen Civilizations*, and the first of my Immutable Laws, which I also refer to as Hanson's Law, reads:

Immutable Law #1
No nation has ever survived once its citizenry ceased to believe its culture worth saving.

The danger to the US which Trump represents, and which the new *Gallup* poll illuminates, can be expressed by the following question - what will happen if the next American president can't, or won't, reduce the cost and burden of America's now hated onerous government?

In November of 2016, a plurality of American voters will hopefully elect a new president who will lead Congress in rolling government back. But what if that doesn't happen? The Greek historian, Thucydides, was the first to observe that history repeats itself. This was because, in his view, the nature of man does not change very much over time. One of his timeless observations was: *Power always seeks to increase itself.*

Students of history would consider it extremely rare, and unlikely, that an all-powerful government, such as the one currently governing the US, will freely give back a substantial portion of its prerogatives to the people it governs. So if that relinquishing of governmental power doesn't happen in the US and soon, how will Americans' growing distrust and hatred for their government impact its ability to defend itself from the threat posed by resurgent militant Islam?

The answer is not reassuring. Consider that the Spanish "Reconquista" took 700 years to rid the Iberian Peninsula of Islamic domination. Greece and Southern Europe were enslaved by the Ottoman Turks for 500 years. The war between the jihadist portion of Islam and the Judeo Christian West will likely last generations with the outcome in favor of the West not ensured. Welfare state Europe will likely be of little help in this building clash of civilizations. The US will need to reallocate resources away from the construction of its own welfare state while marshaling its resolve to wage and win a long terrible struggle.

Therefore, America can ill afford to let its citizenry's hatred for its government to persist because over time it will inevitably morph into a hatred for the country. Soon a new generation will be coming of military age. But what if our sons and daughters, like the Europeans, do not wish to put their lives at risk to save their culture because they hate their government and because they have no memory of when America was still a free country? [End of Essay]

The Trump phenomenon was the result of a growing segment of Americans, many white, working-class men in their 30's and 40's, who still loved their country but had come to hate both their government and America's ruling elites. In 1968, among young white men in their prime working years, the labor participation rate was 96% while 86% of them were married. By 2015, only 79% were working and only 52% were married. These were the Americans who felt squeezed, taxed, fined, penalized and harassed by a leviathan government that was composed of the dependency/entitlement class, the regulatory state and the ruling class. The danger this unholy alliance posed could be summed up in the following question - what will happen when those who have come to hate their oppressive government forget what it was like to live in America when it was still a free country?

Donald Trump

The Expansion of the Tyrannical Regulatory State

Over the previous 13 years, while the US fought, and ultimately lost, the wars in Afghanistan and Iraq, most Americans were not paying close enough attention to notice that the Washington-based establishment had managed to massively expand the tyrannical regulatory state. The number of specific regulatory restrictions listed in the *Code of Federal Regulations* (CFR) topped one million. It had grown by more than 42,000 pages in just the previous 20 years. The print edition contained 174,545 pages - nearly a quarter of which had been added since 1993 when the Clinton administration took office. The print edition took up 238 volumes, and the index alone ran to 1,242 pages. The number of individual regulatory restrictions in the CFR topped one million.

The regulatory state had become a shadow government that Americans had not voted to empower but which more and more Americans had come to hate. It was a complete threat to the constitutional republic, to the country's ability to hold free and fair elections and to every individual's freedom.

As Charles Murray, author of *By the People*, wrote,
> Regulatory agencies operate as self-contained entities that create de facto laws that Congress would never pass on an up-or-down vote. Citizens who have not been hit with an accusation of a violation may not realize how Orwellian the regulatory state has become. If you ran afoul of an agency, you didn't go to a regular court. You went to an administrative court run by the agency. You didn't get a jury. The case was decided by an administrative judge who was an employee of the agency.

In 1964, polls revealed that 76% of Americans stated that they "trusted government to do the right thing most of the time." By 2014, that number had fallen to 13%. Other polls conducted in 2014 revealed that 76% of adults lacked confidence that their children's generation would have a better life than they had lived - an all-time high. Some 71% of adults polled in 2014 thought the country was on the wrong track... and 60% believed that the country was in decline.

While 87% of a citizenry distrusted and reviled its own central government, no pundits on the Right or Left were asking an important question: could the next American Revolution be nigh? Was America losing its ability to produce, in sufficient numbers, a warrior class willing to risk their lives for the love of country?

Financially Destroying the Middle Class

As I chronicle in *Lessons from Fallen Civilizations*, in the decades leading up to the fall of the Roman Empire in the West (in AD 476), the corrupt officials in Rome turned the legions against the middle class. The small merchant and farmer came to hate the government which would confiscate more and more of his private property. Many Roman provincials welcomed the invasions of their new German overlords.

By 2014, the fiscal burden placed upon American citizens by their own government was exploding. A report issued that year by the Center for Federal Tax Policy determined that all American taxpayers worked from January 1st to April 21st to pay their taxes. Moreover, the report revealed that, for the first time, American taxpayers, as a group, paid more in taxes than food, clothing and housing combined.[31]

Five years earlier, at the beginning of Obama's administration in 2009, the official number of government employees was 2,774,000 people. But this was a purposely deceptive number. If one added postal workers, uniformed personnel, those who worked in the legislate branch, the federal courts, contractors and those receiving government grants, such as environmental groups, the number swelled to 14.6 million employees. And during the Obama years, given the massive government overspending on stimulus packages and bailouts, another 4.7 million were added bringing the true size of federal workforce to 20 million. When one added in the state and local government employees, teachers, fire fighters and bureaucrats, the number reached an astonishing 40 million Americans, 25% of the labor force, one out of every four workers, made their living off the taxpayers. And the number was massively expanded during the eight years of the Obama presidency.

To add insult to injury, the vast majority of government workers were paid more than equivalent positions in the private sector and yet they also received generous pensions. Many government workers were retiring with 70% to 80% of their salaries for life. They were receiving pensions that were funded by the private sector workers who largely had no pension plans.

In April of 2016, a document leaked to the international press and dubbed the *Panama Papers,* exposed the fact that left-wing government officials from South America, Europe, Africa, and Russia were stealing vast sums of money from their overtaxed electorates and depositing the funds in secret Panamanian bank accounts. Some of the officials implicated were from the same countries the first openly socialist candidate for the US presidency, Bernie Sanders, regularly touted as the model that America should follow. Immediately President Obama attempted a misdirection play to confuse the issue. He stated that the Panama papers were "akin to corporate tax inversions" where US corporations were setting up foreign corporations to avoid taxes. Corrupt government officials stealing money from their subjects had nothing to do with corporations attempting to avoid high taxes. They were non-sequiturs.

The ploy was a cynical canard. Overtaxed Americans, like their European brethren, instinctively understood that these papers exposed the thieves running governments as hypocrites who were unwilling to abide by the tax levels they created and were hiding their stolen treasure offshore. In light of these revelations, Obama's demand that US companies more fully comply with a 35% corporate tax rate, already the highest in the Western World, was barely noticed it was so typical.

In late April 2016, a report exposed the Obama Administration as having budgeted $17,613 per Central American illegal minor admitted to the United States over the following year. It forecasted 75,000 would arrive over the next year bringing the total cost to the beleaguered taxpayers to $1.3 billion.[32]

Central American Refugees, South Texas

This sum was $2,841 more than the average social security recipient who had paid into the system all his working life.

All of this amounted to a tyranny more oppressive than the one the British imposed on pre-revolutionary America.

Ravaging the Working Poor with Obamacare

By 2015, the tax burden was impoverishing the middle class. From 2009 to 2014, before taxes, median income fell 2.3%. When added to even a modest inflation rate, this was a shocking reduction in middle-class buying power. Recent college graduates were stunned when they received their first paychecks, stunned to see that their state and federal governments had confiscated 10% to 20% of their modest salaries before they even received the funds.

The bottom 50% of wage earners paid almost no state and federal income tax. But because of the costs built into America's vast regulatory and welfare states and the costs associated with a 35% corporate tax (one of the highest of any western country), the once-middle class was rapidly becoming the working poor. It paid huge amounts of hidden taxes built into everything it purchased. Of Obama, I wrote in my first book,

> The middle class was his target. The president's real plan was to extract the money from the middle class in a myriad of ways - fees, hidden taxes, higher Medicare deductibles, penalties and fines, carbon taxes, special assessments to cover failing hospitals and school districts, crony capitalist value-added taxes, and the biggest hidden tax of all - inflation.[33]

This stealthy plundering of the middle class and working poor continued apace on into the waning months of the Obama administration, but a new viscous set of costs and penalties were added - Obamacare. The American public and the economically illiterate news media were sold by Obama and his minions on the fact that the new act was going to actually make healthcare more affordable. Yet shockingly, in 2015, a single hourly worker earning $17,500 a year (150% above the official poverty rate) was forced to buy, at a minimum, a Bronze plan which cost him $1,670. Or if he went without any plan, he'd pay a fine of $695. His fine alone reduced his $8.42 cent an hour wage by 4% or $.33 an hour. Never in US history had a president and his party lied so blatantly about the future costs of a new entitlement. For many in the shrinking middle class, their shock turned to a seething anger.

Ravaging the Working Poor with Climate Change

On the eve of the Paris attacks in 2015, Obama proclaimed that "ISIS was contained" and that climate change "posed the gravest threat to the planet."[34] The next day, France endured the largest attack on its soil since World War II. The attack mounted by ISIS left 130 dead and 500 wounded. Three weeks later, Obama travelled to that same city, Paris, for the climate change talks which would be the world's largest meeting of governmental officials ever. Obama's entourage alone would number 500. Just prior to his departure, he proclaimed, "I will be joining President Hollande and world leaders in Paris for the Global Climate Conference. What a powerful rebuke to the terrorists it will be when the world stands as one and shows that we will not be deterred from building a better future for our children."

A few days later, on December 2, 2015 an ISIS inspired attack in San Bernardino, California left 14 dead and was the deadliest Muslim attack on US soil since 9/11. Given their timing, his ill-advised pronouncements in late 2015 would likely endure as among the most defining of his failed presidency. They engendered fear and loathing.

As the final year of Obama's presidency dawned, the full impact of his "climate con," along with his administration's back-room agreements aimed at drastically reducing American energy consumption, were still largely unknown to the public. Most of the press reporting on the proposed climate treaty was grossly inadequate and vague.

But a few reports surfaced in some Western outlets which exposed the fact that Obama and his cabal of world leaders (those one could call the Climate Hustlers) were attempting to impose a per capita carbon-based energy consumption treaty that would push energy use per capita below that which Americans enjoyed in 1830! If implemented fully, the treaty would constitute the deindustrialization of the West. Modern fossil-based technologies would continue to exist but few ordinary US citizens would be able to afford them and millions in the third world would starve or die of thirst.

Secondly, the treaty would transfer billions of tax-payer dollars annually to dictators, bureaucrats and crony industrialists in those same countries where the poor populations, due to skyrocketing energy costs, would die in staggering numbers. Slowly it was dawning on Americans that the climate change hustle was the biggest con ever. If the horrific costs of this treaty could be imposed by a departing Obama administration, it would disproportionately drive up the cost of fuel and electricity purchased by the middle-class and working poor. If implemented, it was sure to ramp up American rage to new levels.

Both the President & His Heir-Apparent Were Saul Alinsky Radicals

By late 2015, seven years into the Obama presidency, rage against the American government had risen to new levels because it was dawning on ever larger segments of the American public that it was being run by thinly-disguised far-left radical progressives who sought to tear down free-market capitalism and the constitutional republic.

Both President Obama and candidate Hillary Clinton had spent much of their young adult lives in Chicago where they absorbed the teachings of Saul Alinsky, the city's most famous Leftist revolutionary. Much of the domestic chaos which attended Obama's seven years in office could be understood as his implementation of the Alinsky Method, which called for the overthrow of democratic/capitalistic rule.

Alinsky was revered by young radicals such as Obama, Bill Ayers and Hillary Clinton. He was revered because, in the 1950's, he had been able to unify all the disparate Leftist groups, the socialists, the Maoists, the Stalinists by admonishing them to not worry about what sort of system would be imposed after the revolution. His gospel was to "break the system" and "take power." His book, *Rules for Radicals*, was still the secret bible of the American Left. Incredibly, by 2015 at the close of the Obama years, all eight of Alinsky's rules were in play. Patriotic Americans watched with dread as their capitalist system was being torn down by the mandarins of the new utopian order. All of his following initiatives aimed at "breaking the system," were well on their way to full implementation by the Obama government:

Alinsky's rules were better defined as "levers of control."
1. Healthcare - The most important was healthcare. You control healthcare, you control the people.
2. Poverty - Increase poverty to as high a level as possible. The poor will not fight the government as long as they see it providing subsistence handouts.
3. Debt - Increase the debt to unsustainable levels. This way the government can increase taxes creating more poverty.

4. Gun Control - Remove the citizenry's ability to defend itself as you build the police state.

5. Welfare - Take control of every aspect of their lives. Strive to provide to every need: housing, food, employment.

6. Education - Control what people read and listen to, especially the children.

7. Religion - Remove the belief in God (in favor of the earth, in reality, the state).

8. Class Warfare - Divide the people into the wealthy versus the poor. Foment discontent which will make it easier to take wealth from virtually every strata of society.[35]

Unlike much of the poorly-educated, progressive mainstream press, more and more Americans were becoming aware that the radicals were succeeding in their goals of transforming the country and were appalled by it.

Saul Alinsky in Chicago's Woodlawn neighborhood in 1966.

Hatred for the Anti-American Academic Left

More and more Americans who had struggled to afford the soaring cost of "big education," the soaring costs of sending their children to colleges largely run and populated by anti-western and anti-capitalist indoctrinationists, were becoming outraged. As the Obama presidency was drawing to an end, evidence abounded that the education establishment had become successful in turning much of the country's young, impressionable privileged citizens against their own parents.

In April of 2016, one of America's most prestigious universities, Stanford, allowed its students to vote on whether or not it would require a course on Western Civilization. The students overwhelming rejected the idea 1,992 to 347. A student columnist for the *Stanford Daily* explained why, "Teaching Western Civ. means upholding white supremacy, capitalism, and colonialism, and all the oppressive systems that flow from Western Civilization."

Obama Made Common Cause with
Radical Islamists Inside the US

Early in February 2016, Obama shocked and angered many Americans by travelling to Baltimore to visit what was billed as a "peaceful" mosque; except, the Islamic Society of Baltimore (ISB) wasn't peaceful. The FBI had been conducting surveillance there since 2010 when it arrested one of its worshippers, Muhammad Hussain (the terrorist's last name was the same as our president's middle name) for plotting to bomb an Army recruiting center not far from the mosque in Catonsville, MD. And that was not the Mosque's only ties to terrorism. ISB was part of a network of mosques controlled by a Muslim Brotherhood front group called the Islamic Society of North America which, in 2007, was an unindicted terrorist co-conspirator in a plot to funnel over $12 million to Hamas suicide bombers. And finally, the ISB Vice President, Muhammad Jameel, was an outspoken apologist for Osama bin Laden who stated that bin Laden was not the "root cause of terror" but that "US foreign policy"[36] was.

In his speech at the mosque Obama proclaimed, "Muslim Americans keep us safe," and went on to describe the many roles that Muslim Americans play in the nation. "They are our police. They are our firefighters. They're in (the Department of) Homeland Security," he averred. He asserted that Muslims had made "great contributions to our society" and went on to denigrate Republican presidential candidates for their harsh rhetoric linking Muslims to terrorism.

On the day before the president's trip to the mosque, White House press secretary, Josh Earnest, said,

We've seen an alarming willingness on the part of some Republicans to try to marginalize law-abiding, patriotic Muslim Americans. It's just offensive to a lot of Americans who recognize that those kinds of cynical political tactics run directly contrary to the values that we hold dear in this country. And I think the president is looking forward to the opportunity to make that point.[37]

Unfortunately for Obama and Earnest, most Americans were not buying their pitch because they knew at least some Muslim Americans were murdering their fellow citizens as evidenced by the Fort Hood and San Bernardino massacres. By the beginning of 2016, many had heard or read that the FBI had over 1,000 open investigations into Islamic State activity in the US. Americans were appalled by being told that they were the problem, that they were at fault for attempting to "marginalize law-abiding, patriotic Muslim Americans." Like his Iran Deal, they saw their own president's actions and rhetoric as a form of capitulation and they wanted it stopped.[38]

Ravaging of the Working Poor - A Case Study

In a story I wrote for *Townhall Magazine*, I interviewed a member of the working poor: a female bartender employed at a popular Vietnamese restaurant in the heart of downtown Oakland. Like Baltimore, Chicago and so many American big cities, Oakland was a one-party city and had been run entirely by progressives for decades. Yet it had chronic violent crime and high unemployment.

Speaking of fines and penalties run amok, a parking ticket in Oakland then cost the offender $65. But that was if you paid it on time. Failure to do so would quickly bring the overdue penalty of over $100. The woman bartender told me that, while working the day shift, she had amassed so many tickets and overdue penalties that the City of Oakland towed and impounded her car, informing her she could only obtain her vehicle if she paid all her fines in full. To which she told Oakland, "Keep the God-damned car."

That lady bartender was, for me, symbolic of the all the American working poor; impoverished by the supposedly benevolent progressive state, forced to give up her ability to drive, her ability to travel safely to and from her place of work, and was very bitter about it.

Immutable Law #5
If a free people, through taxation, is deprived of its
ability to acquire wealth and property, collapse is presaged.

Much of the American public was distrustful and contemptuous of its own government because they had come to see that it was being run by a cadre of dishonest extreme radicals who were impoverishing the middle class while claiming to champion it.

Losing the War On All Fronts

By 2016, not only was much of the American public enraged by its oppressive government, but the war with resurgent militant Islam was going so badly that it too was a source for Americans' anxiety and deep dissatisfaction. Obama had been elected by not only promising to "fundamentally transform America," but by promising that he would be the president who would "end wars." What he actually meant was that the US, on his watch, would not win but *lose* wars.

In Iraq: He proclaimed that Iraq was the "dumb war," and the "war of choice." Moreover, the Iraq war was merely "a distraction" from the much more consequential war in Afghanistan. In 2011, Team Obama offered the first duly-elected, but completely incompetent, president of Iraq, Nouri al-Maliki, a status of forces agreement which would allow for only 3,000 US troops to remain in country. Al-Maliki told Biden, Kerry, and Obama, that their paltry offer was not even enough to guarantee his personal safety. So he elected to align with his Shiite brethren, the Iranians, and said to them, "Get out!"[39]

President of Iraq,
Nouri al-Maliki

Obama made no sincere effort to reverse al-Maliki's decision. After all, our complete departure from the Iraqi theater would fulfill one of his most fervent campaign pledges which was to end the Iraq war. By doing so, he could also repudiate Bush. Two years later, in 2014, two-thirds of Iraq was in the hands of ISIS, the most murderous regime in the Middle East since Saddam Hussein's Iraq and the most powerful and menacing Islamic terrorist state ever. Obama did not end the Iraq war; he lost the Iraq war *badly*.

In Afghanistan: By late 2015, reports began to surface in even the mainstream press that the rump force of 10,000 U.S troops, which the Obama administration had left in Afghanistan, were in the process of losing that theater as well. The Taliban, a terrorist organization which hosted bin Laden's al Qaeda and colluded in the 9/11 attacks, had come to control more Afghan territory than at any time since that dark day 14 years previously.

By early 2016, much like the ISIS conquest of Iraq, a small contingent of a few hundred Taliban was poised to overrun the Helmand Province, defended by 18,000 Afghan soldiers, and seize all their US weaponry. An exasperated US commander, Army Gen. John Campbell, excoriated the Afghan military commanders for their "utter lack of leadership and the breakdown in discipline." But one of the reasons for the Afghans' lack of martial spirit and their propensity to retreat was that US forces were *also ordered to retreat* when fired upon because their mission, passed down from the Commander in Chief, was only to "train, advise and assist." If the Afghans' American military trainers retreated, why wouldn't they do so as well?

In a shocking breakdown in military protocol, General Campbell reportedly told his Afghan counterparts he was close to "pulling his advisers and throwing in the towel." According to the *Washington Post*, the "US was performing a pathetic charade in Afghanistan" where senior military Afghan officials no longer even pretended that they "could effectively fight the Taliban on their own."[40]

In Syria: After five years of a brutal four-sided civil war where two branches of resurgent militant Islam, the al Nusra Front (an al Qaeda affiliate) and ISIS, fought the secularist rebels and the Assad regime for territory, they were vultures picking apart a dead carcass. The former country of Syria was dead.

Numerous brave journalists, who had ventured into the Syrian war zones and returned alive, were publishing articles and books testifying to the unspeakable atrocities there. Samar Yazbeck, an outspoken critic of the Assad regime who was forced into exile from her homeland in 2011, made several clandestine trips into Syria and reported on the horrors almost too unbearable to process. She wrote, "The only victory in Syria is death: no one talks of anything else. Everything is relative and open to doubt; the only certainty is that death will triumph."

By 2016, the death of Syrian combatants and civilians, including the elderly, women and children reached 250,000. Syria was not just a failed state; it was an apocalyptic state, exporting terrorists all over the West.

In Yemen: As in Syria, by 2015, the country was being dissected by three warring factions. One faction was the Yemeni army and loyalists of the ousted regime, headed by Abed Hadi who was living in exile in Saudi Arabia after having been overthrown by Houthi rebels. This Sunni faction was aided by the Saudi's and the United Arab Emirates. The second faction, the Houthi rebels, was backed by Iran and was Shiite. And the third faction was al Qaeda in the Arabian Peninsula (AQAP) which, seeing its chance during the chaos of revolution, seized a large chunk of the southern coast of the country in the Hadramout province.

While fighting to hold and take new territory, in January of 2015 AQAP had the wherewithal to coordinate the attacks on the offices of the Paris-based satirical magazine, *Charlie Hebdo*, in which 12 Parisians were killed. In addition to the country providing safe haven for international terrorists, Saudi Arabia and Iran were involved in a proxy war in Yemen for power and influence in the Middle East. And finally, a branch of ISIS was established there as well.

In the Philippines: On April 8, 2016 news reached the West the terrorist organization allied with al Qaeda, Abu Sayyaf, killed 18 soldiers and wounded 52 in a firefight on the southern island of Basilan. The terrorist group was strong enough to hold 20 foreigners as hostages and kill Philippine soldiers. Zachary Abuza at the National War College in Washington told the *Wall Street Journal,* "My assessment is that the US training program (in the Philippines) of $50 million a year since 2002, has been an absolute waste of money."[41]

In Iran: After the mullahs running Iran had concluded a nuclear arms treaty with the US in mid-2015, one might have concluded that they would have ordered a temporary cessation of its bellicose behavior issued toward the US and its allies. The Iranians got practically everything they wanted: a guarantee they would eventually be allowed to have nuclear weapons, a guarantee they would be trusted to inspect their own nuclear development sites and a guarantee they could continue building intercontinental ballistic missiles which would be used to threaten the United States. For Obama's part, he got to proclaim that he got a treaty. Any treaty.

The Iranian bellicosity didn't stop. It immediately went up. Since the agreement was signed in July of 2015, Iran test-fired two ballistic missiles, one in October and the other in November. When the U.N. protested, the Iranians countered that their ICBMs were for the defense of their homeland, which is obviously absurd. Then in December the Iranians doubled down. In the international waters of the strait of Hormuz, through which 90% of Middle Eastern oil exports flow, Iranian naval vessels fired rockets just 1,500 yards from where the U.S.S. Harry

Truman aircraft carrier was sailing, nearly missing an American destroyer and French ships. This was full-blown military provocation for what the Iranian media called the West's intrusion into a "forbidden zone."[42] It was clear the Iranians had taken full measure of Obama and found him to be a push-over.

In Israel: By March of 2016, Israel had been suffering under a new intifada where Palestinians as young as 13 were attacking Jews with knives, hatchets and even scissors or were driving their cars into crowds, in one instance, killing two dozen people. Over the previous six months, 90 Palestinian attackers had been killed. 70% of Israelis told pollsters they felt unsafe. Yet by Israeli standards, the violence was manageable. Most remembered the previous intifada when suicide bombers were targeting buses and cafes when almost as many victims would die in a single attack as were killed in this the latest wave of violence. Nevertheless, it was one more reminder that almost nothing in the Middle East had improved under Obama's watch. It had gotten worse.

Far too many Americans were completely appalled by their Commander in Chief because so many of his actions made it appear that he was incomprehensibly *trying* to lose the war with the jihadists. In January of 2016, in his effort to make good on one of his original campaign pledges, that being the closure of our detention facility at Guantanomo Bay, Obama released a new batch of 16 hardened terrorists, most of whom were likely to return to the battlefield. In addition to a close aide to bin Laden, one of the released was Tariq Mahmoud Al Sawah, a 58 year-old gentle-looking killer whose specialty was designing new and innovative explosive devices. He invented a shoe-box bomb which, like the printer-cartridge bombs, was smuggled onto an airliner bound for the US and miraculously failed to detonate over the Atlantic. Al-Sawah was also the father of the IED used to horrific effect in Iraq and is therefore responsible for the death of untold Americans and allied soldiers. He was released into the hands of the very trustworthy Bosnian government.[43]

Obama created a sham board to vet the released terrorists and which has rubber stamped them as "unlikely to return to the battlefield." Intelligence had already shown that 30% of the previously released "Gitmo" prisoners had indeed returned to terror activities. It was obvious that this president planned to release all the remaining 91 terrorist prisoners before a Republican president could take office. And regardless of the loss of American lives that would result from this course of action, the trophy associated with his closing Gitmo was seemingly an important legacy item for this radical president.

In January of 2016, polls revealed that only 37% of Americans approved of their government's handling of terrorism while 57% disapproved. Americans who followed events relative to the wars in Iraq and Afghanistan understood their close connection to the rise of worldwide terrorism and were appalled by the Obama administration's capitulation and their president's willingness to increase the danger to every Israeli, European and American citizen in order to achieve some ephemeral short-term political gain.

With the United States' fiscal operating debt rapidly approaching $20 trillion, a doubling of the debt from all previous presidents combined, the strategically inept Barack Obama and his Democrat fellow travelers had become as dangerous to the survival of the American Republic as were the Bolsheviks to Czarist Russia in 1915. By 2015, military families and those citizens who revered America's warrior class came to hate their government precisely because it seemed to be *trying* to bankrupt the nation while simultaneously losing the war with resurgent militant Islam.

2015 Was a Banner Year for the New Caliphate

For ISIS, and its rival Sunni terror organization al Qaeda in Maghreb (AQIM), November of 2015 was an especially historic month. Resurgent militant Islam launched five spectacular attacks.

- On November 4 an ISIS affiliate on the Sinai Peninsula blew up a Russian commercial airliner, killing all 224 on board.
- On November 12, ISIS detonated a bomb in downtown Beirut, killing 43 and wounding 239.
- On a Friday evening, November 13, eight ISIS-trained and equipped terrorists attacked six separate locations in Paris and, with Kalashnikovs, coldly and mercilessly murdered 130 people in restaurants, cafes and in a concert hall. The wounded numbered 500.
- Not to be forgotten or out done, on November 20, AQIM attacked an American owned hotel in Bamako, Mali, killing 21.
- And on December 2, Sayed Farook and Tashfeen Malik, a newlywed couple who had pledged their allegiance to ISIS, killed 14 people and injured 22 others at their Christmas party in San Bernardino, California.

Some pundits averred that November 13, 2015 was France's 9/11. In response, French Prime Minister, Francois Hollande, characterized the attack as not a police matter, as Obama usually did, but an act of war. He immediately ordered air strikes on Raqqa, Syria, ISIL's headquarters and other targets.

Speaking about the airstrikes, Mr. Hollande said:
Since the beginning of the year, this organization has attacked Paris, Denmark, Tunisia, Egypt, Lebanon, Kuwait, Saudi Arabia, Turkey and Libya.

Every single day they massacre and oppress people. That's the reason why we need to destroy ISIS. That's something which involves the whole international community. I've asked for the U.N. security council to get together as soon as possible in order to mark a resolution for the joint authorization to fight terrorism.[44]

But sadly for the French, they had long lost their power to influence world events, even those which impacted their ability to survive threats to their very existence as a free, sovereign nation. Moreover, the United Nations had no ability to marshal support for the protection of the French homeland either. Two months after Holland had declared war on ISIS, at the beginning of January 2016, France could only muster one aircraft carrier, 26 fighter planes and 100 ground soldiers to engage the enemy in Syria and in Iraq to fight the new Islamic Caliphate. It was ghastly proof that unbridled redistributionism, the fundamental bedrock of Euro socialism, had removed the Euro socialists' ability to adequately defend themselves from barbarous Muslim murderers.

On March 18, 2016, nearly four months after the Paris attacks, one of the ring leaders, Salah Abdeslam, was captured by a Belgian swat team in a raid on his apartment in Molenbeek, a Brussels suburb. When police returned the following day to question neighbors and search the neighborhood they were pelted with rocks and bottles. As one Belgian official put it, "It was clear that a whole lot of people there knew who Abdeslam was and chose not to tell the authorities. He was hiding in plain sight."[45] Four days later, ISIS trained fighters, close associates of Abdeslam, conducted suicide attacks in the Brussels airport and a subway station, killing 35 and wounding 300. It called to mind:

Immutable Law #10
Declining civilizations will always face superior firepower from ascending civilizations because sovereignty is only temporarily uncontested.

ISIS was unafraid to attack Western powers, such as France and Belgium, because it believed itself to be ascendant and its western enemies descendant.

Part Two - To Win Any War is to Know Thy Enemy

As described above; in war, often the first step in reversing a great nation's road to defeat is for its leadership to understand and admit that it is employing a losing strategy and that it must commit to dramatically changing course. The second step is to know the enemy, his history and his present motivations.

Understanding the Meaning of the New Caliphate

To defeat ISIS, its proxies and allies, the first order of business for future US presidents, their top military advisors and the American public would be to first understand a non-whitewashed Islam generally and the power that the new Caliphate had over the jihadist mind specifically. On June 29, 2014, Abu Bakr al Baghdadi, with ISIS territorial gains then reaching an area the size of Great Britain, proclaimed himself the new Caliph and the leader of all Muslims worldwide. In so doing, he had the audacity to do something that al Qaeda, the Muslim Brotherhood and all other jihadist entities had only dreamed of doing over the last century of radical Islam's rise.

As Eric Stakelbeck wrote in his 2015 book *ISIS Exposed*, "…all radical Islamist organizations share the ultimate goal of reestablishing a caliphate, or pan-Islamic super state, that will confront Israel and the West and return Islam to its former glory days."[46] They dream and long for a borderless coalition of Islamic nations, governed by Sharia Law, which controls a large portion of the world's oil supply and which will be armed with nuclear weapons.

In order to counter this threat, future American presidents would need to understand that jihadists know their history and of Islam's lost greatness. As I chronicled in my first book, the modern jihadist is well schooled in the history of the Umayyad Caliphate. This first great Muslim Empire, whose capital was Damascus, was the result of 120 years of conquest which commenced with the death of Mohammad in AD 632 and which came to rule over 5 million square miles. By AD 750 the armies of Allah had conquered two-thirds of Western

Christendom. At its height, the first caliphate controlled the Middle East, North Africa, Spain and even major portions of Italy, reaching the outskirts of Rome.

In AD 732, exactly 100 years after Mohammad's death, Western Civilization was saved in southern France at the battle of Poitiers by the armies of Frankish warlord, Charles Martel. He defeated the invading Muslim hoards and drove them back over the Pyrenes.

Future presidents would also need to know and understand that Islam nearly conquered Europe twice, first at the Battle of Poitiers in AD 732, and a second time at the Battle of Vienna in AD 1683. They would need to know that the Ottoman Caliphate based in Constantinople, at its height, ruled the Middle East, North Africa, the Caucasus, and a large portion southern Europe including Greece, Romania, Bulgaria, Albania, Yugoslavia, and portions of Hungary. But to the benefit of all living in Western Civilization today, in 1683, the Turkic Muslim armies were defeated and routed by a consortium of Northern European armies led by the Polish King, Jan Sobieski. For the next 200 years, Muslim armies continued to lose battles to better-equipped European armies until the final dissolution of the Ottoman Empire at the close of World War I.

Three centuries after the Battle of Vienna was fought on *September 11*, 1683, bin Laden picked September 11 for his attack. It was a commemoration of the exact date when the last great Sunni Caliphate had reached its zenith in terms of ruling the Christian infidel. It was the anniversary of when Islam ruled the most Christian souls.

There was also a terrible irony in the fact that it was in Vienna, through the auspices of the Iran deal of 2015, that Obama and Kerry essentially capitulated to the other branch of Islam, the Shiites.

Future American presidents would need to understand that the average Muslim would know the date, September 11, and what it means in terms of Islamic thought. They would need to reject the belief that "Islam is a religion of peace." Islam had, for nearly all of the fourteen centuries of its existence, attempted to violently conquer the West. Knowing actual, not whitewashed Islamic history, would be critical to marshalling the will and military strength necessary to conquer both houses of resurgent militant Islam.

Secondly, future presidents would need to know that, for ISIS, raping, crucifying and enslaving the infidel or the apostate[47] are not evil acts if conducted in accordance with dictates of the Holy Quran and or other Islamic scriptures. Moreover, a core belief for all Muslims has always been that Mohammad engaged in or endorsed all the above activities. Virtually all Muslims believe that the Prophet's life cannot be criticized. His life is the one by which all others are judged. Therefore, murder and terror are divinely sanctioned if done in the name of advancing their religion. Clearly, Orwell had nothing on Mohammad.

As Eric Stakelbeck wrote in his book, *ISIS Exposed*,

ISIS doesn't just conquer towns - it utterly destroys them, slaughtering men, women, children and the elderly. In January of 2015, survivors of the month-long siege of Kobane, a town in northern Syria located near the Turkish border, described a stomach-churning orgy of bloodletting reminiscent of the Mongols' devastation of the Middle East eight centuries[48] earlier.

When ISIS captured the town, a correspondent on the ground, Sam Greenhill, of the UK based *Daily Mail* wrote,

Headless corpses litter the street...some of the mainly Kurdish townsfolk have had their eyes gouged out...refugees who made it to Surac, just across the border in Turkey, tell of witnessing appalling horrors...Father of four, Amin Fajar, said, "I have seen hundreds of bodies with their heads cut off... they put the heads on display to scare us all. The children saw the headless people," he said quietly, sitting cross-legged on a rug in his tent in a squalid refugee camp in Surac.[49]

For Christians who fell into the hands of ISIS, their fate was even worse. When Mosul fell, the Christian population was given three options, exactly those Mohammad had given the inhabitants of the Arabian Peninsula at the time of his conquest: convert to Islam, pay the jizya (an exorbitant tax levied against non-Muslims under Sharia Law) or die. Chris Mitchell of *CBN News*, on his blog post of November 6, 2014, shared an account given him by Canon Andrew White, the Vicar of St. George's Church in Baghdad, the city's last remaining Anglican Church,

In Iraq at the moment, it is impossible to describe how it really is. It is so awful. Most of our people originate from Nineveh (province) which is where

---

47. A Muslim who fails to be pure enough.

Mosul is located and where our faith started…Things were bad in Baghdad…bombings and shootings…so they fled to Nineveh - their traditional home. It was safer until ISIS came and hounded all of them out. Not some, all of them. And they killed huge numbers. They chopped children in half. They said to one man, "Either you say the words of converting to Islam or we will kill all your children." Then he phoned me, "Abounah, (father), I said the words. Does that mean Yeshua (Jesus) doesn't love me?" I said, "Elias, no, Jesus still loves you."[50]

A few days later ISIS turned up and said to the man's children, "You say the words, that you will follow Mohammad." And the children, all under fifteen, said, "No, we love Yeshua, we have always loved Yeshua." ISIS said, "Say the words!" They said, "No, we can't." They chopped all their heads off.

On August 19, 2014, ISIS released a horrifying video of a black-masked butcher, later dubbed "Jihad Johnny," while he cut off the head of a captured American journalist, James Foley. Two weeks later, ISIS released another beheading video featuring Jihad Johnny, this time cutting off the captured American journalist, Steven Sotloff. Later ISIS released videos of Jihad Johnny decapitating American aid worker, Peter Kassig and two British subjects, David Haines and Alan Henning. The confounding response from President Obama along with John Kerry and British Prime Minister, David Cameron, was that ISIS was, "not Islamic."

In November of 2014, following the Kassig beheading, Obama somehow finally felt obliged to say something about the many ISIS beheadings and doubled down. He said ISIS "represented no faith, least of all the Muslim faith." If his pronouncement were true, then Christians, Hindus, Jews, and Buddhists were all *more likely* to take heads than were Muslims.

Those Americans who saw the videos and listened to their president's pathetic response did so with utter contempt. They longed for a president of the United States who understood that ISIS (also known as IS or the Islamic State) was not just Islamic. It was **very** Islamic.

As the *Atlantic's* Graehm Wood wrote in his essay, *What ISIS Really Wants*,
> Yes, it attracted psychopaths and adventure seekers, drawn largely from the disaffected populations of the Middle East and Europe. But the religion

preached by its most ardent followers derives from coherent and even learned interpretations of Islam.

Virtually every major decision and law promulgated by the Islamic State adheres to what it calls, in its press and pronouncements, "the Prophetic methodology," which means following the prophecy and example of Muhammad, in punctilious detail. Muslims can reject the Islamic State; nearly all do. But pretending that it isn't actually a religious, millenarian group, with theology that must be understood to be combatted, has already led the United States to underestimate it and back foolish schemes to counter it. We'll need to get acquainted with the Islamic State's intellectual genealogy if we are to react in a way that will not strengthen it, but instead help it self-immolate in its own excessive zeal.[51]

Wood was an extremely astute observer of the current Middle East and more and more Americans had come to agree with him that future presidents and their senior military advisors must be fully versed in the ideologies that drive both the Sunni and Shiite jihadist movements. But by 2016, it had become apparent to them that the West could not wait to allow ISIS, as he puts it, "self-immolate in its own excessive zeal."

Muslims from around the world felt great joy when Baghdadi was declared the caliph on June 29. Suddenly, Mesopotamian lands held by ISIS now exerted a tremendous magnetic attraction to them and thousands every month were rushing to its black banner.

As I recorded in *Lessons from Fallen Civilizations*, the last Muslim caliphate to exist was the Ottoman Empire. Its power peaked in the late 16th century and, after losing the Battle at Vienna in 1683, went into decline. Its decline culminated when the founder of the Republic of Turkey, Mustafa Kemal Atatürk, officially ended the Ottoman Empire in 1924. By 2016, supporters of ISIS didn't even acknowledge the defunct Ottoman caliphate as legitimate. This was because it didn't fully enforce Islamic law which requires stonings and slavery, and its caliphs were not descended from the tribe of the Prophet, the Quraysh.

Baghdadi spoke of the significance of the new Caliphate in his Mosul sermon where he proclaimed himself Caliph. He said that for all Muslims, the revival of the caliphate, which had not functioned in 1,000 years, was a communal obligation. "This was a duty upon the Muslims that has been lost for centuries. Muslims sin by losing it. All must seek to establish it,"[52] he said. Holding a doctorate in Islamic jurisprudence, Baghdadi quoted scripture with a command of classical rhetoric. Unlike bin Laden, he claimed to be a descendant of Mohammad's tribe, the Quraysh.

For devout, knowledgeable Muslims, the creation of a new legitimate caliphate wasn't only a political entity but also a vehicle for salvation. Islamic State propaganda regularly reported the pledges of baya'a (allegiance) coming from jihadist groups across the Muslim world. For the devote ISIS jihadis, *true* Islam had been reestablished by the caliphate. Unlike al Qaeda which operated like cockroaches, plotting and hiding in caves and in secret safe houses, ISIS held land: a large portion of ancient Mesopotamia. It was also the largest, richest terrorist state ever. It drew its authority from Muslim scripture and, because the new Caliphate held and governed land, the new Caliph had the authority to command the Muslim world.

This meant that if the residents of Western citadels were ever to be safe again, the lands of the new Caliphate would need be retaken and ISIS destroyed. Future presidents would need to know and understand this.

ISIS Recruitment Video with British Fighters.

Both the inner cadre of ISIS jihadists surrounding Baghdadi, as well as the Shiite Mullahs running Iran, were fervent believers in the coming apocalypse. Both believed they were approaching an end-of-times war and conflagration where millions would die but the armies of "Rome" (Mohammad's term for the infidel West) would be defeated and a great imam would return or arise to rule a unified Muslim world. By their own admission, *both* ISIS and the Iranian regime were actively seeking the apocalypse. And whereas most Muslims were not jihadists, polls continued to show that up to 15% of the world's 1.6 billion Muslims (approximately 240 million souls) were, like the couple from San Bernardino, radicalized and took seriously the Quran's commandment to "slay the idolaters wherever you find them." In a world were weapons of mass destruction continued to proliferate, it seemed that future presidents could ill afford to wait and that preemption was the only rational course for the preservation of the West.

Finally, by 2016, many Americans of both parties were awakening to the fact that they had been denying their own spiritual obligations to join the war against the jihadists. They were finally realizing that it was unconscionable that their president, the supposed leader of Judeo/Christian West, continued to allow some of the very oldest Christian congregations, some dating back to the time of Christ, to be murderously wiped out by radical Islam. It was a crime tantamount to FDR turning his back on the plight of European Jews during World War II when much more could have been done to help them escape the Nazis. Americans were sensing that a new president must also embrace the moral and spiritual component of this struggle and act accordingly.

Part Three - Winning the War with Hard Power & Smarter Power

In addition to fully understanding the beliefs and motivations of the jihadists, future presidents would need to put in place a combination of soft and hard power aimed at neutralizing and ultimately destroying the Islamic threat. The threat would continue to grow and be dire.

As early as 2010, the entire Western World had already dodged a huge bullet. The Yemeni-based AQAP (al Qaeda of the Arabian Peninsula) had managed to develop and smuggle printer-cartridge bombs on board two cargo planes. Due to a Saudi intelligence officer who had penetrated the group and sent word of the plot to western intelligence agencies, the planes were landed in Europe and the bombs removed before

Sana'a, the largest city in Yemen

they could be detonated over their US targets. If the plot had not been foiled, at the very last instant, the planes would have exploded over two US cities, potentially causing a much greater loss of life than 9/11. But more importantly, the terror it could have inflicted on commercial and passenger air travel certainly had the potential to crash the Western economies.

In the summer of 2013, before ISIS had even stormed into Iraq, CIA Deputy Director, Michael Morell, said that civil war in Syria had become the number-one threat to US security in the world. He explained that more fighters were entering Syria at a more rapid pace than had entered Iraq at any time during the height of the Iraq war. He warned that they were likely to wage attacks on the US by capturing Syria's chemical weapon stores.

In January of 2014, Director of National Intelligence, James Clapper, told the Senate Intelligence Committee that the US had obtained evidence of training complexes in Syria that were intended to train jihadists to go back to their home countries and conduct terror attacks. He ominously stated, "Not only are fighters being drawn to Syria, but so are technologies and techniques that pose particular problems to our defenses."[53]

By 2016, in Obama's seventh year as president, most Americans could see that the West was losing its war with resurgent militant Islam. When he first campaigned for the presidency, despite the admonitions from chief strategist, David Axelrod, to give few details, he was forced to discuss national security. He stated that Afghanistan was the "good war" and that Iraq was the "dumb war." In this crude construct he was able to both bash Bush as well as distinguish himself from his contender, Hillary Clinton, as well as the other Democrats, such as John Kerry and Joe Biden who all voted for the resolution of force against Saddam Hussein. Moreover, his vow to send more troops to fight the "good war" was a thinly veiled ploy to show that he was not soft on national security but that he had some strong but secret convictions about the *strategic* importance of Afghanistan.

As mentioned in the *Introduction*, on February 11, 2007, the day he announced his candidacy for president, he fatefully stated, "We ended up launching a war that should have never been authorized... and have seen over 3,000 lives of our bravest young Americans wasted." It would be the first of many of Obama's statements that, while they didn't ring any alarm bells for those of his background and ideology, were grossly dispiriting to those in the military and to those who knew something of war.

In the halls of academia, among the deans of international studies, the concepts of soft power versus hard power were well-established bipolar modes of operation by which the American super power could, and should, conduct foreign policy. For many academics, soft power was comprised of diplomacy, such as the offering of mutually beneficial treaties and trade agreements or offering aid. Hard power was the offer of military action to defend an ally or the threat and use of military force against enemies.

With the election of Obama, the American political and academic Left concluded that his administration needed a new form of power, the name for which was first coined by Harvard professor, Joseph Nye, as "smart power." This construct would be combination of the two powers, soft and hard. This was absurd in that it was hardly new. All great powers dating back to the Roman and Athenian empires used both soft and hard power in their foreign relations. But "smart power" would be different because, unlike Bush who used too much hard power, Obama would emphasize the soft and call it "smart."

As Mark Moyar put it, "The term "smart power" was aimed more at praising liberals and denigrating the allegedly heavy-handedness of the Bush administration, and was meant to convey their conviction that Bush Republicans had been dumb."[54] The Obama administration's overreliance on soft power, characterized by military disengagement and risk-adverse diplomacy, was what proved to be dumb. Over its first seven years the Obama team's "smart power" that they employed in negotiations with Libya, Iraq, Syria, Egypt, Gaza, the West Bank, Israel, Somalia, Yemen, Russia and China, experienced more aggression, war and terrorism; not less. Our faculty-lounge president was forced to narcissistically discard the obvious lessons of past administrations; that is, soft power usually fails when hard power is not present to protect it. Freshman international studies students should know that newly liberated citizens in places like Iraq and Afghanistan can't run schools or introduce more modern farming projects if policemen and judges are wantonly assassinated by jihadists.

How Does the Next President Stop Losing
the War on Terror?
Published by *Townhall.com*, February 13, 2016

PUBLISHED ESSAY BY LARRY KELLEY

In February of 2016, I spoke to Cliff May who is the founder and president of the Foundation for Defense of Democracies (FDD), which he created immediately following 9/11. FDD today is one of the nation's most highly regarded national security policy institutes. Our following interview appeared at *Townhall.com* that month as well.

Larry Kelley: Do you agree with my assessment that we are losing the war on terror which, of course, is a misnomer? Terrorism is a tactic not an enemy. Which measurements would you cite to describe how the West is losing this war?

Cliff May: I totally agree that we in the West are losing this war. I keep coming across new maps that show greater and greater territory now controlled by the jihadists. They are in Libya, Nigeria, Syria, Iraq, Afghanistan, the Indian subcontinent, and the Pacific. It's a threat that is metastasizing rather than being contained. I would add to that list the Islamic Republic of Iran which is about to experience an economic resurgence given the money (approximately $150 billion) that was once frozen and will now be released to them. And Secretary Kerry even admitted that some of that money will be spent on terrorism. They are, and continue to be, the leading sponsor of terrorism in the world. They control Shiite militias in Iraq and the Assad regime in Syria to a great extent. They are more than influential with Hamas. Hezbollah is essentially their foreign legion. If people cannot see what's taking place, they are not looking very hard.

LK: So would you consider that both houses of Islam, Shiites and Sunnis to be at war with the West?

CM: I would put it a little differently. In both those houses of Islam you have

Clifford May

jihadist movements. And here is the key. They are rivals not enemies. Both are at war with America and Israel and in various ways. There are those in this administration who would like to think that Iran has become our ally in this struggle against ISIS. But they are missing a great deal of the nuances in this conflict.

LK: Could you expand on your observation that the two houses of Islam are rivals not enemies? What do you mean?

CM: Jihadism is a two-sided coin, Shiite and Sunni. Iran has, since 1979, under the Ayatollah Khomeini, proudly proclaimed that it was at war with America and the West. Secretary Kerry has been very clear, that Khomeini's successor, the Ayatollah Khamenei, is also at war with us. Kerry admitted this in saying that the Iranian supreme leader often preaches "death to America." For both sides, I would say that there is a long-range strategy to achieve just that over time.

LK: With respect to the recent Iran deal, do you think the Iranians are now less, or are they more, our enemy?

CM: I think that they (the Iranians) feel they are making very good progress toward their ultimate goal and faster than they expected. They see diplomacy as another field of battle. And they believe they've won a very important battle in terms of this newest nuclear agreement. And I think they are correct in that.

LK: So you feel that Sunni and Shiite jihadists are rivals in their attempt to conquer the West?

CM: I do. They both believe the world is divided into two spheres, dar al Islam which is the world governed by Islam, and dar al harb, which is, by definition, a world of war which must be made to submit. And the only question is - Who does the conquering? Is it the Taliban, al Qaeda or Iran?

LK: They are rivals in the conquest of the infidel?

CM: Exactly right. Rivals in the reestablishing the power and glory that the

PUBLISHED ESSAY BY LARRY KELLEY

Islamic world once had and which it is obligated to repossess.

LK: What would be the three or four steps the new Commander in Chief should employ to reverse our losses and what does winning this war look like?

CM: Great Questions.

1. First this war must be the administration's top priority. Not a tertiary but number one goal to contain and ultimately defeat jihadism worldwide. If its top priority is income inequality or climate change, we will continue to lose this war.
2. Second, the last thing we can do is to continue to weaken our military.
3. Third, we need to rely on the Pentagon to determine the methods, manpower and material necessary to accomplish the mission… worldwide.
4. And fourth, while kinetic warfare is necessary so is economic warfare. And this entails building the strongest American economy possible. Because only in this way can we exert maximum economic pressure on our adversaries. Sanctions should not be a symbol but a weapon employed continuously until our enemy surrenders…

LK: Or is overthrown by its own people?

CM: Yes. Economically, we lifted our foot off the throat of Iran at precisely the moment when we were about to get a positive response. Since then we have received no positive responses from them.

LK: Any other tactics we should employ?

CM: There are many. We need to get immigration policy right. We need to fight the ideology as we did with communism. We need a sophisticated war of ideas which will need to stay in place for decades as was the case in the cold war against the Soviets. In summary, all these tactics would need to flow from an administration which makes this war its top priority. Otherwise, we continue to lose.

LK: So assuming that the next president does make this war his top priority, what would indicate to you that we are rolling back this threat and that we are winning?

CM: You would know that we are winning when we were defeating the enemy on multiple battlefields. There is nothing more debilitating to a messianic movement than defeats in battle. If you believe you are divinely endorsed, as do both the Shiite and Sunni jihadists, you faithfully believe that victory will come. If conversely, you are losing troops and territory, as was the case for al Qaeda in Iraq during the surge, you lose your ability to recruit new members to your cause. Our problem was that, having won the Iraq war, we precipitously and completely left Iraq which allowed the defeated remnants of al Qaeda in Iraq split into two entities al Qaeda (in various countries) and ISIS, both of which are much more formidable enemies now. Stop to consider if we had suddenly left Japan and Europe in 1945. What would they look like today?

[End of Essay]

PUBLISHED ESSAY BY LARRY KELLEY

Conquer ISIS Using the Roman Model

Seventy-one years after it was conquered by the US there were still 50,000 American military personnel in Japan. In 2016 the Japanese contributed $2 billion a year to support their own occupation, making it much cheaper for the US to station them there than to keep them at home. Korea continued to host 28,000 US troops on its soil. The two countries had also committed to paying $30 billion to construct four huge American military bases, while the US taxpayer only contributed $7 billion on those projects aimed at protecting our allies' in the Far East. In 2016, Japan, once our mortal enemy, was a staunch ally of the US and lived under the American "nuclear umbrella." That relationship mirrored the Roman Empire's brilliant success at converting conquered peoples into loyal allies. It was a process that historians referred to as "Romanization."

Caesar Augustus, First Emperor of Post-Republican Rome

However, with respect to Afghanistan, in March of 2016, the Defense Department filed a report revealing that, since its liberation in 2001, the US had spent $113 billion there. Adjusted for inflation, this was more than was spent to rebuild Europe after World War II. Most of the money was lost due to waste, fraud and corruption. Some completed Afghan projects, such as dams and irrigation systems, were in the hands of the Taliban which controlled more of the country than it did in the days leading up to 9/11.

Next, Obama sent out Deputy National Security Advisor, Ben Rhodes, to amplify on the equivocations. He said, "The lessons of the last decade show us that a US ground force cannot impose stability or a new system of governance on countries ravaged by extremism and sectarianism - local forces have to do that, with our support."

He went on, "Ground wars in the Middle East are not sustainable, and will ultimately undermine our ability to sustain America's global leadership and ability to accomplish other things in the world that are fundamental to US interests."[55]

His remarks made many wonder: would it not undermine our ability to accomplish other things in the world if ISIS were to release some deadly bio toxins into the New York and D.C. subway systems, or if they were to blow up several key repeater stations, sending a portion of the eastern seaboard into darkness? Moreover, why wouldn't we take seriously their public threats to attack D.C. and New York and resolve to peremptorily destroy them?

In late 2015, a parade of military experts testified before Congress that the US, by itself, could conquer ISIS in 2 to 4 months and could do so with 40,000 to 50,000 *ground* troops. Given that we have the power to do so, the American electorate had to wonder - Wouldn't it be the humane thing to do, given that ISIS will otherwise continue to kill innocents in the Middle East, in Europe, and ultimately in the US? But most of those same experts also offered a cautionary coda by stating that an occupation of *any* Middle Eastern country would, over the long-term, likely prove costly in terms of blood and treasure.

Perhaps the answer lay in adopting some of the features of the Roman model for conquest. Stop to consider that it still confounds our imagination as to how a single city state conquered and held the territory which began in the North of Britain and extended to the Tigris River (in today's Iraq) and all across the whole of the Middle East and North Africa. How the Romans conquered all those realms is better understood than how they held all those diverse populations. What was the glue which kept the empire together for the 200 years that we refer to as the Pax Romana?

In *Lessons from Fallen Civilizations*, I wrote that in 209 BC the great Carthaginian commander, Hannibal, was ravaging the Italian Peninsula. In that same year, a 24-year-old Roman general, Scipio, established a diplomatic template for Roman statesmanship so critical to its success in the consolidation of its empire. He took an army of 30,000 men across the River Ebro and invaded Carthaginian Spain. There he captured its capital, Cartagena (New Spain).

He, like many of the Roman ruling class of his generation, instinctively understood how victory could become a mechanism for building loyalty to Rome.

Scipio made scrupulous lists of his new Spanish prisoners, former hostages of the Carthaginians, and took special care to ceremoniously return them to the emissaries of the tribes from which they hailed. Livy records a number of incidents that have an almost Shakespearean quality. He tells of a sister-in-law of Indibilis, the prince of the important tribe who, when he gained an audience with Scipio, fell weeping at his feet, begging for the return of her beautiful young daughters. Scipio complied and sent one of his most trusted aids to accompany them back to their homeland.

Livy describes another extremely beautiful maiden "...of such beauty that wherever she went, she drew the eyes of everyone." Scipio's fellow officers brought her to him as a gift. When he learned that she was betrothed to a young Celtiberian of noble birth, Scipio summoned the young man, entrusted the girl to him, and said that he wanted no thanks but his pledge to be a "friend of the Roman people."[56]

The Roman System of Patronage

By the time Scipio defeated the Carthaginians in Spain, he was able to implement what became a highly evolved form of diplomacy which historians now refer to as "Roman patronage." Rome's patron/client system was the glue that initially tied the various city states in Italy to their Roman overlords, but eventually tied all its conquered peoples together. It was a peculiar, yet brilliant, system for assimilating new subjects very rapidly and eliciting from them almost instant loyalty. Historians believe that the system grew out of the Romans' keen interest in understanding the people they had come to rule. The system does not appear to be codified. Rather, like much of Roman culture, it was the product of an amalgam of precedents that became traditional policies. The importance of the system defies exaggeration when we stop to consider that, minus the strength of Rome's Italian confederation, Hannibal would have surely destroyed Rome in the third century BC.

The system was multifaceted but the portion which applied to conquered peoples worked as follows: Upon their defeat, the commanding Roman general became their patron. He became those conquered peoples' advocate upon his return to Rome. Immediately upon their surrender, warrior elites of the newly conquered were made to understand that the very same general who had defeated them would become their patron and benefactor. Their patron would use his power to advocate for them and ensure that they would get equal protection under Roman law, no matter which magistrate was ultimately assigned to be their provincial ruler.

As *provincials*, opportunities to share in the burgeoning wealth of the empire, and ultimately full citizenship, was afforded to them. It was a demanding system that necessitated sending embassies to Rome to maintain or renew contact should the patron die and jurisdiction pass to a son. A patron, out of honor and tradition, would advocate for his provincials' public works projects such as the construction of roads, new ports facilities, military fortifications, and aqueducts. These projects produced wealth for the client provincials, lots of well-paying jobs, and a new phenomenon - a rapidly-expanding middle class.

Roman aqueduct still standing

Applying the Lessons of Rome to a
Middle Eastern Occupation

For example, should America be forced to take central Iraq and a portion of Syria from ISIS, wouldn't it be prudent to offer the Sunni occupants of these liberated lands a similar bargain? Instead of making the American occupied area a new independent state, especially given our experience in the region, wouldn't it make more sense for the US to call it a protectorate where local government officials are elected by their peers but where the senior-most official is either a US, NATO or coalition military commander? The position could be something similar to the role General MacArthur assumed in 1945 Japan. Would it not make sense that he be in charge of protecting the new country from foreign threats, training and staffing local police forces, preventing sectarian violence and insuring that the rights of all citizens, Sunni, Shiite, Christian, and other minorities are protected? And most importantly, he would be in charge of standing up and protecting new for-profit enterprises with hard and soft power much as did the Romans.

Safety and stability could be followed by the introduction of multinational companies who would bring in their own senior managers but would also hire local workers to staff new energy, farming, medical companies, public utilities, etc. This could be done with the proviso that some of the tax revenue would flow back to the country where these multinationals are headquartered but some would stay inside the protectorate.

And finally, young men and women would be heavily recruited into the occupation military forces as a mechanism to bring the population out of tribalism and into the twenty-first century fellowship of man.

The Roman model worked extraordinarily well for approximately four centuries. By the first century AD, the average first-century Roman citizen had obtained a level of affluence far above the peasant tribal warrior who lived outside the Empire. Roman patronage became the engine that produced a level of middle-class affluence for the empire's citizenry that was not eclipsed in the West until the middle of the twentieth century. It was this system that enabled a single city-state to command the allegiance of such a vast and diverse realm. Moreover, an American version of that Roman model is still working in Korea and Japan today.

A New "Smarter" Power Could
Begin by Dumping the Palestinians

For seven administrations dating back to the Carter years, the US, along with other nations, poured billions of dollars of aid into the Palestinian-held "West-Bank," an area once part of ancient Galilee, the birthplace of Jesus. In 2014, $793 million, or about a quarter of Palestine's $3.1 billion-dollar budget, came from foreign aid. This represented $176 for every man, woman and Palestinian child; by far the highest per capita assistance in the world. Yet in 2014, $75 million of that aid never got to the development of Palestinian infrastructure which the donor nations had long believed was so necessary to promote a prosperous, and eventually peaceful, Palestine. $75 million went to funding Palestine's terrorists and their activities.

Between 1993, when the Oslo process began, and 2013, the Palestinians received $21.7 billion in aid according to the World Bank. Its leaders had the chance to use all those funds to build infrastructure and promote peace. They didn't. Instead they diverted significant portions to sizable monthly stipends for terrorists, cross-border tunnels and to the purchase of thousands of missiles which eventually rained down on Israel.

A future president could begin by posing the following questions to the country and the world, "Why should the US be funding terrorism?"

"Doesn't it go to a larger moral issue? Can we in good conscience fund the murder of the citizens of our closest ally, Israel?"

Jerusalem, the capital of Isreal

In so doing he could begin a powerful propaganda war against *all* Islamic terrorism, while putting *all* of Islam on notice that the US will no longer be duped into playing its double game. No longer would we be funding, or even be non-committal, about Muslim regimes who are covertly conducting jihadist operations against the US and or our allies.

In February of 2016, Obama's U.N. Ambassador, Samantha Power, traveled to Jerusalem to sell the Israelis (for seemingly the 1,000th time) on why they should accept the vaunted "two-state solution." Her case might have had some merit if the Palestinian State that she proposed was essentially peaceful and democratic, such as Canada or Costa Rica. But nearly everyone outside the sphere of the international Left knows that such a new Palestinian state on the Left Bank would more likely mirror terrorist-run Gaza. A future president could ask the world, "Why should the Israelis be forced to live in very close quarters with a state dedicated to their destruction?

As Bret Stephens of the *Wall Street Journal* writes, "A great power that cannot recognize the dilemmas of its allies soon becomes a useless ally, and it becomes intolerable if it then turns its strategic ignorance into a moral sermon."

For six decades, the Muslim world, along with the American and international Left, had used the supposed plight of the Palestinians as their cause celeb for why the West and its ally, Israel, should capitulate to the demands of the Palestinian jihadists. The Palestinians were the surrogates for all those in the Middle East who demanded that the West pay retribution for colonialism's past sins while they supported terrorist attacks against those same donor nations. A future American president could simply make further aid to the Palestinians contingent upon the following demands, which would prove powerful propaganda plays:

1. The Palestinians make their accounts transparent to the Western donator nations so they can be sure that not one cent is spent on terror.
2. The Palestinians concede that Israel has a right to exist.

If a future president were to do this at the outset of his first term, he would jump-start the reintroduction of American world leadership and put radical Islam on notice that America's new game would be "smarter power," that is, hardball.

The Country Needed a Salesman for Freedom

In order to rally the American electorate to the cause of defeating the jihadists in Tehran, those across the Middle East, and those hiding and plotting within the West, future presidents would need to become accomplished salesmen for freedom. As described above, Americans could only hope future presidents would understand that young men and women would eventually refuse to join the military and refuse to put their lives on the line for a country they saw as their oppressor, which robbed them of their private property and their chance for prosperity.

Shortly after inauguration, the 45th president could begin by pitting the full force of his office against Obamacare and selling the public on why its repeal would return to every American a portion of his or her freedom lost by the passage of this unconstitutional law. He could begin by stating that if this government can force you to buy a product you don't want, then there would be no constitutional protections from an oppressive government.

Moreover, it was a terrible product. It forced the young and healthy to subsidize through higher *mandated* premiums the old, the poor and the sick. The Obamacare individual mandate was an effective new tax on lower and middle class working people, forcing them to pay a higher cost of mandatory insurance premiums. He could also remind the public that the new law violated Obama's pledge to "never raise taxes on the middle class." Repealing it would free workers to buy less expensive insurance in an unregulated marketplace and, ironically, would fulfill one of the Obama's *solemn* pledges to the American people; that being, to never raise taxes on the middle class.[57]

In his role as the chief salesman for freedom, the new president could remind the Americans that in the 1970's the country was similarly in a malaise when freedom and free markets were under assault, and what brought that to a halt was the election of Ronald Reagan. His relentless faith in free markets, fair trade, lower taxes and deregulation was what turbocharged the US economy and as a result western economies. As the economist, Steve Moore, put it, "Reagan and his partner in liberty, England's Margaret Thatcher, adopted a gutsy agenda of tax cuts, sound money, trade liberalization and privatization and, in the case of Britain, a rollback of unfettered and corrupt union power." Together, with renewed economic strength, America and England were able to build a powerful military coalition that allowed them to not just contain the Soviet menace but to bankrupt it.

In order to take land from ISIS and reverse the gains made by resurgent militant Islam elsewhere throughout the globe, the enemy must be named by our future presidents and their motivations understood. Secondly, a dramatic reversal in American resolve and a rededication of resources would be necessary. In order to put the country on this path, the new president would need to be the chief salesman for why a new reconstructed American military would be the catalyst to reverse the tide of world events and the looming dangers associate with the decline of the West. He would need to sell the nation on why we cannot afford to not be the world's policeman, why we must protect our allies from attack, why we must protect the international trading system and shipping lanes and why we must prevent weapons of mass destruction from being acquired by the ever growing armies of Allah.

As Moyar puts it, "Among the most critical objectives are degrading the nuclear programs of Iran and (its close ally) North Korea, depriving terrorist organizations of sanctuaries, and ridding the seas of piracy."[58] The new president would need to sell the nation and the world on why America cannot "lead from behind," as his predecessor did in Libya. To defeat global jihadism, we have no option but to return to leading from the front.

Part Four - The Desperate Need for a Reformation of Islam

In her book, *From Islam to America*, Ayaan Hirsi Ali, a Muslim apostate, wrote "On New Year's Eve, 2007, in a Dallas Suburb, an Egyptian, Yasser Said, shot his 19 and 17-year-old-daughters in the back of his taxi. He then parked it in the driveway of a hotel and absconded, leaving their bodies in the cab."

Amina and Sarah were bright, pretty American-ized girls who both were secretly dating non-Muslim boys, Eric and Eddy. Their father, a man who immigrated to the US in 1983, was enraged having learned of their secret liaisons and was known to have beaten them and threatened to kill them. Their mother, an American from a troubled family, prior to their murders, fled the home with the girls. But she was convinced by the father to bring them to a restaurant where the family could talk. About an hour after they met, the younger daughter, Sarah, called 911 from her cell phone and said she was dying.

In April 2008, in Jonesboro, Atlanta, Chaudry Rashad, a Pakistani man who owned a pizza parlor, strangled his 25-year-old daughter, Sandela, with a cord because she had returned to her parents' house where she told them she wanted a divorce from a man her father had arranged for her to marry against her will. When the police arrived, her father told them he "did nothing wrong."[59]

In February of 2009, in Buffalo, New York, a 47-year-old Muslim businessman, Muzzammil Hassan, who ran a cable TV station which promoted *tolerance toward Muslims*, beheaded his wife who was seeking a divorce.

In my first book, *Lessons from Fallen Civilizations*, my dedication reads:
To the women of Islam,
murdered by their own relations,
deposited in unmarked graves,
that they be welcomed as saints
by the one true loving God.

In that book, I profiled a number of formerly-Muslim women apostates, including

Ayaan Hersi Ali, who had the courage to call out Islam for its fundamentally violent dogmas. Another was Wafa Sultan who now lives in hiding in the US. She grew up a Muslim in Syria and became a psychiatrist there. In 1977, while in her fourth year as a Syrian medical student, Ms. Sultan worked part-time in a gynecologist's office. In her book, *A God Who Hates*, she writes,

> I saw a steady stream of identical family tragedies. A young girl and her mother would arrive completely covered so not to be recognized. They explained that they wanted to ensure that the girl was still a virgin prior to her forthcoming marriage, and that she had a bad fall when she was younger. When the doctor explained, after examining the young girl, that she hadn't just lost her virginity but was also pregnant, the two women would weep and beg the doctor to help solve their problem...[60]

Ms. Sultan went on to explain that, in most cases, the young woman would confess that, since childhood, she had been sexually abused by her father, her brother, her uncle or another male relative. One would think that a doctor's attitude to young women in distress would have been one of care and sympathy. The doctor frequently took advantage of the sensitivity of the situation and demanded fantastic sums as payment. The two women would come back the next day with the money which they might have obtained by selling their jewelry. Watching this whole scene play out, she was just as sickened by the doctor's attitude as she was by the abuse these women were suffering at the hands of their male relatives.

On her visits to clinics in the poorer rural areas, Sultan ascertained that many of the girls suffered a worse fate. Without the money to perform abortions and do vaginal surgeries to simulate virginity, they simply disappeared - killed by their families and dumped into unmarked graves.

Islamic culture visits violence on its own families to a vastly higher degree than any other culture. Hirsi Ali, Sultan and many formerly-Muslim scholars, such as Ibn Warraq, author of *Why I Am Not a Muslim*, wrote eloquently about the fundamentally violent nature of Islamic thought and jurisprudence. Because they lived the life of a Muslim, and are now targeted for death for speaking out against Islamic barbarity, they commanded our attention and authority. They gave us the insight to understand why, in 2015, a young Muslim couple from San Bernardino, living the American dream, would choose to kill their coworkers and die an Islamist's death.

By 2016 it was becoming common knowledge that, in order for future presidents to wage a potent war of ideas against radical Islam, he or she would need to understand that Islamic teaching does not just give rise to domestic violence. As Ali puts it, "Islamic violence is rooted not in social, economic or political conditions - or even theological error - but rather in the foundational texts of Islam itself."[61]

Over his tenure as President, Obama repeatedly informed the world that the horrific violence sweeping across the Middle East by ISIS and its affiliates, and unleashed upon Paris and Southern California, had nothing to do with Islam. On June 29, 2014, ISIS proclaimed its new Caliphate in Iraq and Syria. On August 19 and September 2, for all the world to see on video internet, ISIS decapitated two American journalists, James Foley and Steven Sotloff. So outrageous were these provocations that it forced Obama to reverse his long-held position that he would never continue George Bush's intervention in Iraq and ordered air strikes there in an effort to, as he would later put it, "degrade and ultimately destroy the terrorist group known as ISIL."

On September 10, 2014, the president said, "Now, let's make two things clear: ISIL is not Islamic. No religion condones the killing of innocents. And the vast majority of ISIL's victims have been Muslim. And ISIL is not a state…it's a terrorist organization, pure and simple…"

But as I discussed above, this is not what ISIS professes about its own ideology and motivations. David Adesnik of *National Review* countered the president by writing, "Regardless of how the president balances the imperatives of diplomatic courtesy and analytic precision, the public discussion of the relationship between Islam and terrorism should begin with an emphasis on the school of thought that leading scholars now describe as jihadi-Salafism, radical jihadism, or simply jihadism. The leaders of both al Qaeda and the Islamic State adhere explicitly to this movement."[62]

In a *Brookings Institution* paper, Princeton's Cole Bunzel explained that "while jihadi-salafi thinking might be extreme, it is based on a reading of Islamic scripture that is also textually rigorous, deeply rooted in a premodern theological tradition, and extensively elaborated by a recognized cadre of religious authorities."[63]

A Moroccan convert to Christianity, Brother Rachid, the son of an Imam and host of a Cairo-based television station, wrote this letter to Obama which was published in the *New York Times*:

Mr. President, I must tell you that you are wrong about ISIS. You said it speaks for no religion. I am a former Muslim. My dad is an imam. I have spent more than 20 years studying Islam…I can tell you with confidence that ISIS speaks for Islam…ISIS's 10,000 members are all Muslims…They come from different countries and have one common denominator: Islam. They are following Islam's Prophet Muhammad in every detail…They have called for a caliphate, which is a central doctrine in Sunni Islam.

I ask you, Mr. President, to stop being politically correct - to call things by their names. ISIS, al Qaeda, Boko Haram, Al-Shabaab in Somalia, the Taliban and their sister brand names, are all made in Islam. Unless the Muslim world deals with Islam and separates religion from State, we will never end this cycle…If Islam is not the problem, then why is it there are millions of Christians in the Middle East and yet none of them has ever blown up himself to become a martyr, even though they live under the same economic and political circumstances and even worse?... Mr. President, if you really want to fight terrorism, then fight it at the roots. How many Saudi sheikhs are preaching hatred? How many Islamic channels are indoctrinating people and teaching them violence from the Quran and hadith?... How many Islamic schools are producing generations of teachers and students who believe in jihad and martyrdom and fighting the infidel?[64]

In short, al Qaeda, ISIS and innumerable other jihadist movements, all of whom held the ultimate goal of conquering the West, were very Islamic. And despite their own president's prevarications, by 2016, much of the American public knew it.

The Teacher Who is Ayaan Hirsi Ali

Ayaan Hirsi Ali

As I maintained above, and also in my first book, I believe that in order for the West to win the war against resurgent militant Islam, the US and its allies needed to employ "smarter" power. One way they could employ "smarter" power is for the US and its allies to aid, and give shelter to, those who were Islamic or formerly Islamic and who were courageous and skillful enough to start a small fire which would become the firestorm of Islamic reformation. Of all the voices advocating for Islamic reformation, the one whose voice I believed to be one of the most authoritative, given her Islamic background and her scholarship and fame, was Ayaan Hirsi Ali.[65]

In 2015, her book, *Heretic: Why Islam Needs a Reformation Now* was published. For those who still wondered why terrorism and the civil wars raging across the Middle East and Africa seemed to be the product of Islam and the Muslim world, she made that answer very plain. She wrote:

Now when I assert that Islam is not a religion of peace, I do not mean that Islamic belief makes Muslims naturally violent. This is manifestly not the case: there are many millions of Muslims in the world. What I do say is the call to violence and the justification for it are explicitly stated in the sacred texts of Islam. Moreover, this theologically sanctioned violence is there to be activated by any number of offenses; including, but not limited to, apostasy, adultery, blasphemy, and even sometimes as threats to family honor or the honor of Islam itself.[66]

Ali brilliantly pointed out it was not only undeniable that Islamic sacred texts and Islamic jurisprudence have spawned violent jihadi movements around the globe, such as al Qaeda and ISIS and Boko Haram, but entire Islamic nations also continue to visit violence and cruelty upon their own people. In Pakistan any act, or even a statement deemed critical of the Prophet or Islam by even an unauthoritan

---

65. For her profile, see *Lessons from Fallen Civilizations*, pg. 302

witness, could be labeled as blasphemy and was punishable by death. Pakistani neighbors could condemn their own neighbors to death for speech. In Saudi Arabia, where churches and synagogues were forbidden, public beheadings were common. In August of 2014, public beheadings were held every day in Mecca. In Iran, public stonings for adulterers were common and homosexuals were publicly hanged. In Brunei, where Sharia Law had been reinstated, homosexuality was punishable by death.

The Qur'an has many admonitions to kill the infidel - "slay the unbelievers wherever ye catch them," surah 2, verse 191.[67]

So by the beginning of 2016, there were many Americans, some Muslim Americans, who hoped that a new president would call for a Muslim reformation. There was hope that perhaps history could mimic the events which began in October of 1517. In that year, in the Saxon town of Wittenberg, a relatively unknown monk, Martin Luther, posted his demands that the Catholic Church refrain from its wicked and corrupt practices such as the selling of indulgences for salvation. While the Protestant Reformation would, of course, be vastly different from what could become a Muslim reformation, there was one aspect which each would unarguably have in common. Unlike previous Euro heretics before him, Luther was able to send his message throughout Europe via a new technology - the printing press. Similarly, by 2016 and beyond, as Ali wrote, "I think it is plausible that the Internet will be for the Islamic world in the twenty-first century what the printing press was for the Christendom in the sixteenth."[68]

And while the differences between the two centuries and the structures of the two religions varied so greatly, Muslims of 2016 and Christians of centuries past had one thing in common: they wanted a better life for themselves and their children. Moreover, it was becoming increasingly obvious to millions of Muslims, via the Internet, that jihadists could only murder and destroy but could not build a better future. The tide in favor of the reformation was turning.

Despite the Internet and social media being powerful tools in recruiting jihadists to the side of al Qaeda and ISIS, they were proving also to be powerful mechanisms for sending the good news from Muslim travelers and refugees in the West to their friends and family still trapped in dysfunctional Islamic-majority societies. And that good news was, that in the West, freedom, human rights for all, even women, was a greater source for the realization of happiness than was living under Sharia Law.

Major Muslim leaders were beginning to call out Islam for its essential cruelty and barbarism. This was candidly admitted to by none other than one of the world's leading Muslim clerics and a prominent Egyptian leader of the Muslim Brotherhood, Yusuf Al-Qaradawi. In 2013, he stunningly said, "If they had gotten rid of the apostasy punishment (which is death), Islam would not exist today. Islam would have ended with the death of the Prophet; peace be upon him. Opposing apostasy is what kept Islam to this day."[69]

Islam's unbending position on apostasy directly stems from the Qur'an's unabashed admonition uttered by the Prophet, who said, "He who leaves the religion, kill him." (Imagine how different Western Christendom would be if Christ had uttered the same.) But it is also, in the eyes of the non-Muslim world, perhaps the single most damning piece of Islamic dogma. In my first book, I profile another crusader for the liberation of Muslims, an outspoken author and former Muslim, Nonie Darwish. She brilliantly proved that the dogma which holds that apostates must be killed is not just adhered to by majority-Muslim countries but is as well in minority-Muslim countries including the US. The belief that Muslims who leave the religion should be killed is utterly main stream Islamic dogma. I wrote:

On her website, *formermuslimsunited.org* is a Freedom Pledge that asks Muslim leaders in the US to renounce the portion of Sharia Law that mandates death for apostasy. The pledge was mailed to over one hundred leaders of Islamic Institutions based in the United States, including Ibrahim Hooper and Nihad Awad of CAIR and Dahlia Mogahed, Obama's chief advisor for all things Islamic. Only two signed it. Ms. Mogahed, who maintained an office in the White House, was one of the ninety-eight who refused to sign.[70]

On New Year's Day 2015, the president of Egypt, el-Sisi, chose the citadel of Islamic jurisprudence, the most prestigious center for Sunni religious thought, Al-Azhar, to tell an assembly of Muslim clergy that he was calling for nothing less than a "religious revolution." He asked Muslim leaders to help in the fight against extremism,

I say and repeat, again, that we are in need of a religious revolution. You imams are responsible before Allah. The entire world is waiting on you. The entire world is waiting for your word... because the Islamic world is being torn, it is being destroyed, it is being lost. And it is being lost by our own hands. We need a revolution of the self, a revolution of consciousness and ethics to rebuild the Egyptian person - a person that our country will need in the near future.

It's inconceivable that the thinking that we hold most sacred should cause the entire Islamic world to be a source of anxiety, danger, killing and destruction for the rest of the world. Impossible that this thinking - and I am not saying the religion - I am saying this thinking... This is antagonizing the entire world.[71]

Not since the end of World War I, when Mustafa Kemal Atatürk officially ended the Ottoman Caliphate and established the secular Turkish Republic, freeing it from Sharia Law, had medieval Islam been dealt such a terrific blow. As Ali put it, for a President of Egypt to make this speech at Al-Azhar was highly significant because it had long been a capital of "clerical conservatism, ruthlessly resisting even the discussion of meaningful reforms to Islam." El-Sisi became the most powerful voice in all of Islam advocating for its reformation. Moreover, by the summer of 2016, el-Sisi's military was working very closely with

Mustafa Kemal Atatürk

the Israelis in coordinating attacks on an ISIS affiliate in the Sinai Peninsula called Sinai Province. When the world's largest Arab country is in a military alliance with Israel fighting radical Islam, profound changes are at work.

By the beginning of 2016, for the President of the United States and the leading anti-reformation Muslim across the globe, their ability to continue to tell the lie that Islam was like all other religions, a "religion of peace," was falling apart.

The Forces of the Islamic Reformation

By the beginning of 2016, there was a combination of three powerful forces impacting and enabling the embryonic Muslim Reformation:

1. As mentioned above, the innovation of the printing press was to the Protestant reformation what the Internet was to the new and building Muslim Reformation. Not only was the Internet a recruitment tool for ISIS and al Qaeda but it was also a way for Muslims across the planet to go over the heads of their Imams, to find out the true nature of the Prophet's teachings, his life, the actual verses of the Quran which advocate war upon the infidel and the fundamental cruelty visited upon them by their own faith and culture.

2. Given their access to world events via the internet, it was becoming obvious to many in the Muslim world that the Islamists running places like Central Iraq, Gaza or Northern Mali were unable to make good on their promises of a coming utopia but instead could only impose strict Sharia Law on their subjects.

3. In Egypt, Iran, and elsewhere around the Muslim world, there were major emerging political constituencies advocating religious reform.

The Quran is the central religious text of Islam. Muslims believe it to be a revelation from God.

In Pakistan, during the spring of 2016, groups of Islamic extremists across the country banded together to protest a newly passed bill signed by the Prime Minister, Nawaz Sharif. It was the "Protection of Women Against Violence" bill which effectively criminalized violence against women in Punjab - the country's most populous region.

Before the law was officially enacted on March 1, diehard extremists attempted to block the legislation saying it would "destroy the family system in Pakistan" and "add to the miseries of women." Amazingly, the bill was passed *unanimously* by the Punjab Assembly despite the fact that some the country's eminent religious leaders warned of ongoing protests if it was enacted.

Leading up to the passage of the bill, Pakistan's Prime Minister Nawaz joined President el-Sisi of Egypt in promoting this bill which would be a sea change for Islam. He condemned violence against women and especially honor killings by stating, "This is totally against Islam and anyone who does this must be punished very severely."[72]

Unlike the US government under Obama, the government of the United Arab Emirates also joined the government in Egypt, under el-Sisi, in publicly calling the threat of the "Islamic Extremism" a "transnational cancer requiring an urgent, coordinated and sustained international effort to confront it." The UAE ambassador to the US boldly stated, "The fight against radical Islam must be waged not only on the battlefield but also against the entire militant *ideological* and financial complex that is the lifeblood of extremism."[73]

In Syria, on May 2, 2016, Sam Dagher of the *Wall Street Journal* filed a report entitled *Rescuers Dig as Aleppo Airstrikes Persist*. Accompanying the story was a photo of a building, a portion of which had been shorn away by a missile strike. Standing on what was then an open-air platform, on a place which presumably had been an interior room of their apartment, stood a man, his wife and two white-helmeted volunteer rescuers. The woman's face was bloodied and she appeared to be in shock. The rescuers were both pointing and calling to others on the ground, directing other rescuers who had rushed to the site to evacuate the wounded and to help dig for buried survivors. One of the rescuers was holding the couple's infant in his arms. An observer in Syria told Dagher that the "white helmets," as the Syrian rescuers were known, were credited with pulling close to

41,000 people from the rubble since the bombings began in 2014.

Anyone looking at this photo and reading the story would have concluded that embodied in those two rescue workers was great humanitarianism. It was a photo and a story that proved selfless kindness was not unknown to the Muslim world and that a reformation aimed at tolerance and a Christ-like compassion could take root.

In a poll taken in 2016, in 16 Arab countries, young Arab men and women overwhelmingly rejected ISIS, believed that it would eventually fail, and wanted their government leaders "to improve the personal freedoms and human rights of citizens, particularly women." This poll showed that future presidents of the United States could speak directly to the young Muslim world and encourage their budding desire for individual freedom and tolerance. By doing so, he or she could begin to defang fundamentalist Islam.

While the "Arab Spring" did not produce outbreaks of Jeffersonian democracies all across the Middle East, as some in the West naively hoped, in Tunisia, where a desperate fruit vendor self-immolated and began the movement, in 2016 there was a functioning pluralistic, representative government. A new democratic Tunisia was a testament to the fact that a majority-Muslim country could reject medieval Islam and choose a secular modern alternative.

Here I need to be fair to President Obama, who I have severely criticized for his fecklessness in prosecuting the war with resurgent militant Islam. Jeffrey Goldberg, who was granted great access to this president and is an ideological fellow traveler, in April of 2016, published a 10,000-word piece in the *Atlantic* entitled *The Obama Doctrine*. Goldberg wrote, that despite his endless protestations that Muslim terrorists have nothing to do with Islam, "In private encounters with other world leaders, Obama argued that there will be no comprehensive solution to Islamist terrorism until Islam reconciles itself to modernity and undergoes some of the reforms that have changed Christianity." Therefore, it was important to note that even America's "apologist-in-chief" was secretly attempting to plant the seeds of an Islamic reformation.

Many new Muslim women were joining the ranks of the world-famous female critics of Islam profiled in these volumes: Ayaan Hirsi Ali, Wafa Sultan, Nonie

Darwish and Roya Teimouri. Malala Yousafzi, a Pakistani school girl who the Taliban shot in the face but could not kill, was awarded the Nobel Peace Prize. In her 2015 address to the United Nations, she put on notice the obsequious Islamists sitting in attendance at that supposedly august body called the U.N. She put them on notice that their world would be dying. She said: "The extremists are afraid of books and pens. The power of education frightens them. They are afraid of women. The power of the voice of women frightens them. They think that God is a tiny, little being who would send girls to hell just because of going to school."[74]

Section Three

A Winning Agenda

A Winning Agenda

The List

1. Admit the US Is Losing & Define Victory
2. Build a Reagan-esq Economy – An Arsenal of Freedom
3. Start a Manhattan Project for the Development of Missile Defense
4. Wage a "Smarter" Ideological War – Bring Reformers to the White House
5. Stop Backing Down in the Face of Domestic Islamic Threats & Intimidation
6. Celebrate Our Unique American Culture
7. Enforce the Existing Laws on the Books
8. Call Out Muslim Organizations for Their Treachery
9. Wreck the Iranian Nuke Program with Cyber Warfare
10. Create Middle Eastern Safe Zones for Victims of Genocide
11. Stop Leading From Behind & Lead NATO to Declare War on ISIS
12. Stop Losing the War Domestically by Reducing Muslim Immigration

The first order of business in reversing US losses was for a new Commander in Chief to recognize the country was losing the war with resurgent militant Islam. By early 2016, ISIS had suffered some setbacks such as the recapture of the Iraqi cities of Ramadi and Tikrit, near Baghdad, and Sinjar and Shaddadi in the North of Iraq. But it still controlled, or at least operated freely, inside portions of Iraq and Syria the size of Britain.

Further, ISIS, along with the Taliban, were continuing to carve away huge portions of Afghanistan, causing President Obama to quietly suspend the US departure from that country. Based on this action, it was easy to presume that Obama did this so as to prevent future historians from recording that he managed to lose *both* the wars in Iraq and Afghanistan which he inherited, wars that had mostly been won. Moreover, by 2016, it didn't matter that he reversed his pledge to end all of America's wars because, as the time approached for him to finally leave office, ISIS and al Qaeda were operating in 22 countries. In short, his foreign policy record had already been rendered an abysmal failure.

What follows is concise list of the steps that future presidents should well consider in order for the US to stop losing and to begin winning the war with resurgent militant Islam.

1. Admit the US Is Losing & Define Victory

In addition to recognizing that the US must change course using "smarter" power, future administrations should also define victory, that is, tell the American electorate what victory would look like. And while it would be unrealistic to believe that all of militant Islam be completely eradicated, victory could be defined as a world where there were no more terrorist states, such as ISIS, and no more state sponsors of Islamic terrorism, such as Iran. Without states which sponsor terrorist organizations, the jihadists would lack the things they need to conduct terror: access to the international banking system, legitimate travel documents and passports, and to a large degree, money, weapons and equipment.

2. Build a Reagan-esq Economy – An Arsenal of Freedom

While it would make little sense to attempt to describe in detail a comprehensive plan for economic growth here, Reagan's economic agenda of the 1980's, which served to bring down the Soviet Union, provides a blueprint. In short, that plan should reject the idea that the nation adopt new entitlements such as free education and healthcare. Rather it should be aimed at *eliminating* perverse regulations on business such as Dodd-Frank and Obamacare. It should reduce the corporate tax rate, at 35% - the highest in the Western world - and offer tax exempt status to all US corporations which repatriate their off-shore operations. It should aim at eliminating entire agencies, such as the Education Department and the IRS, in favor of implementing either a flat or fair tax. If this were done, massive job growth would ensue.

US President, Ronald Reagan

In order to implement new Reagan-esq economies, future presidents will need to become super-salesmen for free-market, supply-side economics. This could begin by reminding *Democrats* that it was their iconic president, John F. Kennedy, who was the first supply-side economics president and it was he who said, "A rising tide lifts all boats." President Reagan followed *his* lead and instituted tax cuts across all income categories. And by the time Reagan left office, the US economy had doubled tax revenues to the treasury.

With GDP growth building upon a $17 trillion-economy, future presidents could safely proclaim that American needs, in terms of infrastructure and police protection, etc., would be met. And with GDP growth supplying a commensurate growth in tax revenue, the country could also afford a national defense that no major competitor would want to challenge and no rogue terrorist state could resist.

3. Start a Manhattan Project for the Development of Missile Defense

As described in my story on the electro-magnetic pulse (EMP) threat,[75] the 45th president should convince Congress that a rapid development of not only our missile defenses, but the hardening of our electrical grid, would be of critical importance to the survival of the country. Ignoring the protestations of Russia and China, he could also "go over the heads of Congress," and speak directly to the American people in press conferences and addresses from the Oval Office, alerting them as to why this was not a partisan initiative but a matter of life and death for the nation.

As an on-going feature of his formal addresses, he would want to alert the nation that WMD attacks were not only threatened but *planned* by our enemies and that the US would go back on offense and would seek to destroy radical Islamists everywhere they hide and plot.

"As of this day, we have returned to a war footing because we know that we cannot afford to wait for resurgent militant Islamists to attack us," he could say. "When our enemies openly threaten us with annihilation, we have no other option and a solemn duty to opt for preemption," he could say. And without naming Iran, through this rhetorical device, he could put its leadership on notice that the new Commander in Chief was implementing a much more muscular "smarter power" and that a full-blown preemptive attack by the US and its allies might well be in the Iranians near future.

75. See also, *Blackout, Lessons from Fallen Civilizations: Volume 2 - The Way Forward,* pg. 51

4. Wage a "Smarter" Ideological War – Bring Reformers to the White House

Future presidents could become advocates for those who are working to reform Islam from within the religion. He could make a habit of inviting reformers to the White House for press conferences, lauding them for opposing violent Islamic supremacists. He could invite, for example, Zuhdi Jasser, who is an American doctor and who founded the American Islamic Forum for Democracy. He envisions a "Jeffersonian" Islam where there is a separation of mosque and state and where all blasphemy and apostasy laws are abrogated. And Salem Ahmad who has formed the All Believers Network which promotes interfaith dialogue between Buddhism, Christianity, Taoism, and Islam. And of course, Ayaan Hirsi Ali. He could let the world know that he supports the reformers and the reformation of Islam.

5. Stop Backing Down in the Face of Domestic Islamic Threats & Intimidation

One of my Immutable Laws governing the fall of great nations reads:

Immutable Law #3

Appeasement of a ruthless outside power always invites aggression.
Treaties made with ruthless despots are always fruitless and dangerous.

In addition to putting foreign terrorists and their state sponsors on notice that the US was now on offense, future presidents would want to reverse the trend set during the Obama years which saw an administration acquiescing to the constant charges of "Islamophobia" and backing down to myriad threats from its own resident Muslims living in the US.

Robert Spencer, in his pamphlet, *10 Things America Must Do to Defend Itself Against the Global Jihad*, cites an example of how, in 2011, America-based jihadists allied with a leftist media were able to stymie the FBI from its mission to find and interdict Muslim terrorist plots inside the US. Spencer Ackerman, writing for *Wired Magazine*, got a hold of FBI training material that forthrightly depicted the nature of the jihadist threat as emanating from devout Islamic teaching and thought. In his piece, *FBI Teaches Agents: Mainstream Muslims are Violent, Radical*, Ackerman quoted from the FBI training manual, "Any war against non-believers is justified under Muslim law; a moderating process cannot happen if the Koran continues to be regarded as the unalterable words of Allah."[76]

To this Robert Spencer added, "Like virtually all Leftist and Islamic critiques of anti-jihad and anti-terror material, Ackerman took for granted that such assertions were false, without bothering to explain how or why." Americans who had spent any time at all analyzing the building threat from supremacist/jihadist Islam knew that the FBI's assertion was true.

Nevertheless, based on Ackerman's expose, nearly all indigenous American Muslim advocacy groups vigorously took up the cause to expunge all linkage between terrorism and Islam from US law enforcement training materials and procedures. A letter was sent to John Brennan, then Assistant to the President on National Security, denouncing any and all allusions to Islam and Muslim culture in the training materials as bigoted and false and demanded that they be deleted. The letter was signed by 57 Muslim and Arab organizations up and running inside the US including CAIR, ISNA, MAS, all of which had ties to Hamas and the Muslim Brotherhood.

Brennan complied without a whimper of protest. In November of 2011, he wrote back to them that the Obama administration would create an interagency task

John Brennan, former Assistant to the President on National Security

force to address the problem. It would collect all training materials and purge all references to Islam and, by so doing, purge them of any discussion of how jihadists used Islamic thought and teachings to justify violence. He promised to replace law enforcement's cautious approach with willful ignorance.

Brennan was subsequently promoted to CIA Director after former General Petraeus was forced to resign for providing his lover and biographer some classified information. (His crime was far less egregious than were those of Hillary Clinton's, given that the information was not sent out over an insecure server and because his biographer had a security clearance.) By early 2016, numerous reports surfaced exposing the facts that not only did Brennan play a role in making up and disseminating the false talking points regarding the source of the Benghazi attacks, but that he played a role in the Obama administration's decision to read the Miranda rights to Umar Abdulmutallab, the so called "underwear bomber" who tried to destroy a civilian airliner over Detroit on Christmas day. And finally, it came to light that Brennan was overseeing a plan to base CIA recruitment and promotions on race, gender, sexual orientation, age, religion, and other quotas, rather than on merit and ability.

The future president should signal that he would not be intimidated nor would he attempt to appease *any* foreign power, even if it came in the form of militant, supremacist Islam. Further, all law enforcement and national security materials would be the express property of the American people and not subject to the demands of outside forces. He could further heartily support a bill in Congress which would make it illegal to operate an organization which was linked in any way to the Muslim Brotherhood until it changed its charter which still called for the destruction of Israel, the eventual overthrow of the US by the armies of Allah and the replacement of the US constitution with Sharia Law.

Additionally, the new president could order a top-secret, bottom-to-top audit of the CIA and all other Homeland Security agencies. It would be aimed at uncovering all those employees, agents, and especially agency heads, who held a fealty to multiculturalism and political correctness and who operated under the assumption that it was more important than the protection of the homeland, our overseas deployed soldiers or our allies. All those found wanting in this category would be fired, with Brennan, if he were still employed, the first order of business.

6. Celebrate Our Unique American Culture

In *Lessons from Fallen Civilizations* I wrote that, due to the disastrous 30-year civil war that was the Peloponnesian War, the Greeks lost their desire to defend a brilliant culture which was centered on a free and independent city state, what we refer to as the Greek polis. After losing only one battle to the invading Macedonians, at Chaeronea in 338 BC, the independent Greeks gave up their freedoms to their new overlords and remained a subjugated people for next 2,400 years.

The tragedy that ended an ancient Greek civilization which had produced an incredibly innovative culture, and formed the foundation for our own, inspired me to develop:

Immutable Law #1
No nation has ever survived once its citizenry
ceased to believe its culture worth saving.

A future president, his vice president and his entire cabinet could in unison pronounce the era of multiculturalism and political correctness over. The president could explain that multiculturalism had run amok because it had evolved to the point where it did not celebrate but *elevated* all other cultures above that of America. In its constructs, America was subservient to all other cultures because it was founded on slavery, racism, exploitation and was now destroying the planet. And political correctness had become the code by which the multiculturalists enforced thought control and shut down free speech. By 2016, toward the end of the Obama Administration, multiculturalism, self-loathing and political correctness were cemented into the bedrock of American progressive dogma. In fact, the strange rise of presidential candidate, Donald Trump, owed much of its enthusiasm to the rejection of just this thinking.

The president could task his Education Secretary to work with the nation's textbook manufacturers and university presidents to cajole them into producing curricula which rejected the dogma of the America-haters among us, those whose mission in life was to struggle against what they saw as a brutal blind capitalism. He could take the lead in emphasizing the great accomplishments of this country, such as: its constitution which protects individual liberty; the second half of the twentieth century which saw America lead in winning World War II; America's help rebuilding and setting free the countries which had attacked us; and America's protection of the whole of the free world from totalitarian conquest. And he could emphatically tell the country and the world that Western Civilization was seriously threatened, worth defending and that drastic measures may need to be employed to keep us safe.

7. Enforce the Existing Laws on the Books

As Robert Spencer rightly pointed out, a portion of Section 2385 of the federal criminal code reads: "Whoever knowingly or willfully advocates, abets, advises, or teaches the duty, necessity, desirability, or propriety of overthrowing or destroying the government of the United States…shall be fined under this provision or imprisoned…"[77]

A future president should proclaim that this law, too long ignored by previous administrations, was still on the books and that his administration would not govern as if the rule of law no longer pertained. He could add that unless Congress rescinded the law, he would see to it that it was enforced. And just as mayor Giuliani had done in New York City in the aftermath of 9/11, this future president could order the FBI and other agencies to hire loyal Muslim American officers to infiltrate the Muslim Brotherhood-affiliated organizations and mosques all across the country. And those found to be preaching hatred of the American infidel and advocating the destruction of America would be prosecuted to the full extent of the law or deported.

8. Call Out Muslim Organizations for Their Treachery

As Robert Spencer also pointed out in 2015, "It is remarkable that fourteen years after 9/11, not a single mosque or Islamic school in the US has any organized program to teach Muslims why the al Qaeda/Islamic State understanding of Islam is wrong and should be rejected." A future president could appoint and task an Islamic Reformation czar to find American imams willing to come to the White House and proclaim that they reject hatred of the infidel and all apostasy laws. This should be done to put even more pressure on the US Islamic organizations to either lead the reformation or, if they refuse, disband their US operations.

9. Wreck the Iranian Nuke Program with Cyber Warfare

In March of 2016, a US federal court indicted seven Iranian hackers in absentia for cyber-attacks against numerous US banks and critical infrastructure. On April 4, 2016, on the first anniversary of the Iran deal, the JCPOA (Joint Comprehensive Plan of Action), the ambassador to the US from the United Arab Emirates, filed an article in the *Wall Street Journal* where he quoted Iran's Ayatollah Khamenei as saying, "Those who say the future is in negotiations, not in missiles, are either ignorant or traitors."[78] In other words, the supreme leader was saying to the Obama team: Now that we've out negotiated you and been given a clear path to acquiring nuclear weapons, we are going to keep developing our intercontinental missiles so that we can target your major cities for destruction.

Three years earlier, in 2013, numerous publications corroborated what the NSA whistleblower, Edward Snowden, told a German magazine; that being, Israel and the United States created the Stuxnet computer virus that had just destroyed the nuclear centrifuges at the Natanz nuclear weapons facility in Iran.

Snowden was asked if the US National Security Agency partners "with other nations, like Israel?" He responded that the NSA has a "massive body" responsible for such partnerships called the Foreign Affairs Directorate.

He was also asked, "Did the NSA help to create Stuxnet?" Snowden responded, "NSA and Israel co-wrote it."

Natanz, Iranian Nuclear Site

Then incredibly, in the February 16, 2016 edition of the *New York Times*, an article appeared entitled, *US Had Cyber Attack Plan if Iran Nuclear Dispute Led to Conflict*. It began:

> In the early years of the Obama administration, the United States developed an elaborate plan for a cyber attack on Iran in case the diplomatic effort to limit its nuclear program failed and led to a military conflict, according to a coming documentary film and interviews with military and intelligence officials involved in the effort.
>
> The plan, code-named Nitro Zeus, was devised to disable Iran's air defenses, communications systems and crucial parts of its power grid, and was shelved, at least for the foreseeable future, after the nuclear deal struck between Iran and six other nations last summer was fulfilled.
>
> Nitro Zeus was part of an effort to assure President Obama that he had alternatives, short of a full-scale war, if Iran lashed out at the United States or its allies in the region. At its height, officials say, the planning for Nitro Zeus involved thousands of American military and intelligence personnel, spending tens of millions of dollars and placing electronic implants in Iranian computer networks to "prepare the battlefield," in the parlance of the Pentagon.[79]

The ultra-secret nature of this information was startling, especially given that the *New York Times* had, for the entire seven years of the Obama presidency, diligently supported Obama's "soft power" diplomacy of appeasement and capitulation. That the *Times* would expose the fact that the US, at the beginning of the Obama administration, had the cyber warfare capability to take out the Iranian air defense systems and much of the country's electrical grid, a capability which would have brought the entire country to its knees, begs the question: Why would Obama and Kerry, in 2015, have agreed to a nuclear deal which allowed Iran to keep its nuclear weapons program, albeit in a *phony* state of suspension? In 2013 the US and Israel had already shown they could effectively take an entire facility down through cyber warfare. The US held all the cards! They could have brought Iran to its knees. It will be for historians to determine the motive behind why Kerry and Obama folded their cards, capitulating to a much smaller rogue power which threatened both Israel and the US with annihilation.

To make matters worse for the Obama legacy, despite all its groveling, the Mullahs in Iran clearly did not believe that the US had been humbled enough. In mid-March of 2016, Iran tested two ballistic missiles capable of striking US allies in the region (Turkey, Jordan, the Gulf States, Saudi Arabia and Israel). The Iranian press let the world know that one of its missiles was inscribed in Hebrew with the words, "Israel must be wiped off the face of the earth."

Given that the US already had the capability to shut down the nuclear weapons program through cyber warfare, the 45th president should order that operation to commence the day after his inauguration. Millions of lives might depend upon him doing so.

10. Create Middle Eastern Safe Zones for Victims of Genocide

On March 16, 2016, nearly two years after ISIS began ravaging large portions of Iraq and Syria and killing Christians and other minorities in the most brutal fashion that the Western World had seen since the Middle Ages, Secretary of State, John Kerry, made a statement to a stunned press, finally admitting, "Yazidi's, Christians, and Shia Muslims" were being subjected to "crimes against humanity."

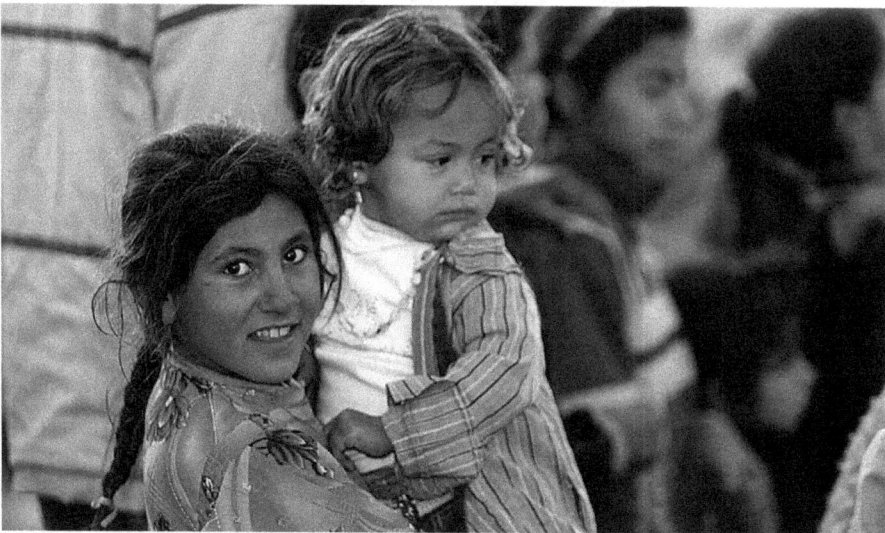

Iraqi refugee children, Damascus, Syria

This was a start, but long overdue. It was yet another example of how President Obama *wanted* to underestimate the depravity of ISIS because he had made clear, since the beginning of his presidency, that he saw himself as a special pleader for misunderstood, mistreated Muslim communities everywhere. Secondly, his long reluctance to act was driven by the implications that it would have on his legacy. It would expose how wrong he had been in characterizing ISIS as a "JV squad" and how wrong he was to order the removal of all US troops from Iraq in 2011, leaving so many innocents to be kidnapped, raped and slaughtered.

A new president could reverse Obama's debacle and order the US military special forces to descend into Christian and non-Muslim minority sections of Iraq and Eastern Syria to set up safe havens. By early 2016, Robert Nicholson, founder of the Philos Project which sought to defend the safety and freedom of Mideast Christians and minorities and Juliana Taimoorazy, founder of the Iraqi Christian Relief Council, were both saying - in the short term, the US need not focus on defeating ISIS totally but rather on creating safe havens where families could go and remain safe in their own homes and communities. Were the new president to do so, it would throw a powerful psychological blow at the heart of radical Islam while, at the same time, be one of the most moral acts the new president could perform.

11. Stop Leading From Behind and Lead NATO to Declare War on ISIS

Shortly after the 9/11 attacks, for the first time in its history, NATO invoked Article 5 of its treaty. The article provided for the collective defense of its member nations in the case of attack. Based on this, a coalition of European countries agreed to aid the US in invading Afghanistan and routed the Taliban and al Qaeda in a matter of a few months.

In early 2016, although ISIS was losing some ground in Iraq, it was spreading into Yemen, Afghanistan, Libya and Nigeria as well as other poorly defended fronts. In a legitimate response to the San Bernardino, Paris, and Brussels attacks, the beheadings of our countrymen and the genocide of Christians in the Middle East, a new president should lead the way in invoking Article 5 again and take the fight to the ISIS *everywhere* it proclaims dominion and where it hides and plots.

12. Stop Losing the War Domestically by Reducing Muslim Immigration

In *Lessons from Fallen Civilizations*, I developed the following Immutable Law governing the fall of great civilizations:

Immutable Law #6
To hold territory, a state must be populated by those loyal to the central authority. When immigration overwhelms assimilation, the fall is predicted.

While the country had not suffered a major attack for 15 years, by 2016 the US was failing its citizenry in preventing future attackers from entering the country. By early 2016, the number of active investigations by federal authorities into suspected Islamic State operatives and other home-grown terrorists numbered over 1,000.

By 2016, the US Muslim Brotherhood had built a vast network in America including mosques, clinics, social and media organizations, legal foundations, medical and trade associations and educational groups, all of which were created to fulfill its stated mission, "Civilization Jihad," to overthrow the US government and replace it with an Islamic State, under which Sharia Law would be the law of the land. All of this was in evidence provided by the Department of Justice and several arms of the United States government. All of this was exhaustively detailed in Muslim Brotherhood writings.

Thanks to the scholars at *www.understandingthethreat.com* and others, it had become obvious to much of the American electorate, despite the obfuscations of the Obama Administration and the left-leaning media, the Muslim Brotherhood was building its forces and was the enemy within. In the early 1980's, the US Muslim Brotherhood created the Islamic Society of North America (ISNA) to be the "nucleus" of the Islamic Movement on the continent. It was formed by many of the same people who created the Muslim Students Association (MSA). ISNA became an umbrella organization for all of the other Muslim Brotherhood organizations created in America afterward.

Once the ISNA was created, the US Muslim Brotherhood created over 100 organizations to serve its mission of Civilization Jihad. These included Islamic

Societies, Islamic Centers/Mosques and other organizations across the United States.

By early 2016, it was unknown the number of American jihadis already in-country, plotting and awaiting instructions. But a Pew survey in 2007 found that 7% of American Muslims between the ages of 18 and 29 had a "favorable view of al Qaeda." And in 2011, another Pew survey found that about 180,000 American Muslims regarded suicide bombings as being justified in some way.[80] Most Americans instinctively knew that they did not want their country to become something like France, where in Paris and in other major cities there are constant ugly demonstrations. Angry Muslims, mostly young men, fill the streets protesting by carrying Palestinian, Hamas and even ISIS flags, shouting "mort aux Juifs!" "Death to the Jews!" Often the demonstrators throw rocks, paint swastikas and surround synagogues, threatening the worshipers while the outnumbered police just look on.

Yet President Obama, in early 2016, threatened to bring to the US thousands of Iraqi, Syrian and other Muslim refugees who were allegedly fleeing the ravages of ISIS. His abandonment of those brave Iraqi's who fought with the American-led coalition to keep the peace after the overthrow of Saddam Hussein, opened the doors to ISIS. The resulting murderous chaos gave Obama the opportunity to bring a new wave of Muslims to the US.

Meanwhile, by the spring of 2016, national security experts were uniformly warning that the US was less safe from a catastrophic attack than in the days leading up to 9/11. Many feared that the next major attack would be a 9/11 cubed and that it would mean the country could be lost.

By the spring of 2016, those Americans unencumbered by political correctness instinctively knew the only sane US policy regarding immigration from Muslim-majority countries was to greatly limit it to those who we could be sure would join us in *reforming* Islam. They knew that admitting vast numbers of new Muslim refugees from the Middle East, as Europe was doing, was both politically correct and suicidal.

Because we knew not all Muslims are terrorists, but nearly all terrorists are Muslim military-aged men; for the foreseeable future, the nation must become extremely selective with respect to admitting immigrants from Muslim-majority countries. However, future presidents should *encourage* immigration from Muslim countries with populations of Christians and non-Muslim minorities who have fled their homes in fear for their lives. They should offer sanctuary to Muslim women who also fear for their lives due to their desire to avoid a forced marriage or their wish to leave the faith.

For Muslim military-aged men, immigration should be limited to those who would sign a document certifying they would never wish to, or agree to, live under Sharia Law in America, that Israel has a right to exist, and that they would, if asked, aid and advise the American effort to reform Islam.

And finally, a consortium of great minds selected from America's private technology firms should be brought together to devise and help implement a world-class, second-to-none Muslim vetting system.

Conclusion

Conclusion

If I were asked to describe what I thought America would look like if all, or even most, of the above initiatives were successfully implemented by a future president reversing the defeatist policies pursued during the Obama years, I would say that the country would continue to look pretty much like a free America. By 2016, only a tiny fraction of the country had actually witnessed Americans lying in pools of blood at the Fort Hood, San Bernardino or Orlando massacres. Only a tiny fraction of Americans are relegated to living in close proximity to all-Muslim neighborhoods, such as now exist in Dearborn, Michigan and elsewhere in the US. Most Americans do not see what is coming if the US government follows the path of Europe. They don't see that with unfettered Islamic immigration to the US, larger and larger segments of the country will be carved out for Muslims-only and become uninhabitable for non-Muslim Americans.

In England, France, Belgium, Sweden, the Netherlands and other European countries, the way they carve out their Muslim-only enclaves is as follows: Once the Muslim population grows to a sufficient size, funds mysteriously become available to build a mosque. The funds are almost always augmented by off-shore sources. Once completed, more Muslims coalesce around the Mosque, relentlessly outnumbering the native-born inhabitants of that neighborhood. Next, the native-born inhabitants are intimidated and made to feel unwanted in their homes. Windows are broken, graffiti is painted on their houses and shops and their young women sexually assaulted. The net result is that the native-born leave and the enclave eventually becomes all-Muslim. Inevitably, the Muslim leaders of that enclave then begin to demand that their people be able to practice Sharia Law, enforcing its code while rejecting their new country's law.[81]

It has been widely reported that there as many as 170 "no-go zones" in France alone. These are all-Muslim areas where crime is rampant and the police are targeted. This may be an inflated number and the existence of "no-go zones" is denied by French and other European officials whose job is to keep the peace. But, as Daniel Pipes reported in an article he wrote about the "no-go" phenomenon, in the all-Muslim area of Marseille, French police were actually fired upon while they made preparations for the Prime Minister to visit the area. In Molenbeek, the all-Muslim neighborhood of Brussels, the known ringleader of the Paris attacks hid in plain sight for weeks without any of his neighbors reporting him to the police. After his capture, the police returned to the area to question neighbors and were pelted with rocks and bottles. And from a strictly visual point of view, suffice it to say, these all-Muslim neighborhoods are gradually failing to retain the look and character that was the product of centuries of European culture. They are deteriorating into something closer to Ramadi and Fallujah.

If we can assume that we will avoid the gradual Islamacization, which the Muslim Brotherhood and all its other sister organizations have in mind for us, and if we can assume that we will prevent Iran and its allies from detonating an EMP weapon over us, America will not become "Ameristan."

Instead, we will continue to look like a free America.

Appendix

Appendix

The editors at the *The Blaze* contacted me in September of 2013, days before the one-year anniversary of the Benghazi attacks, and assigned me to write a piece which would describe what I thought had changed over that intervening year. In short, what I felt had changed was that it was widely known among Americans that President Obama and Secretary Clinton were guilty of dereliction of duty and criminal malfeasance.

What Has Changed One Year After the US Defeat at Benghazi?
Published by *theBlaze.com*, September 11, 2013

One year ago today our consulate in Benghazi, Libya was attacked and our Ambassador, Chris Stevens, was killed along with three other former-members of the US Special Forces who defied orders to stand down and died trying to protect him and his staff. The mainstream media and much of our ruling class has attempted to hide the details and, moreover, the meaning of this event. But much has been begrudgingly divulged.

For example, we now know that it was not a spontaneous attack issued by an unruly mob of Muslims enraged by an obscure internet video, but a coordinated attack by an al Qaeda affiliate armed with high-powered sophisticated weaponry. We also know that Obama, Mrs. Clinton, and various other members of the administration lied repeatedly about the true nature of the attack; and did so just weeks before the presidential election, thereby influencing the outcome of the election. We now know that, at the outset of the attack, desperate calls were made from Libya to the White House asking for help and that Secretaries Clinton and Panetta met with Obama and briefed him on the attack. We even know that while the fighting raged, Obama never once went down to the situation room to see for himself what was happening.

PUBLISHED ESSAY BY LARRY KELLEY

What we don't know is: what was said by Clinton and Panetta to the Commander in Chief, what were his orders, what did he do for the roughly eight hours that remained of the fighting, who gave the order to "stand down," and *why*. Bound up in the reason why Obama and his team lied about the source and nature of the attack is very likely the same reason why this administration, one year later, has made no attempt to kill or capture any of the al Qaeda fighters, some of whom openly hang out in Libyan cafes overlooking the Mediterranean and give TV interviews to al Jazeera.

<u>What are the Wages of Obama's Foreign Policy Failures and Deceit?</u>

Immutable Law #1
No nation has ever survived once its citizenry
ceased to believe its culture worth saving.

Both the independent Greek poleis and the Roman Empire of the West fell because they could no longer muster armies necessary to repel invaders. Now that our president has painted himself into a corner with his rhetorical bravado, with his statement regarding the "red line" that Syria must not cross, and his ridiculous "shot across the bow" comment, members of Congress have been shocked by how few Americans support military action. A Reuter's poll showed support for his military engagement all the way down to 20%.

One could reasonably argue that Americans have not yet given up on American culture but that they do not want their sons and daughters put in harm's way under this Commander in Chief. As Peggy Noonan wrote, "...wrong time, wrong place, wrong plan, wrong man."

After 12 years of war in Afghanistan and Iraq, this president has managed to lose the peace in both countries. Despite thousands of American lives lost for their liberation, Iraqis and Afghans are rapidly becoming our enemies. Given this horrific waste of the lives of our sons and daughters, how can this country continue to ask their younger brothers and sisters to answer the call to arms? How can we ask them to serve under a president who is more concerned with settling scores with his political enemies than consolidating our hard-won gains relative to this nation's security and national interests?

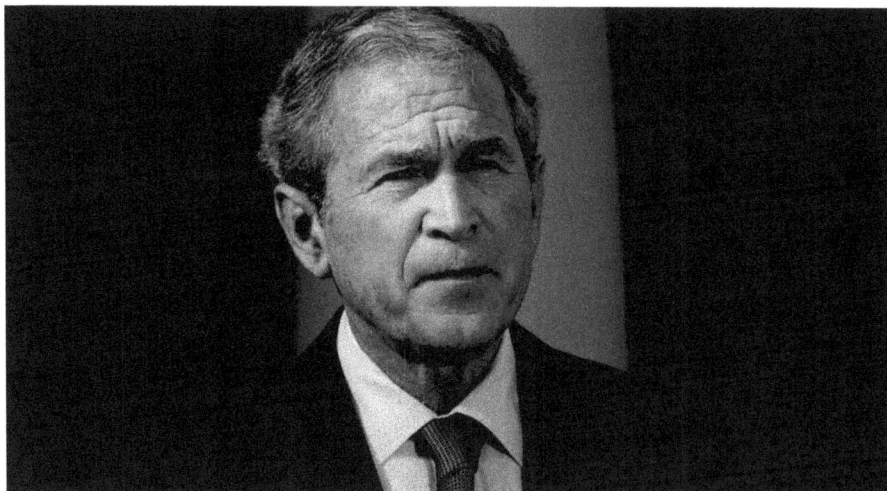

US President George W. Bush while speaking in the Rose Garden of the White House.

<u>Obama's Deceit and Failures Have the Region in Flames</u>

Egypt: President George W. Bush once reflected that conducting American foreign policy was like playing chess in three dimensions. In Egypt, seeing their youth flooding into the squares of Cairo, Obama naively thought he could be the proxy president of the so-called Arab Spring. He decided to throw Mubarak overboard, the man to whom the US had, for decades, paid billions in order to keep the peace with Israel.

Next the Egyptians elected Mohammad Morsi, a Muslim Brotherhood hardline Islamist. He promptly destroyed the Egyptian economy and stood by while Brotherhood loyalists burnt down Christian Churches, schools and homes. In the space of one year the Egyptian military, with the help of millions of secularist marchers, ousted the first duly elected leader in Egypt's 6,000-year history. Good pick, Mr. President. You own it.

Tunisia: Three years after Mohammad Bouazizi set himself on fire, putting in motion what many pundits were once calling the Arab Spring, the Tunisians find themselves ruled by a rabid Islamist, Rashid Ghannouchi, head of the Ennahda party, a Muslim Brotherhood front group. With opposition party leaders being assassinated and the economy in shambles, Tunisians are back out in the streets demanding that the Ennahda thugs go.

PUBLISHED ESSAY BY LARRY KELLEY

Libya: When Gadhafi saw George Bush take down Saddam Hussein's regime, he turned over his entire nuclear weapons program to the US. It seems doubtful that Obama, or anyone else in his inner circle, has considered the fact that when this president blithely backed the overthrow of Gadhafi he has made it highly unlikely that Assad will give up his chemical weapons. Obama's treatment of Gadhafi is just one more reminder that Obama's America can't be trusted.

Today Libya is a lawless country harboring unknown numbers of al Qaeda affiliates.

A Highly Damaged Commander in Chief

What has changed over the year since Benghazi is that, due to Obama's insouciance and duplicity, he is losing his ability to be the Commander in Chief. Photos of American rank and file military holding signs stating that they refuse to fight on the side of al Qaeda have exploded on social media. One post alone generated 16,000 shares on Facebook. The rank and file also know that Obama let it be known that it was SEAL Team Six which killed bin Laden, putting all the men in the unit and their families in grave and perpetual danger.

Major General Robert Scales, former commandant of the Army War College, recently wrote a scathing article for the *Washington Post* in which he describes the growing discontent among military leaders regarding Obama's reckless combination of dithering and bravado.

In the spring of AD 410, a large army of Goths and Roman deserters surrounded the city of Rome. The feckless Roman Emperor, Honorius who had escaped to Ravenna, sent a contingent of 4,000 legionnaires to help defend the city. They never showed up. The city was sacked for the first time in 800 years and the civilized world was shocked. The consequences of highly flawed leadership during a time of war are almost always profound.

[End of Essay]

Secret Muslim Resettlement Inside the US

During the year 2015, here are the cities where the US government secretly imported and resettled the 77,000 mostly male, military-age, Muslims in America.

Listing by state, city, and numbers:

AK Anchorage 125

AL Mobile 125

AR Springdale 10

AZ Glendale 895

AZ Phoenix 1,459

AZ Tucson 935

CA Anaheim 175

CA Fullerton 10

CA Garden Grove 150

CA Glendale 1,420

CA Los Angeles 490

CA Los Gatos 144

CA Modesto 250

CA Oakland 615

CA Sacramento 1,276

CA San Bernardino 65

CA San Diego 3,103

CA San Francisco 5

CA San Jose 142

CA Turlock 120

CA Walnut Creek 90

CO Colorado Springs 138

CO Denver 1,690

CO Greeley 150

CT Bridgeport 100

CT Hartford 285

CT New Haven 205

DC Washington 15

DE Wilmington 5

FL Clearwater 200

FL Delray Beach 95

FL Doral 160

FL Jacksonville 895

FL Miami 1,056

FL Miami Springs 133

FL Naples 115

FL North Port 30

FL Orlando 360

FL Palm Springs 150

FL Pensacola 20

FL Plantation 75

FL Riviera Beach 50

FL Tallahassee 50

FL Tampa 660

GA Atlanta 2,100

GA Savannah 100

GA Stone Mountain 685

HI Honolulu 15

IA Cedar Rapids 55

IA Des Moines 585

ID Boise 720

ID Twin Falls 300

IL Aurora 190

IL Chicago 1,595

IL Moline 200

IL Rockford 300

IL Wheaton 2,660

IN Fort Wayne 200

IN Indianapolis 1,285

KS Garden City 80

KS Kansas City 200

KS Wichita 510

KY Bowling Green 310

KY Lexington 410

KY Louisville 990

KY Owensboro 135

LA Baton Rouge 125

LA Lafayette 30

LA Metairie 185

MA Boston 300

MA Framingham 8

MA Jamaica Plain 100

MA Lowell 275

MA South Boston 260

MA Springfield 230

MA Waltham 10

MA West Springfield 340

MA Worcester 443

MD Baltimore 775

MD GlenBurnie 150

MD Rockville 39

MD Silver Spring 845

ME Portland 350

MI Ann Arbor 80

MI Battle Creek 140

MI Clinton Township 650

MI Dearborn 640

MI Grand Rapids 740

MI Lansing 617

MI Troy 1,215

MN Minneapolis 730
MN Richfield 340
MN Rochester 130
MN Saint Paul 695
MN St. Cloud 215
MO Columbia 140
MO Kansas City 540
MO Saint Louis 725
MO Springfield 75
MS Biloxi 5
MS Jackson 20

NC Charlotte 655
NC Durham 380
NC Greensboro 385
NC High Point 405
NC New Bern 165
NC Raleigh 475
NC Wilmington 80
ND Bismarck 45
ND Fargo 270
ND Grand Forks 90
NE Lincoln 335
NE Omaha 990
NH Concord 245
NH Manchester 445
NJ Camden 100
NJ East Orange 6
NJ Elizabeth 300
NJ Jersey City 506
NM Albuquerque 220
NV Las Vegas 640
NY Albany 360
NY Amityville 20
NY Binghamton 40
NY Brooklyn 55
NY Buffalo 1,442
NY New York 240
NY Rochester 643
NY Syracuse 1,030
NY Utica 410

OH Akron 575
OH Cincinnati 140
OH Cleveland 510
OH Cleveland Heights 190
OH Columbus 1,300
OH Dayton 210
OH Toledo 40
OK Oklahoma City 170
OK Tulsa 395
OR Portland 995

PA Allentown 95
PA Erie 625
PA Harrisburg 200
PA Lancaster 480
PA Philadelphia 750
PA Pittsburgh 470
PA Roslyn 20
PA Scranton 150
PR San Juan 5

RI Providence 210

SC Columbia 160
SC Spartanburg 220
SD Huron 90
SD Sioux Falls 490

TN Chattanooga 85
TN Knoxville 190
TN Memphis 200
TN Nashville 1,225
TX Abilene 200
TX Amarillo 442
TX Austin 930
TX Corpus Christi 5
TX Dallas 1,765
TX El Paso 35
TX Fort Worth 1,503
TX Houston 2,605
TX San Antonio 750

UT Salt Lake City 1,126

VA Arlington 500
VA Charlottesville 250
VA Falls Church 450
VA Fredericksburg 120
VA Harrisonburg 140
VA Newport News 300
VA Richmond 243
VA Roanoke 177
VT Colchester 325

WA Kent 985
WA Richland 230
WA Seattle 714
WA Spokane 510
WA Tacoma 276
WA Vancouver 127
WI Green Bay 20
WI Madison 90
WI Milwaukee 890
WI Oshkosh 135
WI Sheboygan 35
WV Charleston 50

TOTALS 76,972[82]

Mosques in Florida

The Orlando jihadist attack on June 11, 2016 was the largest mass murder in US history. A Google search for Florida mosques brings up a total of 118; including the Islamic Center of Fort Pierce, where the shooter, Omar Mateen, attended and where some reports reveal he heard imams advocating for the death of homosexuals. Yet he was the <u>second</u> suicide attacker to attend the Fort Pierce mosque. The first was American-born Moner Mohammad Abu Salha, who was self-radicalized by watching internet tapes made by Anwar al Awlaki, the same terrorist who inspired the Fort Hood shooter. In 2014, the first American suicide bomber, Salha, drove a truck full of explosives into a government building in Syria.

The large numbers of Mosques in Florida relative to its Muslim population (according to *Wikipedia*: 1,060,000) begs the question - who financed them?

Islamic Center of Ft. Pierce
1104 West Midway Road
Fort Pierce, Florida

After Eight Years of Obama, 70% of Americans Saw America in Decline

In late July 2016, the *Wall Street Journal* ran a cover story with the banner headline: *US in Weakest Recovery Since '49.* The story was an utter condemnation of Obama's economic policies given that, since the recession ended sometime around the beginning of 2010, the average growth rate for economy as a whole had averaged 2.1 %, the smallest since 1949.[83] This rate of growth of the US economy was a harbinger of millions of jobs not created and of great human suffering.

Additionally, in early July of 2016, a Pew Research poll found that a fearsome 71% of Americans were "dissatisfied with the direction of the country." The phrase "dissatisfied with the direction of the country" could easily be interpreted as a euphemism for what the respondents saw as "a decline of America."

The Attempted Coup in Turkey

A lso in July of 2016, Turkey's President Erdogan and his allies put down an attempted military coup of the government. Some alleged that the coup was actually staged by Erdogan as a mechanism for him to further increase his Putin-like grip over his country. The size of his resulting purge was breathtaking. Some 6,300 military officers and soldiers, including 40 generals, were rounded up; 21,000 were suspended from the Ministry of Education; 1,481 judges and prosecutors arrested.

Over the previous decade, as Erdogan was gaining more and more dictatorial powers over Turkey, he had also been inexorably attempting to move the country from a secular state, established by President Atatürk at the conclusion of World War I, toward an Islamist state. He sought to reconstitute the old Ottoman Empire. Experts were predicting that Turkey was a strong candidate for an Islamic revolution similar to the one which swept the theocracy to power in Iran, one which would make Erdogan its supreme leader for life.

However, in the midst of these dire developments in Turkey, there was one bit of positive news. Erdogan wasted no time in blaming exiled Turkish Imam, Fethullah Gulen, who had lived for two decades in rural Saylorsburg, Pennsylvania in the Pocono Mountains. He accused him of inspiring the coup and demanded that the US allow for his extradition. Gulen, who was 77, denied he and his followers had anything to do with the plot. Yet it was important to note that Gulen preached a peaceful, mystical form of Islam. Moreover, by the time of the coup, his movement, Hizmet, set up over 55,000 businesses and ran successful charter schools in 160 countries. In the face of Erdogan's attempt to radicalize Turkey, these were other hopeful beginnings of an Islamic reformation.

An Important New Book on the War with Militant Islam

What follows here is my review of a book written by the highest ranking military intelligence officer in the country, a man who was fired by Obama for speaking the truth to Congress. In my review, I was elated to report that General Flynn and I were in basic agreement in terms of the peril we face and the prescriptions necessary to defeat the enemy – resurgent militant Islam.

Book Review:
The Field of Fight by Lt. General Michael T. Flynn
Published by *LarryKelley.com*, July 29, 2016

As we are in the final run up toward a presidential election where one of the candidates is arguably guilty of criminal malfeasance and very possibly treason, General Flynn's new book, *The Field of Fight*, is an important argument for why America faces an existential threat and why the country desperately needs new leadership. Similar to the purges now taking place in Turkey, the author was one of many senior military officers with stellar life-time military records who were purged from the Obama US military. After thirty years of service, he was dismissed from his position as Director of the Defense Intelligence Agency for the crime of testifying to Congress that the American people were in more danger than just a few years previously.

When fired, Flynn was the senior military intelligence officer in the Department of Defense. Why, with all his stellar experience and intimate knowledge of the world-wide jihadist threat now facing the West, would he be let go? Answer - because he told the truth that President Obama and his capitulationist hopeful replacements didn't want the American public to know…that we are losing the war with militant Islam. The truth is that we are losing to an army of rag-tag cutthroats backed by evil rogue regimes such as Iran and Russia, and we are losing due to our current regime's bad management of the war effort.

I was gratified to read Gen. Flynn's book because my forthcoming book also makes the case that the West is once again losing ground to resurgent militant

PUBLISHED ESSAY BY LARRY KELLEY

PUBLISHED ESSAY BY LARRY KELLEY

Islam. Whereas my new book frames the current struggle as a continuation of the 14-centuries-long war waged by Islam against the West, a war where the armies of Allah took control of large portions of Europe, Greece, the Balkans and Spain, Flynn's account is filled with fascinating new intelligence-related revelations about the internal workings of the Muslim jihadist world.

Flynn peppers his narrative with fascinating historic analogies and observations as well. For example, in describing the terrorist alliance - Iran, Russia, and the jihadists networks, Boko Haram, al Qaeda, ISIS, etc., he characterizes them as vulnerable. "Machiavelli insisted that tyranny is the least stable system, because the people can quickly turn against the tyrant."

Flynn makes a startling observation and condemnation of the Obama presidency, Iranian leaders…know they were very nearly overthrown in the summer of 2009, when millions of Iranians associated with the "Green Movement" filled the streets with more demonstrators than in 1979, when the Shah was overthrown." The mostly young Iranian demonstrators even held up signs and chanted, "Obama, where are you?" Sadly, in early 1979, during Obama's first few months in office, he had already established a secret channel of communications with Iran's Khamenei through Oman. As US military officials pressed him to back up and support the movement, his response was "let's give it a few days."

His "giving it a few more days" turned into his giving his blessing to the Iranian regime's rounding up, imprisoning and murdering of thousands of Iranian advocates for freedom. As Flynn writes, "Removing the sickening chokehold of tyranny, dictatorships, and radical Islamist regimes must be something our nation stands for…If we don't stand for this, we stand for nothing."

Today the Iranian freedom movement which, with our help, could have toppled the largest terrorist-sponsoring Islamist state, one which will soon have nuclear weapons and the long-range nuclear missiles necessary to destroy New York City and Washington D.C., is dead. Flynn quotes one imprisoned Iranian freedom fighter as describing Obama's unwillingness to back their movement as a "historic opportunity missed." I might add - it may also prove to be the largest strategic blunder by any US president ever.

ISIS itself may be far less stable than they appear due to the barbarity it turns upon its own fighters. Flynn reports that when ISIS fighters who had given up the fight to hold the city of Ramadi returned to Mosul, they were made to stand in a circle in the center of a city square and were set on fire, burnt alive for all who dared to watch.

Most of Flynn's prescriptions for how we change our warfare tactics from defense to offense are also present in my book but, given his thirty years in military intelligence, his are developed in greater detail. We both believe that a major component of our attack must be psychological war. Flynn points out that *all* the terror networks work with the big drug cartels based in Latin America but which operate globally. He points out that, in his experience, fully three-quarters of the terrorists apprehended on Middle Eastern battlefields were found to be in it for the money, not religious convictions. This should be an ongoing story aimed at repudiating militant Islam.

There is only one point on which General Flynn and I disagree. He states that it was a huge strategic mistake for the United States to invade Iraq militarily. He goes on to write that if our basic mission was to defeat terrorists, our target should have been Tehran not Baghdad.

I disagree. Three of the plotters of the 1993 World Trade Center bombing were Ramzi Yousef, Abdul Rahman Yasin, and Mohammed Salameh, who were implicated in the attack which killed six Americans and wounded over one thousand (it was an attack which could have killed 200,000 had the first tower fallen against the second. And it was the largest terrorist attack on US soil up to that date). They were discovered to be in constant contact with Iraqi handlers prior to the attack and escaped to Iraq after the bombing. Yasin went on to live in Baghdad and was an employee of the Iraqi government.

The harboring of these men by Iraq was an act of war. Add to that, Saddam Hussein attempted to assassinate President Bush (the elder) on his visit to Kuwait, he was known to have maintained development programs aimed at producing all three classes of WMD's, chemical, biological and nuclear, he was the only leader to have used chemical weapons on his own people, and finally he murdered more of his own people than did the Serbian dictator, Milosevic. After 9/11, history will record that he should have been targeted for removal.

PUBLISHED ESSAY BY LARRY KELLEY

I agree with General Flynn that Tehran should be and *should have been* the target of a US regime change. But in my view, the dye should have been cast quickly in those terrible weeks after 9/11 when Mayor Julianne was working 18 hours a day and attending all those funerals for the fallen New York firefighters, police and civilians. Long before the American Left could wake up to its nefarious mounting of its anti-Iraq war propaganda effort, the Bush administration should have gone to Congress and asked for a declaration of war on all terror-sponsoring states. That in place, Afghanistan, Iraq and Iran would know that they were among those regimes targeted by the US and its allies, given that the wording of that declaration would include the admonition that the prosecution of the war on terrorism would be conducted in the time and manner of the allies' choosing. If that declaration had been made, the American left would have been neutralized and the world would be safer now.

[End of Essay]

Death by a Thousand Cuts

As I record in my previous book, often a feature of a dying civilization is its destruction of its middle class through taxation. It also forms one of my immutable laws governing the fall of great civilizations:

Immutable # 5
When a free people, through taxation, is deprived of its ability to acquire
Wealth and property, collapse is presaged

Quietly, on January 1, 2016, without a single vote from one Republican member of Congress, here's what happened to the American taxpayer:

- Medicare tax went from 1.45% to 2.35%
- Top Income tax bracket went from 35% to 39.6%
- Top Income payroll tax went from 37.4% to 52.2%
- Capital Gains tax went from 15% to 28%
- Dividend tax went from 15% to 39.6%
- Estate tax went from 0% to 45%
- A 3.5% Real Estate transaction tax was added

These taxes were all passed in the Affordable Care Act, also known as Obamacare.

End Notes

End Notes

Preface

1. Center for Immigration Studies, *Ice Released* 19,273 Criminal Aliens I 2015, April 27, 2016.

2. www.westernjournalism.com/new-reports-highlight-isis-related-activity-along-u-s-me, Aug 13, 2016

3. www.investigativeproject.org/articles/Funding Terrorism - The Buck Stops Here, IPT News, December 6, 2016 Special Report: What the Alarming Increase in Lethal Islamist Terror Means Going ...

Introduction

4. abcnews.go.com/Politics/story?id=2872135 Feb 13, 2007 - Obama Apologizes for Saying Troops' Lives 'Wasted $400 billion, and have seen over 3,000 lives of the bravest young Americans wasted."

5. Mark Moyer, *Strategic Failure*, Threshold Editions, a division of Simon and Schuster, New York, 2015, p 202.

6. Ibid, p217

7. https://books.google.com/books?isbn=1476713278 2015 *On October 18, New York Times correspondent David D. Kirkpatrick chatted on the with Ahmed Abu Khattala, a known Ansar al Shariah leader.*

8. www.wsj.com/articles/the-end-of-the-arab-spring-dream-1450297624 Dec 16, 2015 - The End of the Arab Spring Dream. By Sohrab Ahmari.

9. www.rasmussenreports.com/.../war_on_terror/war_on_terror_confidence_falls_ Jan 26, 2015 - *Belief that the United States is winning the War on Terror has fallen to yet another...*

10. www.cnn.com/2016/11/16/world/global-terrorism-report/ Wed November 16, 2016 *There was a 650% increase in fatal terror attacks on people living in the world's biggest economies in 2015...*

11. www.wsj.com/articles/remember-irans-role-in-9-11-1473290470 Sep 7, 2016 - Joseph Lieberman

12. All citations appear as they did in the text of my published articles. They are the standard format of political commentary columns.

Section One

13. An EMP, or electromagnetic pulse, is a short burst of electromagnetic energy. This burst is disruptive to electronics and electrical systems.

14. www.cbsnews.com/.../president-obama-north-korea-challenge-south-china-sea-agres...Apr 26, 2016 - In wide-ranging conversation… with Charlie Rose…

15. There were human rights abuses committed by the military against his Muslim Brotherhood supporters in Morsi's deposition. But relative to what has occurred in Syria and even our own revolution, the loss of life was comparatively small.

16. Amazingly, like Benghazi, the downing of TWA 800 was an act of war carried out by terrorists, using a surface-to-air missile, a couple months before a presidential election and covered up by a sitting president.

17. Muslims know that September 11, 1683 was the high point of Muslim domination over the Christian infidels and that it is the reason bin Laden selected that day for his attack.

18. Interview with James Carafano, Vice President, Heritage Foundation, December 1, 2013

19. *Country Report on Terrorism*, 2012

20. Currently there are nearly no experts on Islamic jurisprudence who disagree that under Sharia law, apostasy is punishable by death.

Section Two

21. Mark Moyer, *Strategic Failure*, p295.

22. www.washingtoninstitute.org/policy-analysis/view/iraqs-dire-situation Jun 17, 2014 - *Knights, a Lafer Fellow with the Institute, has worked extensively with around 60 of 243 Iraqi army combat battalions cannot be accounted for...*

23. www.theatlantic.com/magazine/archive/2016/05/the-hell-after-isis/476391/The Hell After ISIS, Anand Gopal.

24. www.nationalreview.com/.../state-department-iran-didnt-sign-iran-deal-joel-gehrke Nov 24, 2015 - *"The Joint Comprehensive Plan of Action (JCPOA) is not a treaty or an executive agreement, and is not a signed document," wrote Julia Frifield, ...*

25. Michael Oren Ally –*My Journey Across the American-Israeli Divide*, Random House, New York, 2015, p 271.

26. Ibid p. 278.

27. Ibid p 280.

28. www.theatlantic.com/magazine/archive/2016/04/the-obama-doctrine/471525/

29. Michael Oren, *Ally*, p121. (see above)

30. www.weeklystandard.com/reading-obamas-mind/article/1042845 Oct 19, 2015 | By Lee Smith.

31. www.taxpolicycenter.org/statistics/amount-revenue-source Feb 3, 2015.

32. www.washingtonexaminer.com/obama-budgets-17613-for...illegal.../2590078 May 2, 2016 - *President Obama has budgeted $17613 for each of the estimated 75000...*

33. Larry Kelley, *Lessons from Fallen Civilizations*, Hugo House Publishers, Englewood, CO 2012, p 323.

34. www.breitbart.com/.../2015/.../22-times-obama-admin-declared-climate-change-great...Nov 14, 2015

35. www.vcn.bc.ca/citizens-handbook/rules.html, Saul Alinsky 1971

36. https://www.jihadwatch.org/2016/.../obama-at-islamic-society-of-baltimore-mus-lim-a...Obama at Islamic Society of Baltimore: "Muslim Americans keep us safe". February 3, 2016 By Robert Spencer.

37. www.upi.com/Top_News/US/2016/02/...Muslim-Americans/2611454509080/Feb 3, 2016 - *White House Press Secretary Josh Earnest condemned the rhetoric ... marginalize law-abiding, patriotic Muslim Americans"*

38. www.washingtontimes.com/news/.../elite-fbi-surveillance-teams-tracking-48-isis-susp/ Nov 27, 2015 - *The FBI has roughly 1000 active Islamic State probes inside the U.S. and new reports have revealed that at least ... FBI tracking 1,000 ISIS suspects in the U.S.; 48 considered high-risk ...*

39. http://www.nationalreview.com/corner/380508/no-us-troops-didnt-have-leave-iraq-patrick-brennan

40. http://www.investors.com/politics/editorials/taliban-expansion-exposes-us-af-ghan-strategy-as-charade/ Dec 28, 2015 - *The U.S. is performing a pathetic charade in Afghanistan, a Washington Post report reveals.*

41. http://www.wsj.com/articles/soldier-deaths-raise-questions-about-effectiveness-of-phil-ippines-counterterrorism-1460285852

42. http://www.nbcnews.com/news/world/u-s-carrier-harry-s-truman-has-close-call-irani-an-n487536

43. http://www.washingtontimes.com/news/2016/jan/21/obama-releases-al-qaedas-most-skilled-explosives-e/

44. https://www.theguardian.com/world/video/2015/nov/14/president-hollande-paris-at-tacks-act-of-war-video

45. http://www.businessinsider.com/the-captured-paris-attack-suspect-was-hiding-in-plain-sight-2016-3

Section Two

46. Erick Stakelbeck, *ISIS Exposed, Beheadings, slavery, and the Hellish Reality of Radical Islam,* Regnery Publishing, Washington D.C. 2015, p92.

47. A Muslim who fails to be pure enough.

48. Erick Stakelbeck, *SIS Exposed, Beheadings, slavery, and the Hellish Reality of Radical Islam,* Regnery Publishing, Washington D.C. 2015, p. 53. (see above)

49. http://www.dailymail.co.uk/news/article-2790296/blood-curdling-screams-headless-bodies-siege-town-mail-man-sam-greenhill-reports-frontline-jihadi-squads-lie-wait-western-hostages.html Sam Greenhill, October 12, 2014.

50. https://books.google.com/books?id=uOkHDAAAQBAJ&pg=PA57&lpg=PA57&d-q=mitchell+st+george+baghdad&source=bl&ots=cQE1IMsUDC&sig=u_ubz8c-bEN8ckSyAQhWYQ5K4S9I&hl=en&sa=X&ved=0ahUKEwitmoOs-b3RAh-Upr1QKHVV3D20Q6AEILzAD#v=onepage&q=mitchell%20st%20george%20baghdad&f=false

51. http://www.theatlantic.com/magazine/archive/2015/03/what-isis-really-wants/384980/

52. http://www.telegraph.co.uk/news/worldnews/middleeast/iraq/10948480/Islamic-State-leader-Abu-Bakr-al-Baghdadi-addresses-Muslims-in-Mosul.html

53. http://www.washingtontimes.com/news/2015/sep/9/james-clapper-islamic-state-could-infiltrate-us-we/

54. Mark Moyar, *Strategic Failure*, p 54.

55. http://www.spiegel.de/international/world/interview-with-ben-rhodes-about-paris-attacks-and-syria-a-1063687.html

56. Larry Kelley, *Lessons from Fallen Civilizations,* pgs 94-8.

57. http://www.politifact.com/truth-o-meter/promises/obameter/promise/515/no-family-making-less-250000-will-see-any-form-tax/

58. Mark Moyar, *Strategic Failure*, p 177.

59. Ayaan Hirsi Ali, Nomad, *From Islam to America*, Free Press, New York, 2010 p.223.

60. Wafa Sultan, *A God Who Hates – The Courageous Women Who Inflamed the Muslim World Speaks Out Against the Evils of Islam*, St. Martin's Press, New York, 2009 p. 28.

61. Ayaan Hirsi Ali, *Nomad*, p, 93.

62. http://www.nationalreview.com/article/428638/islamic-extremism-islamic-terror-islam-linked

63. https://www.brookings.edu/research/from-paper-state-to-caliphate-the-ideology-of-the-islamic-state/

64. https://www.youtube.com/watch?v=QxzOVSMUrGM

65. For her profile, see *Lessons from Fallen Civilizations*, pg. 302

66. Ayaan Hirsi Ali, Heretic – *Why Islam Needs Reformation Now*, Harper Collins, New York, 2015, p101.

67. See also, *Lessons from Fallen Civilizations*, pgs. 196-204

68. Hirsi Ali, *Heretic*, p. 190.

69. https://www.jihadwatch.org/2013/02/qaradawi-if-they-had-gotten-rid-of-the-apostasy-punishment-islam-wouldnt-exist-today

70. http://formermuslimsunited.org/the-pledge/cover-letter-pledge/

71. https://www.youtube.com/watch?v=MIcsmfJPRxo

72. http://www.dawn.com/news/1241751

73. http://www.uae-embassy.org/news-media/statement-ambassador-yousef-al-otaiba-challenging-extremism-0

74. https://www.malala.org/malalas-story

Section Three

75. See also, *Blackout, Lessons from Fallen Civilizations: Volume 2 – The Way Forward*, pg. 51

76. https://counterjihadreport.com/2015/12/29/robert-spencer-10-things-america-must-do-to-defend-itself-from-jihad/

77. http://www.frontpagemag.com/fpm/264783/president-trump-now-what-robert-spencer

78. http://www.reuters.com/article/us-iran-missiles-khamenei-idUSKCN0WW0PT

79. https://www.nytimes.com/2016/02/17/world/middleeast/us-had-cyberattack-planned-if-iran-nuclear-negotiations-failed.html?_r=0

80. http://www.cnsnews.com/news/article/michael-w-chapman/pew-144000-us-muslims-say-suicide-bombings-civilian-targets-often-or

Conclusion

81. http://www.danielpipes.org/16322/muslim-no-go-zones-in-europe

Appendix

82. http://www.wnd.com/2016/12/secret-refugee-resettlement-transforming-america/

83. http://blogs.wsj.com/economics/2016/07/29/seven-years-later-recovery-remains-the-weakest-of-the-post-world-war-ii-era/

Photographs

Photographs

Cover

f11photo (Photographer). Iwo Jima Memorial Washington DC USA at sunrise. [Photograph], Retrieved September 27, 2016, from: https://stock.adobe.com/stock-photo/iwo-jima-memorial-washington-dc-usa-at-sunrise/64928433.

Introduction

Odriography (Photographer). monde arabe "5 calques propres" [AI/EPS], Retrieved July 01, 2016, from: https://stock.adobe.com/stock-photo/monde-arabe-5-calques-propres/66515251.

danhowl (Photographer). (2011). 'World Trade Towers Burn in September 11, 2001 Attack' [Photograph], Retrieved July 01, 2016, from: https://secure.istockphoto.com/photo/world-trade-towers-burn-in-september-11-2001-attack-gm458127767-17598120.

Section One

chrisdorney (Photographer). Sir Winston Churchill Statue in Paris [Photograph], Retrieved July 01, 2016, from: https://stock.adobe.com/stock-photo/sir-winston-churchill-statue-in-paris/69269236.

Gallup, Sean (Photographer). (2011). Merkel Meets With Egyptian President Mubarak [Photograph], Retrieved July 01, 2016, from: https://secure.istockphoto.com/photo/merkel-meets-with-egyptian-president-mubarak-gm97431060-16842914.

Sullivan, Justin (Photographer). (2012). President-Elect Obama Meets With the Transition Economic Advisory Board [Photograph], Retrieved July 01, 2016, from: https://secure.istockphoto.com/photo/president-elect-obama-meets-with-the-transition-economic-advisor-gm83601967-18969396.

Rashad, Jonathan (Photographer). (2011). Over 1 Million in Tahrir Square demanding the removal of the regime and for Mubarak to step down [Photograph], Retrieved August 17, 2016, from: https://en.wikipedia.org/wiki/File:Tahrir_Square_-_February_9,_2011.png. *This file is licensed under the Creative Commons Attribution 2.0 Generic license.*

www.kremlin.ru (Photographer). (11 April 2015). Abdel Fattah el-Sisi [Photograph], Retrieved 17 August 2016, from: https://en.wikipedia.org/wiki/File:Abdel_Fattah_el-Sisi. jpg. *This file comes from the website of the President of the Russian Federation and is licensed under the Creative Commons Attribution 4.0 License.*

Furian, Peter Hermes (Photographer). Iran Political Map [AI/EPS], Retrieved July 01, 2016, from: https://stock.adobe.com/stock-photo/iran-political-map/70003539.

Sedmakova, Renata (Photographer). Vienna - philosopher statue for the Parliament - Herodotus [Photograph], Retrieved July 01, 2016, from: https://stock.adobe.com/stock-photo/vienna-philosopher-statue-for-the-parliament-herodotus/14156602.

sadikgulec (Photographer). (2014). Kurdish Soldiers in Arbil.[Photograph], Retrieved July 01, 2016, from: https://secure.istockphoto.com/photo/kurdish-soldiers-in-arbil-gm499333655-42721356.

James Foley a moment before his gruesom beheading. Digital image. *Catholic Online.* Catholic Online. Web. 01 July 2016.

Free Kurdistan (Photographer). (4 August 2015). YPJ fighters [Photograph], Retrieved 17 August 2016, from: https://en.wikipedia.org/wiki/File:YPJ_fighters_3.jpg. *This file is licensed under the Creative Commons Attribution 2.0 Generic license.*

kundir12 (Photographer). Ala Kurdistan kurdische Flagge [JPEG], Retrieved July 01, 2016, from: https://stock.adobe.com/75817013.

BillionPhotos.com (Photographer). Military. [Photograph], Retrieved July 01, 2016, from: https://stock.adobe.com/stock-photo/military/103118192.

Guilane-Nachez, Erica (Photographer). Asian Barbarians - 5th century [Photograph], Retrieved July 01, 2016, from: https://stock.adobe.com/stock-photo/asian-barbarians-5th-century/39439557.

Wong, Alex (Photographer). Senate Commerce Committee Holds Gas Pipeline Safety Hearing [Photograph], Retrieved July 01, 2016, from: https://secure.istockphoto.com/photo/senate-commerce-committee-holds-gas-pipeline-safety-hearing-gm104515256-18927735.

Kollidas, Georgios (Photographer). Karl Marx [AI/EPS], Retrieved July 01, 2016, from: https://stock.adobe.com/stock-photo/karl-marx/44798993.

seyyed shabodin vajedi (Photographer). (17 October 2006). Ali Khamenei leader of Iran

[Photograph], Retrieved 17 August 2016, from: https://en.wikipedia.org/wiki/File:Abdel_Fattah_el-Sisi.jpg. *This file comes from the website of the President of the Russian Federation and is licensed under the Creative Commons Attribution 4.0 License.*

Pozzebom, Fabio Rodrigues (Photographer). (18 August 2011). The president of the Syrian Arab Republic, Bashar Al-Assad during a visit to Congress [Photograph], Retrieved 17 August 2016, from: https://commons.wikimedia.org/wiki/File:Bashar_al-Assad_(cropped).jpg. *This file is licensed under the Creative Commons Attribution 3.0 Brazil license.*

www.kremlin.ru (Photographer). (2006). Official portrait of Vladimir Putin [Photograph], Retrieved 17 August 2016, from: https://commons.wikimedia.org/wiki/File:Vladimir_Putin_-_2006.jpg. *This file comes from the website of the President of the Russian Federation and is licensed under the Creative Commons Attribution 4.0 License.*

Florida DMV (Source). (2001). Mohamed_Atta [Photograph], Retrieved 17 August 2016, from: https://en.wikipedia.org/wiki/File:Mohamed_Atta.jpg. *This work was created by a government unit (including state, county, and municipal government agencies) of the U.S. state of Florida. It is a public record that was not created by an agency which state law has allowed to claim copyright and is therefore in the public domain in the United States.*

US Army (Source). (2 February 2004). Mugshot of Abu Bakr al-Baghdadi taken by US armed forces while in detention at Camp Bucca in the vicinity of Umm Qasr, Iraq, in 2004 [Photograph], Retrieved 17 August 2016, from: https://en.wikipedia.org/wiki/File:Mugshot_of_Abu_Bakr_al-Baghdadi,_2004.jpg. *This image is a work of a U.S. Army soldier or employee, taken or made as part of that person's official duties. As a work of the U.S. federal government, the image is in the public domain*

Concept W (Photographer). Hexacopter drone flying in the sunset [Photograph], Retrieved July 01, 2016, from: https://stock.adobe.com/stock-photo/hexacopter-drone-flying-in-the-sunset/75964820.

Section Two

Gallup, Sean (Photographer). (2012). Zu Guttenberg Meets With ISAF Commander General Petraeus [Photograph], Retrieved July 01, 2016, from: https://secure.istockphoto.com/photo/zu-guttenberg-meets-with-isaf-commander-general-petraeus-gm107089642-18933752.

Cullen, Cherie (Photographer). (25 March 2011). Defense.gov photo essay 110325-D-XH843-010.jpg [Photograph], Retrieved 19 August 2016, from: https://pam.wikipedia.org/wiki/File:Defense.gov_photo_essay_110325-D-XH843-010.jpg. *This image is a work of a U.S. military or Department of Defense employee, taken or made as part of that person's official duties. As a work of the U.S. federal government, the image is in the public domain.*

Walker, Andrew H./Getty Images (Photographer). (2006). Donald Trump [Photograph], Retrieved July 01, 2016, from: https://secure.istockphoto.com/photo/donald-trump-gm157728158-19285025.

Vichinterlang (Photographer). (2015). Central American Refugees, South Texas, Summer 2014 [Photograph], Retrieved July 01, 2016, from: https://secure.istockphoto.com/photo/central-american-refugees-south-texas-summer-2014-gm470907732-63229253.
Saul Alinsky in Chicago's Woodlawn neighborhood in 1966. Hillary D. Rodham noted his "exceptional charm" but questioned his effectiveness. Digital image. *AP.* NBC News. Web. 17 August 2016.

Sherrill, James (Photographer). (13 June 2006). Nouri al-Maliki meets with George W. Bush [Photograph], Retrieved 19 August 2016, from: https://en.wikipedia.org/wiki/File:Nouri_al-Maliki_with_Bush,_June_2006,_cropped.jpg. *This image is a work of a U.S. military or Department of Defense employee, taken or made as part of that person's official duties. As a work of the U.S. federal government, the image is in the public domain.*

ISIS Recruitment Video with British Fighters. Digital image. *Rampages.* RampageUS.com/ISIS. Web. 19 August 2016.

Kilinson (Photographer). yemen sanaa [Photograph], Retrieved July 01, 2016, from: https://stock.adobe.com/stock-photo/yemen-sanaa/65932988.

Skidmore, Gage (Photographer). (10 February 2012). Cliff May by Gage Skidmore.jpg [Photograph], Retrieved 19 August 2016, from: https://commons.wikimedia.org/wiki/File:Cliff_May_by_Gage_Skidmore.jpg. *This file is licensed under the Creative Commons Attribution-Share Alike 3.0 Unported license.*

Crisfotolux (Photographer). Caesar Augustus first emperor of Ancient Rome [Photograph], Retrieved July 01, 2016, from: https://stock.adobe.com/stock-photo/caesar-augustus-first-emperor-of-ancient-rome/90296059.

Avraham, Kushnirov (Photographer). The bridge was built in Roman times [Photograph], Retrieved July 01, 2016, from: https://stock.adobe.com/stock-photo/the-bridge-was-built-in-roman-times/113440386.

SeanPavonePhoto (Photographer). Jerusalem Old City Skyline [Photograph], Retrieved July 01, 2016, from: https://stock.adobe.com/stock-photo/jerusalem-old-city-skyline/54912281.

Skidmore, Gage (Photographer). (05 March 2016). Ayaan Hirsi Ali by Gage Skidmore.jpg [Photograph], Retrieved 19 August 2016, from: https://en.wikipedia.org/wiki/File:Ayaan_Hirsi_Ali_by_Gage_Skidmore.jpg. *This file is licensed under the Creative Commons Attribution-Share Alike 3.0 Unported license.*

Unknown (Photographer). (29 October 1923). Ataturk.jpg [Photograph], Retrieved 19 August 2016, from: https://commons.wikimedia.org/wiki/File:Atatürk.jpg. *This work is in the public domain in Turkey because it has been expropriated as national heritage or its copyright has expired.*

meen_na (Photographer). Koran - holy book of Muslims [Photograph], Retrieved July 01, 2016, from: https://stock.adobe.com/stock-photo/koran-holy-book-of-muslims/79271405.

Section Three

Unknown (Photographer). (08 April 1983). Official Portrait of President Reagan 1981.jpg [Photograph], Retrieved 19 August 2016, from: https://en.wikipedia.org/wiki/File:Official_Portrait_of_President_Reagan_1981.jpg. *This image is a work of an employee of the Executive Office of the President of the United States, taken or made as part of that person's official duties. As a work of the U.S. federal government, the image is in the public domain.*

Souza, Pete (Photographer). (04 January 2010). John Brennan [Photograph], Retrieved 19 August 2016, from: https://commons.wikimedia.org/wiki/File:John_Brennan.jpg. *This image is a work of an employee of the Executive Office of the President of the United States, taken or made as part of that person's official duties. As a work of the U.S. federal government, the image is in the public domain.*

Saber, Hamed (Photographer). (22 June 2006). Natanz nuclear.jpg [Photograph], Retrieved 19 August 2016, from: https://en.wikipedia.org/wiki/File:Natanz_nuclear.jpg. *This file is licensed under the Creative Commons Attribution 2.0 Generic license.*

Gordon, James (Photographer). (24 June 2012). Iraqi refugee children, Damascus, Syria. jpg [Photograph], Retrieved 19 August 2016, from: https://en.wikipedia.org/wiki/File:Iraqi_refugee_children,_Damascus,_Syria.jpg. *This file is licensed under the Creative Commons Attribution 2.0 Generic license.*

Appendix

Smialowski, Brendan (Photographer). (2008). Bush Addresses The Economic Crisis From The Rose Garden of White House [Photograph], Retrieved July 01, 2016, from: https://secure.istockphoto.com/photo/bush-addresses-the-economic-crisis-from-the-rose-garden-of-white-gm83210165-16850517.

Index

Index

About the Author

About the Author

Larry Kelley earned his BA in English Literature from the University of California at Santa Barbara. Upon graduation, he led surfing explorations to North Africa and Central America, until he went to work in high-technology sales. Since 9/11 he has written articles on terrorism and resurgent militant Islam for the San Francisco Chronicle, Human Events, Townhall Magazine and other publications. His favorite musician is cowboy bard, Pete Charles, whose beautiful country western ballads include the Kelley Compilation.

www.ingramcontent.com/pod-product-compliance
Lightning Source LLC
Chambersburg PA
CBHW062203270326
41930CB00009B/1626